QUANTUM-THE SCIENTIFIC PROOF OF ESOTERIC

By Cihangir Gener

ESOTERIC

Mankind has sought the answers to 'why' questions for as long as he has known himself. Why is he here? What is the purpose of life? Why does the world exist? What are the stars and the universe and why are they there? Do all existences have a purpose? It is these 'reasons' which have prepossessed his mind ever since the first day and have pushed man to search for answers in his own way. There must be a reason for his existence and an explanation for the events which take place around him. Man, whose brain capacity has expanded throughout the process of evolution, has realized that there must be an initial reason for everything. This initial reason has firstly been natural events, and then it has been thought that the sun and other celestial bodies have been responsible. Mankind, who has realized that these may not be the reasons for the beginning of everything, has begun to search for the answer in more subjective beings and the Gods he has created in his own imagination. Gradually these numerous gods have become A Single God and the idea that this Single God is responsible for everything has been accepted in general. Today, even in the root of religions regarded as polytheistic, there is the idea of 'Creator God' and 'Father God'. Gods are in fact the manifestations of the different characteristics of this Single God.

The polytheistic point of view has left its place to the belief in a Single God, who is responsible for everything and created everything, with the Hebrews. With Judaism, Christianity and lastly Islam, the idea of Creator God has spread to a majority of the world. A different view on the existence of God, which remains outside this general knowledge, exists as well. This different point of view is the 'God that Brings into Existence'. In terms of historical developments, this point of view goes back a much longer way, to the periods during which mankind has first appeared. God is not the Creator, but whom things Come Into Existence from. Everything has come into existence from him and everything is him. All beings together form the entirety of God. The universe is a manifestation of God. Man is a manifestation of God as well. Therefore, the God-Universe-Man sameness comes into question. The expression used in the Western languages for the 'Unity of Existence' discourse is 'Esoteric'.

Esoteric has been acknowledged as one of the many beliefs throughout the centuries and due to its relatively difficult to understand context, the number of its advocators among the human masses has not ever exceeded certain limits. However, the scientific inventions of our time show that Esoteric is not solely a belief and that it is a discourse which explains all kinds of existences and phenomenon in the universe, a fact. The latest inventions of the last century, such as The Quantum Theory, The Theory of Relativity, all verify the realities Esoteric has been advocating for thousands of years. All these scientific developments and new inventions, which support these and are continuous, point out that the coming centuries, will be the Esoteric Age.

Esoteric is the most competent answer mankind has found as to why mankind exists. In this light, Esoteric is an expression of the oldest Single God belief in the history of mankind as well. It is not possible to isolate Esoteric thought from the history of mankind. No matter which point and which stage of the history of mankind is looked at, Esoteric has always appeared there. (See, Esoteric Anagogical Doctrines Encyclopedia – Cihangir Gener).

The word Esoteric has been derived from the Greek adjective 'Esoteric'. Exo means 'inner-esoteric' in Greek. Esoteric thus means the science of things which is inside, hidden and secret. Esoteric is a system of doctrines. It is the expression of the Pantheist world view in a single word. Initiation in turn is the initiation ceremony for those who attend schools which give this information, in order to have this hidden and esoteric knowledge. In Ancient Greece, the initiated people were called Esoteric and those who could not pass the initiation were called Exoteric (those who remain outside). Pythagoras used the word Esoteric for his own students and Exoteric for those who were not his students. In Greek, the word 'Pan' means whole and 'Theos' means God. The root of the word Theos goes back to the word 'Tau' which is much older. Pantheism is a philosophical view which advocates that all gods in fact are the supplementary aspects of a Single God. The Word Pantheon comes from the same root and is the expression of the structure which shows all gods together. The pantheon of Greek gods in Greece means all gods which are believed to exist.

The word Esoteric passed to Greek from the Luwian language. The word Esoteric has first been used by the Luwians who have lived in Anatolia in the 8 thousand B.C.'s. These oldest settlers of Anatolia were a community who called themselves 'Luwi'. The word 'Luvi' means 'People of the Light' in this peoples' language. The Word 'Ezo' means 'Essence' in the Luwian language and has passed to Turkish with very little changes phonetically. The word 'Ter' means 'Head, Mind' in Luwian. Therefore, Esoteric as a single word may be expressed as 'The Science of Godly Essence and Intuition under the Leadership of the Mind'.

Esoteric is a belief system, which is based on the idea of the sameness of God, Universe, and Man, where everything emanates from God and is a part of God. The purpose is for every part that lives different experiences to bring these together and thus reach awareness in a higher level. Esoteric is the expression of the Unity of Existence in the Western languages. This belief is expressed in the Eastern languages as Mysticism-Spiritualism and Esoteric-Sufism in Islam. The Western thought is a structure which has always kept the mind in the foreground. The Mind and Rationale has been aggrandized ever since Ancient Greece, which is accepted as the beginning of the Western civilization. In particular with the Age of Enlightenment, intellectual thought and scientific advancement have found their expressions in the upper most level. The same point of view lies beneath the belief of Unity of Existence being expressed as Esoteric in the West.

In terms of Eastern doctrines, mysticism is the general name given to the methods by which one's soul unifies with God through love and meditation. The cognition of the knowledge of that is limitless through the methods of love and intuition is called mysticism. While the Eastern point of view advocates that man's immortal soul continuously finds body for evolvement, the Western thought claims that the Creator places a soul to the body and after death, the soul is either awarded or punished. Materialism, which is another consequence of the same Western thought advocates that the soul does not exist, what is essential is the body and that the mind exists to meet the wishes and needs of the body and the consciousness ends as a result of the separation of all atoms after death. However, it has been found out in the weight measurement of the body right before death and after death that, the weight decreases 7 grams after death in comparison to prior to death. If there is no soul as materialism advocates, what could be the reason for this weight decrease?

In terms of philosophy, Galilei states in his work titled *Le Opere* that: "Philosophy is written [nature] in that great book whichever is before our eyes -- I mean the universe -- but we cannot understand it if we do not first learn the language and grasp the symbols in which it is written. The book is written in mathematical language, and the symbols are triangles, circles and other geometrical figures, without whose help it is impossible to comprehend a single word of it; without which one wanders in vain through a dark labyrinth". In monotheistic religions, while there is the creator-created duality, we do not see this in Pantheism. Everything which exists has emerged from God and is identical to God. The Universe and the God are one. God is not the creator, but ne which exists and the sum of the universe. God, who is timeless and eternal, exists both in the Macro cosmos and the Micro cosmos.

The representative of existence in the upper most level is Man. Man, just like every living this which lives on our World Today, is the result of an evolutionary process. Evolution, in other words the Law of Evolvement is a law which continues from pre-eternity to eternity. In the first moment of the beginning, the Emergence, or The Big Bang, the law of evolution has begun to take place and energy created the Universe by transforming into matter. The law has continuously taken place throughout time and has resulted in the emergence of Man in our world. The law of evolution is based on the effort spent by everything that exists to develop itself. The ultimate target of every particle which has separated from God is to return to the main source it has separated from. Every part which separates from God gradually grows distant from the main source in the environment of the universe which is made up of matter and hits the bottom in the full sense of the word. The single way for matters which hit the bottom to be able to return to the main source is the law of evolution. All kinds of matter in the universe exist through four main powers and continue their lives. There are Fire (Energy), Air (Gas), Water (Fluid) and Soil (Solid). Through the various combinations of these four main elements, each particle which has emerged from God goes though different experiences and jumps to a higher step of existence with the gain these experiences bring. Evolution continues even today both in physical and spiritual terms. Man's continuous effort to reach what is better has brought with itself not only physical advancement, but also intellectual advancement and the advancement in thought has reached the conclusion that everything has a reason of creation-being brought to existence (See, *Dear God, I'm Returning to You* – Cihangir Gener).

Man has emerged from the coming together of both the soul and matter. The soul and matter are one, a whole. One is the visible, while the other is the invisible side of existence. However, they are one and single. The most perfect evolutionary process may be attained in an environment, where the unity of both is kept in balance. Putting one or the other in the foreground and neglecting the other are processes which prevent evolvement. The most important aspect is balance in life. It is mandatory to be balanced with the universe, keep the same resonance, vibration and resonance state continuous.

Esoteric advocates that eternal awareness without a past is God. The life lived by each individual is the physical materialization of the power of the eternal creativity. Humanity is capable of leaving both the dogmas of science and religion. The realities of both areas have the capacity to clear the way for humanity together. Einstein stated that "Science without religion is lame, religion without science is blind." The father of quantum physics Max Planck stated in his work titled *The Universe in the Light of Modern Physics* that "Modern physics is related to the realities of old teachings which teach the realities that exist beyond our senses" and has shown how true the ancient esoteric knowledge is. The writer of *God Theory*, Bernard Haisch believes that the seemingly irreconcilable differences of divine religions are of an esoteric level. According to Haisch, who states that each religion shares common denominators in the esoteric level, the world is in fact a center of esoteric wisdom. Haisch, who believes that modern science ignores Esoteric, states that science does not even take into consider including the Esoteric subjects in its research and avoids taking the responsibility of removing its own dogmatism. However, the area of scientific questioning will not be arbitrarily limited and Esoteric will resume the respectability it deserves as always. In fact, quantum physics displays the connection between quantum experiments and the Higher Awareness.

Soul, which is a fragment of Divine Light, never dies and its sole purpose of the return to the main source it has separated from, that is, God. The only way this could be achieved is through evolution which is a universal law, in other words, evolvement. What really matters is the soul and its advancement. Matter, or the body, is what the soul uses to step into a higher level and its expression of its existence in time. Man, whose beginning took place as a result of Divine emanation, but who will come to an end when he returns to it in this life, is the highest level of known expression of Divine existence. Man, who embodies the soul -body trilogy, is Micro cosmos. Micro cosmos is identical to Macro cosmos, that is, God, which embodies father-mother and son, or essence, ore and life.

God is always in motion. Emergence or Divine emergence is continuous in the spiritual level. The Divine particulars which emerge in the spiritual level become apparent in the physical World. This ascent and passing onto the apparent state takes place in two steps. The first state is in the form of vibrations and overflow movement which are intrinsic to the Divine structure. Arabi has called this first step the Feyzi Akdes. Feyzi Akdes is the breathing in and out of a sort of Divine breath which is necessary for the continuation of existence. This vibration movement cannot be felt in the physical world. It is totally ambiguous and without rule. However, quantum science has identified the existence of these vibrations within the energy area and has called these 'Quantum Fluctuations". In order for the existing things to be apparent, the first movement that is needed is these Quantum Fluctuations. Arabi called the second ascent Feyzi Mukaddes. The formation of beings which become apparent through this second step, which may be expressed as Divine Lighting, takes place within the framework of certain physical laws and rules. With Feyzi Mukaddes, the soul's unification with the body and being's starting its divine journey is expressed. Man, like all beings, has to carry certain characteristics. Feyzi Mukaddes embodies the death and rebirth cycle. All beings will die and will be reborn as a new being. The only thing which does not die is the part which comes directly from God, that is, the soul. In each birth, the soul is given a body and in each death, the soul gets rid of the body. Meanwhile, in each being the capacity to reach perfection exists as a secret power. General evolvement and laws of change are the indicators of this power. The evolvement of Divine Higher Awareness is possible only through when matter gains body and with the continuous evolvement of the soul.

God lives in the physical world through all its creations and experiences new things. The experiences of each star, or individual, are in fact God's own experiences. The purpose of God is to carry his own evolvement to higher levels with the awareness of his own creations. Paul Davies asks the question "Why would mankind have the ability to understand on which principles the universe evolves?" The answer in terms of Esoteric is simple enough: "The whole universe behaves in accordance with the law of evolution. We humans are beings who have evolved in the highest known level and by raising our level of perception, are continuously increasing our chance to live very different experiences".

Evolvement is nothing but the transforming of hidden potentials into active powers. The universal law which allows the evolvement of the soul, that is its return to the main source it emerges from, is the rebirth law. The rebirth chain, which allows the soul's development from the inanimate beings that are the expressions of existence in the lowest level to the Perfect Man who is situated in the highest level, is only possible if the soul reaches perfection and returns back to God. The physical world for the soul is like a school attended to learn and gain experience. In this school, everyone experiences the sparks of enlightenment which show why people have to accept this test or another. The law of rebirth pushes the soul into embodiment. As a consequence of these embodiments, the world appears as a place where the spiritual energy is renewed. In other words, the soul which is incarnated experiences a different aspect of life and develops this.

Unification with Divine Light is not possible with a body. The body consists of matter and matter is the initial level of the journey to God. There is a long distance matter has to cover in order to be able to reach God. The body is only a tool used by the Soul in its effort reach God. As a result of these efforts, the soul of a person who has become the Perfect Human can only unite with the Divine Light after the last death of the body. However, to be able to understand that death is not an end and that it is the beginning of new journeys, a majority of esoteric schools have realized that experiencing death before death should be lived. Symbolically, it has been fund suitable for humans to go through experiences in which they are supposed to have died, to express that a new life begins and with the purpose of overcoming the fear of death. This experience has been accepted as a stage of maturation to attain knowledge of reality and to reach the true path. Esoteric secrets have been given to the new participant only after going through this death before death experience. The expansion of this symbolic discourse is that, the journey to reach reality may only begin before dying for the last time, which is experiencing death countless times before reaching God and for a person who is search of this to experience real death many times.

According to the Esoteric point of view, emanation is without a past and eternal. There is no beginning or an end. The evolvement of the Divine being will continue until eternity through the experiences of its each particle it has brought into being. Within the framework of quantum laws, since each particle which exists in the universe communicate with each other, there is no event God is not aware of. Since the universe is God, each galaxy in the universe are its small cells, each star system in the galaxy is a small cell of the universe and other planets are a small cell of the star systems, humans and other beings are a small cell of the world, atom is a small cell f humans and other beings, atom's parts are a small cell of the atom and this goes on in the same manner until eternity.

The Deist philosophy which the Western civilization is based on claims that not a single atom has lessened and not a single atom has increased. According to Lavoisier, the universe is the way it was created. It does not decrease or increase. The universe is only an energy totality which is in a state of continuous change and transformation. The age of all atoms is as old as the universe. However, the ages of the combinations they form together are young. A decrease or an increase in their number does not take place as a result of them coming together. Just as humans grow with the food they eat and add them to their bodies after they are born, they mix their body with soil when they die. Increase or decrease is against the principles of divine will. According to Deism, coming into being out of nothing or disappearing out of being are against the principles of creation. Beings only reproduce and spread. The Creator has created the whole universe as a whole and has put forward certain principles. The universe is deterministic. Everything functions in accordance with these predicted principles. God's interference with this formation is not in question. God has completed the job and has taken a back seat. The issue will be further dealt in detail.

Some scientists dwell on the question of who has created God if God is the first reason and the creator. This question takes us to the result that for each creator there must be another creator. When the beginning and end of time is puts forward a similar question. It is not possible for these types of questions to have an answer. The answer will get caught on an eternal cycle paradox. Therefore, we need to limit our answers as the beginning, end and creator of our own universe. The God image on people's minds displays differences within the framework of acquired information. Monotheistic divine point of view is the product of 4 thousand years. However, it is known that humankind has been on Earth at least for 200 thousand years. According to divine religions, the greatest sin is not to believe in the Creator God. Then, were all generations which lived before the Monotheistic religions came sinners? The change in the perception of God has even continued during the hegemony of Monotheistic religions. For instance, while according to Kepler, who lived in the 16th century, God was a geometry engineer, according to Newton, who lived in the 17th century, God was a physicist. Newton thought that God created laws of physics together with the universe and stood aside. Planck proved that this was not so and Einstein expressed God as a relative concept. Today, our latest perception is that, God is a Quantum Computer designer. However, mankind has looked within himself even on the first day of his emergence and found the answer. God is inside him. The universe and humans like all other creations are a part of God. The name given to this point of view is Esoteric and the end the Quantum Computer Designer is taking us will show that we need to understand this to everyone.

Renowned scientist Stephen Hawking, who is sometimes an Atheist and sometimes stands close to Deist Materialism, asks what God was doing before creating the universe. According to Esoteric, the answer would be that God dealt with the previous universe. God will be dealing with the next universe after this universe disappears. Therefore, it is timeless and eternal. However, in our age, science has been built on reductionism, randomness and materialism. If this is the situation and we are merely physical beings who have emerged by chance within a random universe, then we cannot possibly say that any of the goals we have in our lives have any value. According to materialism, the past of the universe definitely determines its present time and its present time definitely determines its future. This point of view does not lend any credence at all to free will; in fact, man is also totally subject to the laws matter is subject to. The materialist point of view claims that the universe will be definitely given an explanation for someday, if not in the present time. In fact, the universe is mechanical and deterministic. On the other hand, Esoteric rejects the idea of a mechanical and deterministic universe right from the beginning. The function of science and the importance of intellect should always be kept in the foreground; however this pair should never be imposed as a dogma. Esoteric also seeks the answer to the 'Why' question Materialism never asks. According to Esoteric, none of the answers humanity would give to the Why question should be imposed as dogma. In fact, where there is dogma, advancement, or evolution stops; however, development show that evolution never stops.

The Esoteric point of view suggests that evolvement and emergence are a never ending process. Everything that matures returns to Him every moment and everything leaves Him to experience brand new things every moment. In other words, His commands come every moment and become reality in the universe. The God of Esoteric is not like the Deist God who has completed his job and stood aside. Within the framework of esoteric understanding, God is timeless and eternal. Beginning, ending or standing aside cannot be in question. The Quantum universe is the scientific expression of this formation. The universe is continuously in communication with flows of energy. Nothing is disordered in the universe. Everything continues its existence in accordance with a certain order and laws. Even the smallest disorganization that may take place is intervened with and precautions are taken to rebuild order. Entropy's (disorder) being low shows the existence of an orderly structure. The entropy of all kinds of material existences being very low is an ordinary situation. There is a harmony, an order within life. The law of entropy is one of the greatest proofs which displays the order in the universe. Although the great explosion which constitutes the beginning of the universe seems like it has created chaos, it is understood that there is a great order within this chaos and four forces which have immediately become active with this explosion and put the universe in order. Contrary to what is believed, the universe has been formed in accordance with a certain purpose and certain order. Although the universe is continuously expanding right now, it has been calculated that its entropy is quite low. This shows that the universe is one with the harmonious building blocks which complete each other and it is a holistic organization of life. In other words, the universe has a holistic intelligence. There is never an end in the universe. There is always a beginning. Each end is an expression of another beginning. Divine emergence and evolvement are eternal.

The emergence of the universe and all its beings from God is not disengagement. Emergence does not mean a separation of distancing from God. We may resemble emergence to an ocean. Just as the separation of water from the ocean due to freezing or vaporizing does not create a decrease in the volume of the ocean, beings which separate from God are not an expression of a decrease either. All water which separates from the ocean still carries the characteristics of water. The only difference is the different manifestations of water. It is ice, vapor, rain and returns to the ocean after it goes through various experiences. The return takes place within the framework of certain physical and spiritual laws.

God's acceptance as only a first reason as Deism claims causes the questioning of the reason of this first reason as well. All Monotheistic beliefs answer this question with the theory that God is Without a Precursor and Eternal. Taking the reality that everything has a beginning and an end in the universe as the starting point, it is not possible for an eternal existence without a precursor is not possible with the materialist point of view. Paul Davies, who is a scientist, explains his thoughts about Materialism in his work titled *The Mind of God* as follows: "I belong to the group of scientists who do not subscribe to a conventional religion but nevertheless deny that the universe is a purposeless accident. Through my scientific work I have come to believe and more strongly that the physical universe is put together with ingenuity so astonishing that I cannot accept it merely as a brute fact, it seems to me, to be a deeper level of explanation. Furthermore, I have come to the point of view that mind conscious awareness of the world is not a meaningless and accidental quirk of nature, but an absolutely fundamental facet of reality." The observation of the universe shows that everything is in a state of change and evolution. Everything is born, lives and dies. The thing that is without a precursor and is eternal is this continuous cycle. The universe was also born at some point, still lives and will die at some point. However, this birth is not a beginning, as death is not an end. As many births take place before birth, there will a new birth after death. Today's universe is made up of the building blocks of the ones in the past. The future's more advanced universe is being built today.

However, in today's World, almost no individual has the chance to view issues generally and as a whole. Each subject being accumulated with information that requires expertise in itself is one of the most important reasons for this. Almost everyone does limited researches on the subject they choose as their career area. No scientist has sufficient information about the other's knowledge and area of interest. The basic laws and basic subjects not being understood sufficiently in a way prevents going after reality. It does not seem possible for a person to have knowledge in all subjects. Especially, minds who receive a reductionist education to be aware of the fact that knowledge is one and whole is not possible. In fact, the knowledge of astronomy for instance, is also the knowledge of medicine and mankind's new evolutionary plane makes it mandatory for this point of view to be developed. As much as the chain of evolution between the precursor soup and the thinking man is understood, the quantum leap will be realized as well.

Today, science is speedily evolving towards the holistic universe hypothesis of the quantum world. The new dogma developed together by scientists, who advocate the Deist or Materialist point of views, in order to put a stop to this as follows: "Matter and Energy, the two areas analyzed by the Quantum science are both a part of the material World. Everything that can be seen and felt can be explained in a definite manner through physics, chemistry, biology and techniques of genealogy. All spiritual ideas are nothing but old fashioned superstitions and mythology". This point of view is frequently used as a definition which proves everything by the science circles. According to this view, energy is a derivative as matter and it has absolutely no connection with metaphysics' interest areas such as emotions, thoughts and even liveliness. However, science itself shows us that emotions, thoughts and even liveliness each have an electromagnetic wave dimension. Electromagnetic waves are expressions of energy. Since the electromagnetic frequency man spreads while alive ends with death, it may easily be stated that the Soul, which provides liveliness, is a kind of energy. Many cultures defined the Soul as 'Life Energy'. The Soul is pure energy and pure consciousness. The Soul cannot be destroyed. Although it is a part of a great union, each individual soul preserves a perfect record of its own eternal existence.

There are two types of birth for each soul. While the first of these is the soul's separation from God and passing onto the material universe, the second is the rebirths which take place for evolvement. Each embodiment in the universe is both a testing place within its own scope and a suitable place to test the beings it carries within. While a planet spends effort for its own evolvement, it is the living area of beings on their path for evolvement as well. The human body has the same status. Humans both advance in their own path of evolvement and constitute the suitable environment for the evolvement of all the cells and all the atoms in their bodies. Cells die in our bodies every moment and new cells are born. Each body is a place to obtain information to reach a new life. Testing is not performed only in a single life, but with an infinite number and variety of lives. Each death does not ever mean reaching God, as each birth does not ever mean separation from God. Until the last stage where the soul reaches perfect balance, second births of infinite variety take place in the universe of consciousness. Therefore, no death is a separation and no birth is a reunion. Each separation and return is solely a journey around the world and back and it is a situation which repeats infinitely.

God's blowing his soul to Adam is a symbol. What is meant by Adam is the whole of the universe. It is God who gives a life and soul to the universe. God's transferring his own characteristics to those who come to being from him is a natural result. God's divine light is reflected on the whole universe. The universe consists of his reflection from the visible to the invisible. When Adam had a good grasp of the secret, he passed from the Divine dimension to the consciousness dimension. Therefore, Adam is the first initiate. He is immortal, because the environment he passes onto is a tangible body. The tangible environment has rules and these rules are valid for everything. He begins to get to know the environment he is in with his limited consciousness and the completion process. No matter how many lives this process continues, his duty is to complete the process and return to the essence he belongs to, that is, to God. Man acquires a richer consciousness as he experiences. His consciousness will increase as he knows himself, the divine light will expand as his consciousness increases and he will finally find God. Sometimes, this journey may take up an infinite timeframe with stumbling and comebacks. However, this is not important. What is important is that, the person knows himself. He will be able to return to his infinite perception when he knows himself, although he is a mortal. This is the evolvement process.

At the beginning of emergence, what separates from God is Essence. Essence is the expression universal life. It is the proof of the liveliness of the universe as a whole. Everything that separates, is renewed, reproduces and creates difference and variety is a part of Essence. Since emergence is of infinite continuity, Essence's disengagement and return to God continue infinitely as well. Essence embodies both the Divine Soul and Matter. The unification of these two constitutes liveliness which finds its definition in the various layers. Djan is the phenomenon used in the development, experiencing, following and management of new formations. All experiences acquired through what is lived are then the expressions of being crowned with the universal evolvement.

The only difference between humans and other beings is the existence of a consciousness in the higher level and a very extensive free will, which are the characteristics of human soul. God has given soul, consciousness and free will to all his parts and has aimed at increasing his evolvement process as a result of these souls' experiences. Emergence is an expression of a divine world which extends until eternity. It is without a precursor and eternal. It has neither a beginning, nor an end. Evolvement is a process that is to be lived until the final end. The purpose is for beings to transmit the experiences they live to the divine light and to gradually increase the awareness of the divine Higher Consciousness.

The concept of trueness exists in each world and each particular. The right direction has been determined with laws and principles which carry a divine validity. However, difference is necessary for the increase of awareness and the beings who experience this difference in the highest level are the Perfect Human Beings. Beings begin their chain of evolvement from inanimate matter, which are the expressions of the lowest frequency of matter. These evolve through millions of years and lastly reach the Perfect Human Being, who is the expression of the densest frequency of matter. However, at this stage, they have completed their return journey to God.

Humans have soul, whereas objects have ores. This common resource shows the ore, that is the energy area. Ore is the energy area which exists in each being and which emerges. Both living beings and objects are derived from the same sources. As human beings have soul and body dimensions, objects have matter and wave dimensions. These dimensions have a characteristic to supplement each other. Without one, the other cannot exist. The Quantum theory has proved that matter and wave as in fact the same thing. The bodies of living beings and the matter of inanimate objects are equal to each other. In the same manner, the souls of living beings and wave characteristics of inanimate objects are equal to each other. Each existing thing appears temporarily. No being is permanent. In the end, they will all return to the main source they emerged from, to the universal soul, in other words, to God. Each existing thing has a spiritual component. However, this spiritual component is of different power and degree in each being. For the eternal soul, living-inanimate differentiation is not in question. Every existing thing originates from God and has equal importance and value.

Through the Esoteric point of view, it may be questioned whether God is perfect or not. The advocates of The Creator God envision that God is perfect and that He is of a nature that does not need anything. However, there is no answer to the question why this perfect Creator God, who does not need anything, has created humans and other beings. God, from the Esoteric point of view, is of a most perfect structure in terms of His essence. However, He is open to constant development due to His essence and any kind of universal experience allows this development to continue in the eternal level. Just as the God of the past being relatively left behind from today's God, the God of the future may be said to be more advanced from the God of the present time. God is not exempt from the Law of Evolution which has universal validity. In fact, since God and Universe are the same, then all kinds of evolution in the Universe means the evolution of God as well.

Man who has understood the reason for creation, that is, the reason for God, has created religions as a method of reaching this most glorious being. It is observed that two understandings of God have been acknowledged in the history of mankind. The first is the Creator God thought. God has created everything. Besides the Creator, there are the created as well. The philosophical expression of this point of view is Theism. The purpose of the created is to serve the Creator by being good subjects and be awarded with an eternal and perfect life-style as a result. What does man become when he is awarded with an eternal and perfect life-style? What is the ultimate purpose? According to Theism, there is no answer to this question. The reason for the ultimate purpose, which is attempted to be attained with the conclusion, can only be known by God who knows everything. Man has no answer to give to this question. The second discourse is the understanding of God, which has been explained previously in detail, which everything emerges from. The purpose of emergence is to create the Perfect Man, who is the being that can most influence the Godly consciousness with his own experiences. The ultimate target is the evolvement of the highest possible number of man and transform into Perfect Man. it is the main target of Esoteric discipline that the Perfect Man, with all his experiences and awareness reaches God and increases the awareness of Super Consciousness by emerging with Him.

This endless continuity of this development makes the continuity of the creation process mandatory as well. This process extends to endless time with the continuity of emergence for development, spreading of beings to the universe in multitude and each spreading resulting in the feeding of the whole by the evolvement of this multitude. The continuity of evolvement and new experiences being lived necessitates that beings have free will. The will of beings are subject to the law of evolvement as well and the will of beings which evolve in the physical dimension increases in direct proportion to their level of evolvement. However, as the free will gets stronger, each being may be damaged due to what this process takes away from it, as well as benefiting as much as possible from what it brings. Beings who decide with their free will should endure the consequences of these decisions. Everyone will see the remuneration of the things they do in proportion to their will. The reason for returns and repetition of experiences due to spiritual evolvement are solely free will. However, the whole of all experiences mean new experiences and each of these feed the

Godly Super Consciousness. The laws which are valid in the universal level are indications of the principles of godly will.

Where are the soul, love, emotions and thoughts hidden in the creation process? How are these powers placed in the program and codes of evolution? The answer to these questions points out to a conscious being. If there is a state of absence in the beginning, then how has this absence transformed into being? Since the whole universe, which has faultlessly continued its evolution for billions of years from the micro cosmos to the macro cosmos with a definite purpose has not transformed into chaos, then it becomes more plausible to accept the idea of order and existence rather than coincidence and absence. There are two indispensable beliefs in Esoteric: 1- The belief in God's existence and 2- The belief in the immortality of the Soul. The existence of God is a belief acknowledged by a majority of us. The belief in God's existence is not a dogma. Although Atheism regards the existence of God as a dogma, the atheists do not have an answer besides "coincidence" to this extraordinary order of the universe. However, it is a very interesting coincidence that this mechanism operates within a perfect order from the largest to the smallest part. According to Atheism or materialism, there is no reason for existence. The process of existence is not a reason, but a natural consequence. IF consequence is mixed up with reason, then it becomes inevitable to accept the existence of a transcendent creative power. The universe has not come into existence in order to embody life. The natural conditions of the universe have created a suitable environment for the formation of life coincidentally in our world. Although it is not impossible to say that the same environment can emerge in other world, this possibility is very low.

According to the materialist point of view, knowledge should limit what the 5 senses and science can measure. The materialist scientific approach attempts to prove the absence of God through scientific. This materialist approach puts forward the view "if God's existence cannot be proved through scientific methods, then there is no God". However, the issue of the existence of God is outside the research area of materialist science. This discourse does not carry any other meaning than putting a cover on another belief, a scientific cover that there is no God. The approach "If it cannot be proven, then it does not exist" does not take a reasonable and verifiable information as its basis. In addition, regarding the unknown outside the limits of knowledge is not being scientific, but scientific. Scientific means the dogmatization of today's scientific laws and suggestions. It is in fact a model of belief. Just like fundamentalism, there is an extremely rigid and conservative point of view in scientism.

The subject of Esoteric is humans. Its purpose is to open the path to answering the basic questions in relation to the reasons of life. Everyone walks on this path alone and answer the questions by himself. A dogma or a doctrine is not suggested on this path. It is not possible for a person, who depends on a doctrine, to think within the limits of certain models and does not question his own truths to perceive Esoteric. Where suspicion and questions ends, Esoteric ends as well. The cornerstones of initiation are not to be blindly depending on any doctrine or dogma. However, this line of thought does not directly reject belief. On the contrary, it is the glorification of the beliefs of people who believe after questioning and are always ready to re-question their beliefs. Therefore, all initiation schools have always been homes of enlightened interpretation and advancement. It is not possible to think about concepts such as enlightenment, secular thought, brotherhood, universality, quality and freedom, independent from Esoteric and the process of questioning it brings along. As much as all humanity comes close with these values, the possibility of success for humanity will increase. The single characteristic of esoteric schools is that they are full of people who have thirst for reality. However, the solutions these individuals attempt to find to problems consist solely of sharing their own methods they use in their effort to search for reality.

Esoteric is the method of awakening what is inside. There are no guides, gurus or a magical formula that can take man to the targeted point to be reached. Esoteric is the philosophy of those who look for wonder in man; in the essence of man and Esoteric schools are the home of these people who are in search of this. Esoteric is not a rival to either philosophy or science. It goes parallel with then and aims at brings people to a point where they do what they do in the best possible manner. Esoteric philosophy has given a fight against those who have attempted to shape people into certain formation throughout philosophical history. The weapon of those who have imposed their truths has either been religion, or nationalism or class consciousness. These are all artificial differentiations. Humanity as a whole is above all these differentiations and it is universal. The aim of Esoteric is to teach free thought and questioning and to fight against every type of dogma.

A majority of esoteric schools have explained the secret that God, Universe and Man being identical to only those they have accepted into their circle and have never given this explanation to those who remain excluded from this circle. With the exception of Indian and Chinese schools, this method is valid from almost the whole world. According to the believers of the esoteric schools, a person who knows the secret should keep it to himself and only share it with those who have the merit to understand and share it. It has been envisioned that a majority of the public is not at a level to grab the meaning of this secret and they can reach this secret after they receive a certain education. In line with this method, which we may call elitism, individuals who are thought to reach the target of Perfect Man have always been selected among the well-educated people with good morals and the secrets belonging to the organization which are thought to help the evolvement of the individuals have only been given to those step by step after they are initiated to the organization. Through this method, it has been envisioned that, the person is to be given knowledge as much as he deserves, digests this knowledge, develops it through thinking and increases his individual evolvement with this method to reach the level of Perfect Man. The power of this method comes from the fact that it carries the teaching to upper levels by educating individuals who already have reached a certain level of advancement upper levels, benefiting from the results they reach and making use of the synergy which is created by the coming together of intellectual people. However, this method has caused only a limited number of people to be aware of the teaching and has left the majority bereaved of learning about the opportunity of evolvement envisioned by Esoteric.

People who are attempted to be gained by initiation are those who are free of all kinds of prejudice and dogma. They are people whose minds are completely enlightened, free from preconceptions and open minded enough that their point of views are able to perceive the reality of humanity. For these people, Reality is one. It is the whole of an inseparable whole. Initiation is a process. Initiates know that they can only reach reality through research. An initiate is a person who does not know, but seeks to know and is aware that he has to search. Only through this method can he reach the reality he hopes for. Initiation is a tool and no a purpose and beginning and not an end; it is a process which continues throughout life. Initiation embodies the idea of dying in past life and being born into a brand new life. Death and being reborn is the common characteristic of all esoteric schools. Man will be born into an enlightened and new life and will get to know himself in this new life. At the bottom of this ritual lays the wish to descend to the depths of one's own self by oneself and finding God in oneself.

The only way of reaching wisdom is knowing oneself. By doing this, life and the universe are understood and one may reach reality. Man is formed with the coming together of numerous elements and these elements which are independent of each other may sometimes contradict with each other. Initiation is the method of transforming this chaos inside of us into harmony. Esoteric schools bring together people who feel some kind of inadequacy, deficiency in themselves and have certain basic questions about life. The answers to these questions are sought in line with the common mind. With the reality of this common mind being superior to the individual mind, the answers humanity has found in the past are continuously brought to the table and effort is spent to find more efficient answers. By this means, it becomes possible to continuously attribute new and contemporary meanings to the used symbols. People in general look at life under certain patterns. These patterns are some belief, sometimes ideology and at other times, religion and traditional values taught during childhood. However, it is not possible to reach reality through glasses worn by prejudices.

Esoteric belief of God is a teaching that has been fictionalized based on the attempt to bring rational explanations to man's basic questions about God. The rationale used is directly opposite of rationale based on belief. While rationale based on belief prohibits the questioning of all kinds of dogma, Esoteric is a method which aims at reviewing information newly acquired by the common mind of humanity and allowing humanity to be free of all kinds of dogma. Esoteric envisions that information based on intuition should be used where the Mind and Rationality are left helpless. In other words, esoteric discourse is intuitionism which is based on the mind. According to this point of view, an individual's finding the answers to the basic questions about himself is possible by filtering the consequences he has arrived at through his intuition from his mind. While Esoteric develops an individual's intuitive powers through the initiation teaching method, it also teaches the continuous questioning of the acquired consequences and keeping these under the control of the mind. There is no place for dogma, prejudice and readymade forms. Through intuition under the control of the mind, everyone will be able to find their own reality in their conscious. Everyone will use their own free will to reach reality. If there is no free will, then individual development does not make any sense.

In Esoteric, the answer to the question 'Why' is always sought for within symbolism. In fact, Symbolism is an art of interpretation which is open for advancement and does not bring a definite judgment. Using the language of symbolism is to strengthen intuition.

Esoteric means to use the power of intuition under the leadership of the mind. The language of Symbolism is Geometric. Geometrical concepts do not have equivalents in reality. They are each idealizations which exist in our minds. However, due to these idealizations, it is a fact that intuitions gain power. Symbolism is a language which only makes use of symbols, by which people transmit the accumulated knowledge they reach through intuition to the future generations. This language is a teachable language. The schools which teach this language are initiation schools and the people who take the lessons are initiated persons. These people walk on the path of understanding the basic realities. Their purpose is to increase their capacity of seeing the esoteric facade of events. The reason for the existence of initiation is the freedom of the human mind. The most basic characteristic of esoteric is that, it does not have unchangeable principles and dogmas. The purpose is to establish the harmony and peace within the individual and thus to transform the individual into a smooth functioning part of the universal harmony. When each person understands this, they will become a part of the unique harmony of the universe and feel that they have taken their destiny into their own hands. As a consequence, man will experience the extraordinary joy of being integrated with the universe he is a part of and contribute to the process of universal development. To achieve this and to be able to awaken the already existing divine light within is possible for everyone.

On the other hand, the only way of reaching the Perfect Man is not through Initiation schools. As there are belief systems which explain their final goal as bringing up the Perfect Man, such as Brahmanism, Buddhism and Zoroastrianism, it can be observed that there are many schools within monotheistic religions, which explain their purpose as man's evolvement and believe in the creator-created duality. Kabala schools under Judaism and Sufi schools which develop under Islam are good examples of this. It can be seen that, throughout the history of mankind, numerous thinkers who are not members of any esoteric organization have reached the conclusion that the final goal within the systems of thought they have devised themselves, is to Evolve. Therefore, the only way of being Perfect Man cannot be expressed as being a member of an esoteric school. In fact, there are hundreds of schools and ways and this is an indication that a single way is not in question esoteric is a method of steering towards intellect, the good, the truth, the beautiful, tolerance, love and all other virtues and advancing on this path every single day. Esoteric means to be hard-working in taking the world towards enlightenment and fertile in the spreading of esoteric ideals to humanity. Esoteric ideals are open to everyone. People can walk on this path without being a member of any organizations that are Esoteric in origin.

Retiring into seclusion, contemplation, meditation, invocation and similar activities have always been used by the advocators of Esoteric as methods of finding God within themselves. However, the claim that to find God, one needs to leave the intellect aside and dive only to the depths of the consciousness will only allow man to strengthen a single aspect and this is not in line with esoteric understanding of 'unity'. Each individual should contemplate from time to time, relax by getting away from every day worries and listen to his inner voice; however, he should also find a way of doing this without leaving his intellect aside. Only through developing the skill of directing emotions and thought to intellect, a person may reach both spiritual and physical evolvement and may reach the desired level of

Perfection. It is almost impossible for a method which only gives importance to either the spirit, or the body to be successful. Individuals need to succeed in suing all kinds of scientific and technological development of his times to develop the spiritual advancement of himself and his environment. Only turning to consciousness cannot be accepted as a way of obtaining the true knowledge in reaching God. Another method is to teach what He has created to get to know Him. This is the scientific research method.

The intellect is a mental skill, which allows man to obtain knowledge in a verifiable manner; in other words, it allows man to obtain knowledge which he is able to explain to the others how he obtained it and to evaluate this knowledge in a manner that will make it possibly for him to obtain other knowledge. Science is the method of acquiring knowledge which has taken as the intellect as its basis. Mankind has made it possible for science to emerge within the evolutionary process, by involving the intellect in his efforts to find reality. Other methods of knowing within the scope of searching for reality are inspiration and intuition. Intellect's difference from these is that, it is systematic and provable. People who use their intellect and intuition are always able to have the opportunity of finding the true way through their personal efforts.

Rationalism claims that the human intellect and the ability to reason are the only foundations of achieving knowledge and that questions which cannot be answered through the use of intellect and reason remain outside the scope of the area of science. The area of science is limited with what we can perceive only with our senses. However, is it not true that great inventions and scientific development have been achieved by people who live with their faults, superior sides and emotions, act with their prejudices and weaknesses, dream and while they try to reconcile these with reality, involve all the facts left outside by science to their studies? Therefore, the scale for everything is humans. In other words, both reality and truth should be defined in relation to it. It is also Man who will decide what is right and what is wrong. Science is one of the most powerful tools used by individuals who use it in their search for reality. However, it is not the single tool we have to reach this goal. It is quite apparent that only science and the intellect are not sufficient in man's adventure to search for reality. Science always embodies the unknown. In the language of ancient symbolism, science is pictured as a woman witting between two columns. The woman figure is black to indicate the secret and unknown character of science. The position of her hands is totally esoteric. Her right hand looks to the sky and her left hand looks to the ground. This symbolic stance whose roots go back to Egypt is also used in Mevleviyeh. It means that, man is the mediator between the macro cosmos, the universe and the micro cosmos, the world. The union between the world and the universe is an expression of unity.

Today, the science that is taught in our universities only takes into consideration things which can only be perceived with our senses. This knowledge is indispensable for the evolution of humanity; however, it is not sufficient to reach reality on its own. To reach reality, we need to go beyond these external meanings which address our five senses and grab Inner meanings which cannot be perceived with the five senses. All the basic messages of life are not hidden in the external, but the internal. Seeing with the heart's eye, the civility of discovering the Inner is esoteric. Esoteric is not a mystic or metaphysical path.

The basic aim of esoteric is to reach inner awakening and the idea of unity. Esoteric does not only deal with science. Metaphysical subjects are also in esoteric area of interest. The concept of Metaphysical knowledge can be defined as knowledge which can be understood and perceived beyond that which is perceived with the five senses. Thoughts, emotions, vitality, spirit, intuition, God which cannot be proven with science, but whose lack is considered to unable the continuity of the existence physical universe find a common explanation in Metaphysics. Esoteric suggests that metaphysical experiences are necessary in the path to learning God as well; however these metaphysical experiences should have rational explanations. All kinds of experiences which cannot be explained through intuition and assumed to be 'spiritual' are outside esoteric area of interest. For instance, Spiritualism as some claim is not an Esoteric teaching, because its applications do not need to be based on methods which can be explained by using the intellect. In all stages of history, all Esoteric schools have preserved that period's scientific knowledge in the highest level, defended these and spent effort to develop them. However, they have not seen any harm in advancing with intuitional thoughts based on intellect, in areas where physics remained insufficient and not only with physical findings.

Quantum physics lacking determinist inferences has resulted in this scientific area to be defined as irrational by some people. These people cannot stand the idea that their world, which is used only to make observations, form connections between these observations and deduce practical applications from these, is slipping through their fingers. The corruption of rationalism seriously turns a significant part of traditional thinkers upside down. The science of the 18th and 19th centuries has resulted with the victory of a mechanic materialism, which explains everything through arrangement determined with the carious forces of interaction between the particles of miniscule and inseparable matter. The inference of this extremely primitive vision which many biologists are still trying to hang onto is the redundancy of philosophies which make a reference to the existence religions and entities without substance. However, the scientific findings of the Quantum world have caused this materialist chain to break. The location of all physical parts cannot be located and the reality that these are mathematical abstraction which can spread to all places has delivered a great blow to determinism. For instance, the speed of though which is assumed to be an abstract concept is the great speed in the universe. It is not possible to determine the speed of thought through a physical data. The speed of thought is even beyond the speed of light, which is the great physical speed known to man. Despite this, it is not possible for a materialist scientist to accept that 'thought waves' are faster than light, before it is proven that this is a documented and acknowledged scientific theory. However, this approach does not change the reality that thought is a quantum information transmission tool. In the classical meaning, Materialism is in the throes of death today. The extremely dark materialist vision, which claims that we are nothing but the meaningless and temporary results of random shocks and coherences which little substances are subject to while hanging about in space, is not a scientific vision that is valid anymore.

The teaching of Esoteric has maintained its existence and reached the present time all over the world, from the east to the west, in hundreds of different schools. Today, each of these esoteric knowledge which are the subject of a university, owe their survival and reaching the present time to these esoteric schools. A majority of these both External and Internal knowledge which make up our present civilization have reached today by being preserved in these schools. Once upon a time, as a result of spilling out of occupational secrets which were the teachings of these schools, with the Enlightenment period and becoming sciences which in turn became a branch of universities each, esoteric secrets have transformed into the commodity of all humanity. While doctors emerged over the thousands years of accumulation of knowledge of Shamans who trained their apprentices in line with the Secret Doctrine, today's chemistry has emerged from the common ground of hundreds of chemists who shared the same secret doctrine. The most known example is architecture. The secrets of construction, which has remained under the responsibility of masons for hundreds of years, are now in the interest area of universities. All occupational secret knowledge of esoteric is now the commodity of humanity. Therefore, we may say that these schools have played an important role in the history of mankind as educational institutions, which have allowed the emergence of today's civilizations, by sharing the occupational secrets within the context of all kinds of esoteric schools. Enlightenment is shaping humanity's new evolutionary stage through the increased power of information sharing.

However, the only secret the esoteric schools embody is not occupational secrets. The coming forward of the God-Universe-Man sameness which is the main expression of esoteric, its emergence just like occupational secrets, its opening up to the common use of all humanity, is the inevitable result of the 21st Century Enlightenment Age. As a result of this historical development, the word 'Esoteric', which has only been whispered to the ears of selected individuals until the last quarter of 20th century has turned into a word cried out by everyone in the first quarter of 21st century and hundred, thousands of works which explain this concept have scattered all over the world like a volcanic explosion. Esoteric means being hard-working in taking the world to light and being fertile in the spreading of esoteric ideals to humanity. Esoteric ideals are open to all humanity. People may walk on this path without being a member of institutions that are Esoteric in origin. The reason for individuals' coming together under the same roof in esoteric schools is to provide education for those selected individuals who are considered to be able to be educated in a speedy manner. Thus, brains which have thoughts that may be dispersed and lost in society, come together under roofs where they can sow their potentials, be affected and affect others, educate each other. Within these kinds of structures, they are taught how to handle inborn human weaknesses and it is possible to prevent these weaknesses from coming to the fore.

The goal of individuals who walk on the path of esoteric is to become a coherent part of the harmonious universe. In line with this thought, the goal of individuals has become to look for what is right and beautiful. When individuals see ethical values as a part of universal harmony and determine their main goals as becoming a part of this harmony, ethical rules turn into absolute values for each person. Concepts such as justice, love, compassion, benevolence are each building blocks of esoteric teaching. The glorification of these values for everyone is only possible by individuals' purging themselves of their faults.

In an environment where individual development is regarded as meaningless, it is not possible for esoteric to be effective. Individuals' purging themselves of their faults and the harmony of the universe are related to each other. Each person is responsible for transforming into a building block which reflects this perfect harmony. The individuals' inner world and the external world, the individual and society in fact mean the same thing. A person who thinks in this manner and as long as purges himself of his faults, contributes to the infallible order of the universe as well. Each individual who trains himself in this path is an expression of God on this world.

If there is an absolute thing, it is that ever since his existence, man has feet that his own mortal existence is connected to the immortal reality beyond him. Call this reality infinity, absolute knowledge, perfection or universal mind. The name given to it is God. It is this idea of God which exists in man since the beginning. It was there before the appearance of monotheistic religions and exists today in those do not believe in monotheistic religions. This God is not far from us, He is inside of us. As soon s man discovers God within, reality shows itself as a product of an incontestable ability of institution.

The most powerful took in each person is their life energy. It is this energy which determines a person's future. Both the individual's personal evolvement and humanity's general evolvement will only be possible with the increase of individuals who will spend an effort to realize a great cause of rightness, kindness and beauty. It is in each person's hand to make his own destiny and humanity's destiny better. Each individual is a part of that glorious whole called humanity. In other words, each person is a cell in a magnificent organism. The survival of the cell depends on the organism's carrying out the function it is responsible for, that is, to act in accordance with its reason of existence. Humanity as a whole is a living entity and man owes everything he own to this entity. However, the evolvement of humanity is in direct proportion to the evolvement of each person separately. For an individual to realize certain high ideals, as long as he provides power for humanity, he will not only carry himself but whole humanity to higher levels. It has always been this way and will continue to be so.

The universe has not been created and completed at once. Creation is universal and still continues. Life is made up of a continuous evolvement. Esoteric teaching members see themselves as the representatives of God in the continuity of creation. The relationship of esoteric philosophy is through the intermediary of individuals who are the basic unit of the society. The enlightenment of individuals, their achieving mental freedom, decorated with ethical values and each person turning into Perfect Man as a final result is the single goal of esoteric. Through these values of esoteric, exalted individuals should have their place in society and it will allow the society to get closer to these values as a whole and allow Esoteric values to become the values of the whole humanity. This has been the case in history and it will continue to be that way in the future.

Are the hypothesis about the universe and the structure of the world are to be left only to the monopoly of select scientists? IF Quantum mechanics extremely complicated as they claim and are they the only ones who have the capacity to grasp the structure of Quantum? No. Quantum gives answers to numerous questions humanity has sought for thousands of years and embodies the seeds of a huge cultural revolution. In fact, we may say that the interest areas of Quantum present us with the opportunity get rid of the complicated stack of semi-scientific beliefs, which are mainly the work of 19th century and take up space in the mind of contemporary man. Quantum, which is a brutal, defeatist and destructive science, has overthrown a structure, which has been tamed through development by traditional science. All Theist, Deist or Materialist systems, are face to face with the risk of losing their meanings in the face of Pantheist structure of Quantum. God can only be found inside of us and by living in all entities everywhere, He can experience the reality of substance. Laws of nature, which lay under the universe, point out to the existence of a God who has an infinite variety of ideas and has purpose.

Quantum science associates everything, matter and soul to an unknown absolution, whose existence can easily be inferred from the extraordinary appearances of new physics. Religious structures spend effort to achieve results, which can enliven their traditional structures from this concept of absolution. However, Quantum science remains closer to a God figure, from which everything emerges and everything including Himself forms a whole, rather than a father God figure that creates his own subjects. They have proven that the founding aspects of the universe have overlooked the distances which separate us from them in our view and that they are connected to each other. However, these basic data are still trying o be overlooked by a great deal of people, whether they are physicists or not. The basic philosophy of the world of science still remains as mechanical materialism. Great masses of people are uninformed about the existence of the latest scientific realities due to the influence of traditional religions. Those who are informed attempt to hide these and act as if these do not exist, with the concern that their order might be destroyed. However, regardless of the reason, history has taught us that, no one has the power to stop scientific developments. For Galileo's scientific finding related to the spinning of the world to receive acceptance from the scientific circles tens of years and for the decision to execute him for his discovery to be cancelled by the Catholic Church hundreds of years had passed, but this has never stopped the world from spinning. As a result, the common mind of humanity has always prevailed.

Esoteric has always kept the intellect in the foreground. Even in the explanation of metaphysical subjects which cannot be proven with scientific approaches, it has not accepted claims which opposed rationality and has acted extremely sensitive in terms of these claims at least to be plausible. Therefore, in esoteric teachings, it is not possible to see any statements besides metaphysical discourses which can be highly likely supported with scientific findings. For instance, Esoteric greatest claim, the philosophy of God-Universe-Man union, has reached a point where it is approved of by science. Contemporary scientific explanations such as the Quantum Theory, The Theory of Relativity, the Hologram Theory all display discoveries which verify the unity of Existence. In the same manner, the existence of four basic elements (fire, water, air, soil), which have come from thousands of years from the past and transformed Chaos into Order (Ordo Ab Chao), is defined as "Four Basic Forces" by the science of physics today. Therefore, this book is not only based on scientific data, but on intuitional senses under the leadership of the mind. For this reason, this book is not based on "the theory of civilization" which is the prerequisite of today's science; it begins with civilization which existed prior to the flood; because all remnants, findings and oral traditions which cannot be explained by science but whose existence cannot be denied, can now be expressed with "Rational" explanations, with the theory that humanity ha at least created one great civilization before the flood.

It is time for the universe to be seen as a Quantum Computer. Our own realities are constantly evolving. This book claims to be a part of this evolutionary process. When some aspects of the program used by humanity until now to define reality started to hinder, the program started to be redesigned in line with new knowledge. When it is seen that the model taken as basis is faulty, or that a part of the model is decayed, the decaying part is thrown away and the program is updated. As a result, the dimension of the perception of reality changes as well; because all kinds of updates mean that there is new information being transmitted to the system and the meaning of reality is changing.

QUANTUM AND ENTROPY

The Quantum Theory has shown that the predictions of esoteric have been scientifically proven. Things which have been expressed for thousands of years by the esoteric discourse are being proven by Quantum science one by one. It has been seen that God, Universe and Man are one, all kinds of information are shared immediately by each particle, Big Bang is in fact Divine Emergence and the events which take place in the Universe and the events which take place in the subatomic world are the same. Hermes had expressed the sameness of the macro cosmos and the micro cosmos are "Whatever is above, is the same as below". Contemporary discourses such as, the communication of electrons and tachyons mean the union of soul and matter, all show that Esoteric has been proven in the scientific level by the Quantum.

In Latin, Quantum is a compound word which may mean "How much?" and "A Lot". Again, in Latin, the word "Kuanta" means package and the word Quantum may be expressed as "Information within the Package". The Quantum Theory has first been brought forward at the beginning of 20th century for the first time by physicist Max Planck. Plank, in the hypothesis he published in 1901, stated that objects are made up of small units with carry a finite amount of energy, which vibrate like a bow. Planck, who argues that the vibrating units make up objects and these vibrating entities are atoms, has written his name in history as the father of Quantum Theory.

After Planck, Einstein claimed that light spread through photons which are small energy packages. According to Einstein, light beams are made up of photons and each photon carries energy that is in direct proportion with the frequency of light. Photon energy cannot be divided. It is not possible to break photons into pieces and divide them into smaller units. Through scientific research which take these explanations as the basis, it has been proven by the Quantum Theory that light is both particle and wave. As a result of the studies conducted by Ganow on the Quantum Theory and its derivative Standard particle model, the reality of quantum has been reached and through the analysis carried out on the micro world, the quantum reality has been carried to the macro world. The understanding of the Quantum Theory as different from all scientific reality known until that day has transcended the boundaries of science and started to influence man's daily life by turning gradually into the Quantum Philosophy. The Quantum reality reaching daily life means the speeding up of the evolvement leap in both individual sphere and the social sphere.

Classical physics, which has been used since Newton, has been used to explain the behavior of tangible and visible objects in daily life. However, after the discoveries of Planck and Einstein, it has been understood that these physics laws cannot be used to understand the sub-atomic world and thus, the formation of matter. Quantum physics, which emerged in the 1930's, has caused the classical physics laws to lose their importance. Newton physics is based on the idea that matter is a solid and rigid reality. At first, this reality seems right. However, when we use an electron microscope to look at the solid reality of matter, we will see 99& emptiness and 1% light. Quantum physics has proven that matter which seems like a solid reality is in fact made up of condensed light clusters and not solid particles. In the same manner, each atom particle inside of us contains 99% emptiness and 1% energy. The interesting point is that, mankind has first discovered how quantum mechanics operates and then just like the electron microscope has achieved the technology which proves quantum laws.

The Quantum Theory analyses the behavior of atoms and sub-atomic particles. Although its area of interest seems only like the sub-atomic world, it embodies the whole universe; because every being in the universe is made up of atoms. The particles in atoms display behavior which does not fit into any rule or formula. These strange behaviors constitute the basis of Quantum Theory. According to Quantum mechanics, heat, light and all other radiations spread in the form of small packages. Planck has discovered that, all electromagnetic radiation, including light, are not only waves which continuously spread, but that they are also a flood of very small energy packages which he named "Quanta". In line with Quantum's meaning of "knowledge within the package", these packages which embody all sorts of information have been called "Quanta". Later on, Einstein has called these light packages "Photon". Photon particle is a quanta of light, the knowledge of light. Each matter has electrons and each electron has photons. These photons preserve all information about matter within.

Photons, which are light particles discovered by Einstein, emerge as a result of the quantum leaps of light electrons. While photon is a secret energy, is transforms into action from power through electrons. Energy is transmitted in the form of quanta, or information packages. The communication of electrons with Tachyons through photons is the proof of this transformation from power to action. This subject will be dealt with further detail. This transformation of power into action is the transformation of potential energy into kinetic energy. What transforms matter from power to action is energy. The essence itself has transformed into action from power through electrons and Tachyons by energy oscillation. What makes this transformation possible is God himself. The existing things merge from the existence. Quantum is a science which verifies Pantheism.

In Quantum physics, "Planck Time" is accepted as the smallest slice of time. Planck time is the light overcomes the smallest distance. The smallest point today's science has reached in distance measurement is "Planck Length". Planck Length for the present time is the smallest unit of length which cannot be divided into two. This measurable smallest distance is -33 cm over 10. Planck length is the quantum of length. Planck length which is expressed as -43 over 10 is acknowledged as the beginning of the expansion process which emerged with the big bang. A slice of time prior to this time has no meaning in quantum physics. To ask what was there before is meaningless in terms of the Quantum Theory. In the same manner, the intensity of the smallest area in the upper most level, the intensity prior to Big Bang, is called "Planck Intensity". Planck intensity is a space that is compressed in the maximum level. Within this intensity, the whole universe has shriveled in a dimension smaller than an atom.

Within the framework of the physical explanation of Quantum, Photon is a unit of energy which carries particle characteristic. Light beam consists of photon particles arranged in tandem. However, energy flows as a whole and not intermittently. It can be understood from this habit that light also has a wave structure. Therefore, light is a structure which displays both wave and particle characteristic. Light is both matter and energy. The Quantum Theory has proved that all matter carry both wave and particle characteristics on the basis of light. Light is the most significant structure which shows that matter has both wave and particle characteristic. Light has the characteristic of spreading in emptiness. The experiments conducted on the electrons of atoms of different matter have also shown that they carry a wave structure. Broglie has applied Einstein's formula on electrons and proven that electrons act as both wave and particle just like light. As a result, it has come out in the open that all objects which make up matter act as both waves and particles.

Therefore, each existence has two different characteristics which complete each other. The first is matter which belongs to the physical world, that is, the body and the second one is energy which belongs to the metaphysical world, that is, the soul. Matter or particle flows intermittently. Due to its structure, it is limited and finite. Energy flows constantly. Due to its wave structure, it is limitless and infinite. While matter or the body dies, energy or the Soul is immortal. The immortality of the soul asserted by Esoteric is a scientific reality. The Quantum philosophy has shown that it embodies a holistic view which completes each other and does not contrast with each other, instead of opposition.

Quantum mechanics is also used in explaining objects in the universal level and events which have a great distance between them successfully, besides objects in atom dimension. Through Quantum science, it has been discovered that the ability of transmitting information between distances is inherent in the structure of the universe. As quantum information increase, our understanding of the universe changes dramatically and this causes new views on the essence of the universe to be put into words in the scientific world as well. Esoteric, which has predominantly been in the area of interest of philosophers in the past, has gradually begun to grab the interest of the science world as well. A light cluster actually means an energy bundle. When light bundle crashes with an object which is not transparent, most of its energy turns into heat. All objects in nature emit light. Since the wave length of light emitted by cold objects is longer, no one can see this light. When an object is heated, its wave length becomes shorter and the light emitted by this object can be seen. For instance, when a mineral is heated, the resulting ember is the light of that object. Energy and mass are different versions of a single thing. Energy equals mass. The maximum distance light covers in one second is 300 thousand kilometers. This shows that the speed of light has a limit and no object which has a mass can exceed this speed. In fact, it is not possible for an object with mass to even come close to the speed of light. As long as mass does not transform into pure energy, it cannot reach the speed of light. The speed of light is absolute constant. No object with mass can go faster than the speed of light. In fact, no object in the universe can even reach the speed of light. As speed increases, time slows down and that is the reason why no object can reach the speed of light. Wince reaching the speed of flight for mass means that time will stop; it is not possible in the physical universe which has four dimensions. Only when an object transforms into energy, it can come closer to the speed of light. Only Tachyons can go faster than light. These are claimed to display particle characteristics. The nature of tachyons will be dealt with in the coming parts.

When two electrons clash, photons appear. In the sub-atomic world, it is impossible to detect the actions of a photon. The more we try to measure it, the more it escapes. When we find its location, either its speed remains unknown, or when we detect its speed, its other characteristics are not able to be measured. This condition which guides the movement of photons is called the uncertainty principle. No physical power influences the movement of photons. The assumption of positivity makes the measurement of objects mandatory. However, in line with the laws of the quantum, an object's location and its movement directions cannot be measured at the same time. In order to be able to determine the exact location of objects, we should look at it as particle and to determine its movement direction and speed, we need to measure it as wave.

No matter how much a whole shattered, its energy cannot be lowered under a certain quantum limit. There is an unbreakable communication between the particles which make up the system. This communication between electrons preserves its existence no matter what the distance between them is. This scientific reality has been proven with many experiments. Maxwell and Dirac in their separate studies have shown that, particles which are applied pressure communicate with other faster than light and in an instant with each other and as a result, particles which move synchronously emerge. This ability to move synchronously takes place even if two photons are directed to two opposite directions, are polarized in the same direction, or vibrate like a pendulum. It is definite that, even particles in the furthest corner of the universe are informed about all kinds of pressure applied on any given particle. Due to this relationship and communication, a pressure to be applied on a part of the system will spread immediately to all of the parts within space and time. The Hologram Theory which will be explained further on is another proof of this. Therefore, separating an object into pieces will cause the object to assume another structure which is different from the previous one; however, nothing about the information on the particles' essence will be lost. Sub-atomic particles clash with each other only through an intermediary particle. This clash means wave Exchange and wave Exchange means communication. Scientists have presented information whose reality can be proven about the trueness of the supernatural through Quantum physics.

Energy in the science of physics is defined as "the ability to do work". Energy is evident in all particles of the universe. It is apparent in all places of the infinite and limitless are of existence at all times. In other words, God himself is Energy. Energy becoming apparent locally is an expression of existence. Energy losing this characteristic of being apparent, or missing universal energy is an expression of destruction. Energy may become apparent both as wave length and matter. A limited and fixed frequency emission points out to matter and a wide and variable frequency points out to wave. Each object carries the characteristics of being both wave and physical particle. This is a reality proven to us by the Quantum Theory.

The structure consisting of two different structures in beings is not only unique to living being. All inanimate matter also carries the characteristic of being both wave and particle. Continuity and limitlessness create each being's metaphysical dimension and finiteness and limitedness creates the physical dimension. Each being is of a complex structure which is both finite and infinite, both limited and limitless. The whole of these characteristics are each a part of the universal evolution program. The body which has a limited structure and the soul which has a limitless structure owe their existence to God. However, body disintegrates when it reaches the end of its life span and turns either into matter or energy and contributes to the universal material structure or the continuity of mobility. The soul which emerges directly from God either continues its journey of evolvement by reincarnation or after it completes it duty, goes back to the Universal Soul and feeds it with knowledge and experience.

All objects in the universe are in the form of a holistic wave which is inside a single area of energy. The experiments conducted on the Quantum Theory have shown that any kind of interference on the holistic area of energy are sufficient to collapse the wave. When any object living or inanimate is made subject to observation, an independent particle behavior can be seen. With a holistic approach to an object, seeing a similar wave structure or with a limited approach, seeing it as a particle is totally up to us. According to the Quantum Theory, matter appears to us both as particle and wave. It depends on the observer's condition at that time which one of the duality is valid. When an observation is made, the observed object displays particle, and when it is not observed, it displays wave function. They exist simultaneously and are changeable in accordance to the style of observance. Energy, matter, particle and wave cannot be located definitely. This is world where certainty does not exist. A dynamic infinity which depends on time, the present moment is lived. In Quantum Theory, the dynamic aspect of matter emerges as a result of the wave nature of particles. The Theory of Relativity has shown that the existence of matter cannot be separated from the movements the matter makes. The universe is a dynamic, vibrating, interactive, and changing and a holistic structure at the same time. The basic aspects of this dynamic universe are not its matter particles, but each a dynamic probability model.

The Quantum Theory, due to its wave function, can predict the evolution of a microphysical system at any moment. However, according to quantum physics, dealing with the future of a particle also means influencing the natural flow of that particle and as a result of this, the evolution of the particle goes under change. In other words, each step taken in the direction of evolvement causes changes in the universe and these changes come back for evolution to take place. In fact, in case an observation is made (in the interaction), the same function is reduced only to one of the probabilities it is depicted. When the new formation process is over, new probabilities where many paths are open until the new quantum observation come into question.

Quantum science has shown that everything consists of energy. Although the universe seems as if it is only made up of matter, in fact it is alive in the dimension of energy. Einstein has proven with a formula that the essence of everything is energy. With Einstein's scientific point of view which he formulated as "The essence of everything is energy, everything interacts with everything", the fixed, inanimate universe model has been destroyed and the Quantum Universe, which shows that everything is an energy which is alive, mobile and vibrating in different dimensions, has been born. God breathes out his soul to the universe and has transformed fixed energy into a living form. After the discovery of the Quantum, it has been understood that, in fact matter does not exist, everything is possible through energy and this energy formation has a meaning. All knowledge is in line with the period it emerges in. Today's science has once again proven what the esoteric discourse has been saying for thousands of years. This scientific reality of the past civilizations has been forgotten by humanity due to the historical turnabout (flood) and the reality has been brought to the light once again in our time. Yet, the advocators of Esoteric have never forgotten this reality.

In classical mathematics, 1+1=2. However, in Quantum mathematics, 1+1= Eternal 1. Each individual, besides being an existence by itself, is a part of Eternal 1, that is, God, as well. Each individual has reached its present life as a result of numerous lives. Therefore, two individuals who come together mean the togetherness of an eternal number of lives. However, besides being an existence by itself, each individual is a part of Eternal 1, God. Thus, the union of two individuals is a Godly union. Every matter in the universe is made up of molecules, every molecule is made up of atoms and atoms are made up of nuclei and electrons. It is possible to interfere with the atom nucleus and separate the atom particles. However, this process of separation does not take place in the level of a single atom; it can be seen that the existence's other parts are also subject to the same influence. Separation, disengagement from the material whole is impossible in the Quantum world. Each part is connected to the material whole with an invisible energy in the upper most level. Interference made on a part of the whole results the whole to go through the same change. In the Quantum world, everything is a whole both in the material dimension and metaphysical dimension. Nothing disengages or separates. It is not possible to take something out, to break something away from the circle. Everything is intertwined and whole. When a material interference is made, the whole is completely and immediately informed about this interference. In the Quantum universe, each action definitely creates a reaction. In the same manner, each reaction gives way for a new effect and this cycle continues until eternity. Eternity is also an expression of the uncountable One.

In the universe, each matter seems different, however, this difference and variability, does not spoil the essential characteristics of atoms. In Quantum physics, it is impossible to separate, break an atom away from the whole. Each part of matter are connected to each other with invisible ties, in the upper most level with their energies. Each atom is in communication with the other. None of the parts can be separated from the whole. There is no breaking away and separation. However, transmutation takes place. Variability penetrates to each particle. And each particle of the universe immediately is informed about this change. Distance and space can only be seen. Each change which takes place in a person, a star, a galaxy becomes known in the whole universe. Whatever the particle is, it is also the whole. In other words, the Formula "whatever the particle is, it is also the whole" Formula has been proven with Quantum science.

In the Quantum world, there is no material disengagement or separation. However, there is place or shape changing. The most basic part of matter known for the time being is Quark. It still has not been discovered what is inside a quark. Quarks and leptons, which are sub-atomic particles, interact with electron particles which carry power and give mass to the whole of the visible matter in line with the interference made. Death is changing either place or shape. Nothing dies and everything lives. Distance is a relative concept. Any change which takes place in any way causes changes to be experienced in the whole universe in accordance with the new conditions. Variability penetrates in each cell. Whatever happens in the particle, arrangements which are necessary for the Whole to adapt to that change emerge as well. Free will, metaphysical law of attraction and the law of evolvement all operate in line with this reality. Even if change takes place in personal existence, the universe automatically makes all arrangement suitable for this new condition. In the Quantum world, everything is a whole. Nothing disengages or separates.

According to Quantum physics, two existences cannot occupy the same place at the same time. No energy can contact any other energy. This means that, two existences cannot be at the same place. In line with the Quantum Theory, no being can say I am here; He is here, at the same time, simultaneously and at the same place. The expansion of this theory might either be that there is no God, or that God is the whole of everything. As Theism claims, a Creator-Created duality is impossible according to Quantum. In addition, as Atheism claims, if there is no God, then we need to provide a plausible answer to the question how the extraordinary rhythm and order of the universe happened, as this cannot be explained only as coincidence. There is an infallible order within eternity. This order is a mathematical order. There are no deviations. According to Quantum Theory, there is an orbit for each particle and its free will in return. No particle ever touches the other. Free will is free as long as it is not opposed to the orbit, or the envisaged duty. Therefore, the only satisfying explanation according to Quantum is that, everything is a part of a whole.

Quantum mechanics has shown that 99% of matter is emptiness. The name of the energy which fills this emptiness is Vacuum energy. The definition 'emptiness' is only a definition in the minds of mankind. Vacuum is not possible in any way. Even if vacuum environments which are attempted to be created in laboratories, it is a fact that there are uncountable particles. There are no places which are empty in the universe. In other words, every place is filled with the creator's eternal existence. From the Esoteric point of view, all creation is full of life and in every place, there are existences suitable for the conditions of that place. The distance between atoms is protected with this "vacuum energy". Since there is no disengagement or separation in the Quantum world, all existences are only made up of different combinations of atoms. Today's science shows that everything is made up of atoms and atomic particles. Differences and variability can be defined as the variability of the density of energy. However, this variability does not spoil the characteristics of atoms. In time, the infinity of the sub-atomic universe will be better understood. Still, the same reality's existence will not change. Just as in micro cosmos, the same laws are applicable in the macro cosmos. A majority of the universe consists of emptiness. It has been proven that this emptiness is not nothingness and that it is a sort of energy area. The characteristics of this energy defined as Dark Energy have not completely been understood yet. However, it is highly possible that Dark Energy and Vacuum Energy are the deviations of the same phenomenon.

God's existence as an organizing aspect and the arrangements made, or universal laws being both applicable in macro cosmos and micro cosmos and they are all a whole has been proven once again by Quantum. The claim that God 'does not exist' is a claim which lacks a rational proof. Since there is no explanation and proof for God's lack, there remains a single choice: God is everything. Since everything is a part of God, God is everything and exists everywhere. Thus, it is not in contradiction with Quantum science. Two existences cannot exist at the same place at the same time, but a single existence can exist everywhere at the same time. The distance seen between particle and whole, difference and variability is only in the energy dimension. The differences are caused by the density and vibrations of energy. Mankind perceives the universe as shown by his own consciousness and brain as different energies and different matter. This reality put forward by Quantum physics expresses that, the atoms which exist in the macro cosmos and the micro cosmos communicate and interact with each other. The material universe, in which humans also exist, is the union of beings which communicate and interact with each other in infinite seconds.

The material world is the world of balance. It has unchanging laws. The universal laws are the physical hands of the invisible in the visible world. Laws are tools of providing continuity and order. It has been these laws which transformed chaos into order at the beginning. Today, the same laws continue their functions to transform any kind of chaos which may take place into order. Although laws seem as if they have different rules and formulas, they all exist for a single purpose. They all act and give service within a whole and know each other. Each being has a free will as much s it is allowed. Each being continuing its existence with its own free will is a universal law. However, although each being has the capacity to act with its own free will, this free will cannot be used to break away from the orbit, or duty it is bound to. Each existence's orbit has been determined in accordance with the duty assigned to it. These orbits never get intertwined. There is a distance between all existences. There is a distance between each whole and each particle. Both in the macro and the micro level, each existence has a definite orbit. Various matter can come together and form an infinite number of different formations, however the building blocks never get intertwined or merge with each other. Each one continues to move in its own orbit with a certain distance. Each existence has been formed within the framework of a certain plan, through the coming together of energy in different frequencies.

In the universe, nothing can be repeated twice in the same manner. If an experience lived has not put forward the necessary development for evolvement, the events will repeat themselves in order to provide a chance to give the required lessons; however, the experiences lived are never the same. Each time, the formation takes place in a different manner and the reactions given are different as well. Life energy always flows by being renewed. The science of physics shows this to us. In physics, existences may stand next to each other, on top of or above each other or to the left or right of each other. However, they can never stand in an intertwined manner as a whole. Each matter which is seen as a whole is an illusion and it is only made up of various particles which attract each other. In both macro and micro worlds, although all particles attract each other, there is a certain distance between them. Therefore, no event which takes place in the universe can be the same with another. Events may be very similar in line with the universal laws, but they can never be the same. Each formation carries differences in itself.

In the universe, all events takes place between the 3rd dimension space and time, which is the fourth dimension. The 4th dimensional space-time structure which covers the whole universe is called Holistic Energy Area. Although the Holistic Energy Area constitutes all the existence as a holistic structure, it cannot be reduced to only those which exist. The Holistic Area is of a more transcendent, different and complex structure than those which exist. It is both continuous and discontinuous. It seems as if there is emptiness between objects, but this emptiness is filled with energy. Holistic Area continuously vibrates with this energy and prepares a ground for new objects to emerge. These vibrations seem disorderly and irregular. These vibrations are called Quantum Vibrations. In the holistic energy area, there are crucial points and connections which tie these points to each other, which make it possible to calculate quantum interactions numerically. Existences are the crucial point in the energy area. As the distance between them increases, the attraction power between them also increases. Therefore, we may say that each existence in fact tries to return to the holistic energy area. Electrons, which are the cause of quantum leaps, have a tendency to return to their precious positions in the shortest possible time. Just like electrons, basic particles also have a tendency to return to their natural states to continue their existences. This law is a proof of the order of the universe. On the other hand, each matter which exists is bound to perish and lose its finite existence. However, the holistic area which is an infinite energy area is ready to create new existence at any moment. The main source of all live and inanimate things which appear independent to us is the universal energy of the Holistic Energy Area.

According to Quantum Theory, man may be defined as an energy package. If man is an energy package, it will transform into an orderly, single wave when he reaches the critical point. This orderly wave will in return suddenly merge with the universe. An individual who reaches perfection merges with God. This union may be defined as the ability to reunite with a forgotten whole. All beings are separated from the infinite holistic energy area as intensified energy balls. Since both the universe and humans are parts of this holistic energy area, they have a close relationship with each other. According to the entropy principle, man has a holistic relationship with the universe. Man is never a being which has been formed coincidentally. If the constant numbers which explain the universe had been a little different, it would not be possible for atoms, living or inanimate existence, or the universe to be formed. The existence of constant numbers and their effects will be explained further on. Man, just like all other beings, is the product of these constant numbers being between certain values. All beings provide change through energy transforming on itself and make evolution possible.

Just as there is a measurable and observable physical world, there is also a metaphysical world which cannot be measured and observed. Metaphysics means "beyond physics." Metaphysics has a different area of reality which cannot be measured and observed. This inability to measure or observe it does not mean that it is not real. The human mind has the tendency to define everything and reject those which it cannot define. Metaphysics is the area of undefined things and that is the reason why people who especially deal with positive (?) sciences, who have been educated in this area and try to prove everything for years, either completely reject everything that has to do with metaphysics, to at least remain silent. However, energy itself is also undefined. Still, it is impossible to reject the existence of energy. God may also be defined as "the holistic oneness which is undefined". Within this holistic oneness, there cannot be a concept such as far or close. Each point within this area of oneness is in constant interaction with another point. For the existence of communication, the farness or closeness of a point is not important. Because area is the identical oneness are within a holistic connection. Existence units are nothing but local energy densities. Their connection with the holistic energy area is never broken. By time, some of these connections may become thinner, or gain strength by getting thicker. This change is evolution. Man is also within the same scope. Man is also a local energy density according to this definition. The only difference is man's ability to determine and change his own path, through his free will which is more in comparison to many beings due to the dense energy vibration. Man has the capacity to both develop his psychological and social structure. Experiencing the most efficient and unique experiences for evolvement is possible through man's free will. The individual soul, as long as it constructs a balanced structure within responsibility, forms a dense interaction with the holistic soul and the more it forms stronger connections, the more it becomes peaceful and balanced. One of the basic requirements of wisdom is being responsible and using this responsibility justly and appropriately.

Science prior to Quantum is founded on four basic aspects. These are objectivity, localness, positivity and reductionist assumptions. Objectivity claims that the universe consists of structures which are disconnected to each other and that it is possible to determine the characteristics of objects by isolating them from their environments. Locality foresees that the interaction between objects is only possible in limited environments and that an interaction with far distances is not possible. Positivity assumes that the universe is measurable. According to this point of view, all kinds of scientific approaches can be expressed by can be expressed by being put down as numbers. Reductionism advocates that in order to understand the structure of objects, they need to be divided into small pieces. The smallest parts of objects are the most basic building blocks of the universe. Today, scientific studies which are based on these four basic assumptions still continue. According to this point of view, biological structures can be reduced to chemical interactions and chemical structures can be reduced to physical interactions. These approaches which have a very significant part in the development of today's technique and technology are regarded as almost non-touchable taboos by the scientific circles. However, the Quantum Theory has proven that these approaches are not valid and they have been refuted.

Western science wants proof and evidence for the acceptance of a hypothesis. In order for something to be accepted as scientific, it requires for that thing to be repeatable. This scientific method anticipates that observation, testing of the observed model to be approvable. Western science is based on the assumption that only the tested and approved theories can be laws. This kind of an understanding does not have an explanation for the One who is everywhere. Since God cannot be proven scientifically, approving His existence scientifically cannot be possible. It is not possible to trust something which cannot be proven. This distrust also embodies loveless as well, because existence of love cannot be proven either. Some Western scientists believe that God is an illusion created by man's mind. Although the Quantum Theory has been proven many times and has corrupted the Deist thought structure, it is still approached with suspicion in some scientific circles and there is an attempt not to put it into words that much. If it were possible, the Quantum theory would be regarded as non-existing; however this is not scientifically possible. This kind of an approach is bound to create a civilization full of limited minds. Science cannot explain the reality of objects with the help of only physics, chemistry, biology, mathematics and geometry either. Scientific theorems which derive from binary logic need to begin with "in accordance with our current knowledge". New knowledge and experiments may show that the current knowledge is wrong at any moment. It is not possible for man to get to know himself through a binary method. Knowing oneself is only possible through Quantum.

According to the materialist point of view, the universe is a finite system. There is no basic reality underneath anything. Therefore, infinite cycle cannot be possible either. To think the contrary would be expecting infinite knowledge from a finite universe. Quantum physics has proven that there is nothingness underneath microscopic objects. It is not possible for any object to come with a priori knowledge. They have all come into existence in a random manner, depending completely on environmental developments in accordance with the laws. No object shares any kind of information with the other. The first event has taken place without any reason. It is completely coincidental. All that is taking place today are randomness which is the continuation of these first coincidental events. Once the formation of the universe has begun, a chain reaction started and these reactions gave way to rules. Then, the rest of the universe acted in accordance with these rules. Quantum physicists who have a materialist point of view claim that there is no single and basic reality independent of us and all our perception changes in accordance with our point of view. Therefore, each individual defines his own reality as a result of the observations he makes. Quantum physics shows that the behavior which appears when a photon is observed is coincidental and variable. This claim may at first glance seem right. In fact, it contains some reality in the context that there is no Single Reality independent of us. However, Materialism remains silent in terms of there being a single reality which continuously acts with us and is not independent of us; because an independent material does not remain to be defended. The advocators of materialism have gradually refrained from using this concept, because matter itself has ceased to be 'materialist' itself. Pure and rigid materialism of 19th century has totally collapsed in the face of Quantum science. Therefore, the materialists of the past prefer to define themselves as "Realists" now.

The mechanical world view which classical physics explains is very beneficial in terms of daily life and production of technology. However, limited mechanical world view in the sub-atomic area had to leave its place to the holistic organic world view. Quantum science and mystical narrations are in fact the expressions of the same thing. As we go into the depths of matter in physics and consciousness in mysticism, totally different realities appear beyond the surface appearances of daily life. The physicist acquires his knowledge from observation and experiments, while the initiated people acquire it from inner observation, experience, enlightenment and intuition. He experiences through intuition that the mind and the body are one, the whole universe is one and whole. In the world of particles, the unity and wholeness of events is valid as well. Scientific developments have given results which verify the Ancient Esoteric Discourse until today. It is highly possible for future science to prove that the process of existence still continues. Providing the mutual interaction of mystical institution and scientific analysis will make it possible for brand new paths to appear for individuals.

Cosmos means "Universe which has order". Chaos on the other hand expresses conflict. It is generally acknowledged by today's science that the universe was created as a result of a massive explosion. However, what is it that lies underneath the big bang? How has the cosmic egg which begun to spread with big bang been formed? Contemporary science is not able to provide a plausible answer to this. Monotheistic religions search for the answer to this question in the Creator. According to this point of view, there is a perfect creator above everything else and the universe has suddenly appeared in line with its wish. Meanwhile, science only puts forward various plausible hypotheses about the expansion of the universe from the moment of its formation. According to Esoteric, there is only one cosmic egg at the beginning of everything. Since space and time did not exist then, matter and energy which transformed into each other are not in question. Matter and energy did not carry quant characteristics then. The electrons taking of the permitted values turned them into quants. However, it is possible to talk about the existence of a wise and loving soul inside the cosmic egg. God breaks this cosmic egg and creates the quant world by forming billions of degrees of heat. Thus, within a very small fraction of that first second, sufficient number of electrons is created which can organize and maintain the evolutionary program of the universe.

The universe is shaped like a sphere. Galaxies are generally also shaped like spheres. The stars and the planets are shaped like spheres. When a system takes on a spherical shape, the need for energy is reduced to the minimum level. A small impact may influence a great environment. Sometimes, the combination of forces resulting from the environment guides the system. Just like these forces put into action by the spherical shape providing the maximum amount of benefit, being regard acting compliantly and orderly as a maximum amount of benefit for themselves. Order is the expression of beings' existence form. When the water mass reaches zero degree which is the sub-critical point, water molecules suddenly take on a significant order and form a crystal structure. They no longer change places by slipping. Therefore, the ice crystal is semi rigid and semi-transparent. No matter what the type of the element is, all atoms become orderly when they reach their own critical points and this order is not changeable. All this order shows that the universe is active within the framework of a certain program.

In our galaxy the Milky Way, there are about 300 billion stars. In the whole universe, it is estimated that there are 10 over 23 planets. If we assume that there is life in only 1/100 billion, then we may conclude that planets on which there is life should be tens of billions. These numbers are not only estimations. This issue will be dealt with in detail in the section about the Universe. It is shown more and more each day by science that a universal program is effective. Taking our own world as a starting point in order to determine this programming will take us to more accurate results. Just as in the universe, in our world not coincidences but a planned and programmed order is dominant. God seems as if He has squeezed the greatest secrets of life into tiny DNA-RNA molecules. It is these molecules which give the life matrix, program code and evolution message, transmit information storage of a living being from one generation to the other, solve all problems within the structure, program and administer them.

To be able to understand the universe, we need to study in-depth the relationship between Chaos and Order. In the universe, there cannot be chaos without order and vice versa. Chaos theory explains the essence of uncertainty and brings a different interpretation about life and death. Man, who tries to understand the world and the universe within the framework of the principle of causality, has the tendency to call everything he does not know the reason for, events which he cannot find answers for with his mind, 'coincidence' and forget about them. Believing in coincidences is a natural result of a local and reductionist point of view. The more man looks at events from a wide perspective and perceives the holistic unity in the universe and stays away from reductionist approach in his interpretations, there is more of a chance that he will reach the realities behind those coincidences. The most basic finding mankind has ever made until now is the reality that there is nothing that does not change in nature. Everything is in a constant state of change. The only thing that does not change is change itself. Everything continuously dies and is replaced by new things. Although change seems as if it is constantly giving way for the formation of new structures, there is actually a repetition. This is not a one-to-one repetition. It is rather a similitude and a relatively more advanced version of the previous. This advancement is an expression of evolvement. Differentiation at first is slow and increases gradually, but the building block is always similar. Variety is born out of differentiation. If this development is evaluated over time, we may talk about the creation of species and the transformation of simple structures into gradually complex structures. At the beginning stage of life, it is possible that all animal and plant species were derived from a single being, because the same DNA structure is seen in all living beings.

The materialist scientific approach states that, the emergence of the human species as a result of the evolutionary process which took place in the world can be completely coincidental. According to this point of view, even if life is possible in the universe, due to similar conditions to the world being present in other planets, it is impossible. Therefore, it seems very unlikely that the other living beings in the universe have similar conditions and these living beings to be similar to humans. However, it should not be forgotten that, the universal intelligence has a certain program and it may well be possible for species in certain stages in the universe to reach similar results within certain durations. Of course, there may be differences, but it is inevitable that there may be similarities as well. According to the materialist point of view, the probability of other humans to be in the universe is not even one in billions. However, the esoteric point of view states that a different species of humans might have been present in the universe; because God has an evolutionary program which has definite results and perfect experiments can only be experienced through perfect living beings. Since humans are the most evolved living beings are humans, the same plan may be repeated under different conditions. The evolution theory which has been advocated by esoteric for thousands of years has been put forward in the scientific world for the first time by Darwin in 1859 and made into a book.

While Western thinkers asserted various theories about the universe and humans, they have always sought ways of separating humans from Godly completeness. The leading person who shaped this kind of Western thought is Kant. In Kant's moral philosophy, it is advocated that belief in God and the concept of immortality of the soul are a result of moral values inoculated to man externally. Kant wishes to see the relationship between the general laws of nature and intelligence and the mind in order to grasp the reality. However, this can only be valid for the expression of a materialist reality. According to this point of view, every reality needs to be proven with experience. Russel, who had the same views, stated that the concepts of oneness and plurality do not agree and that individuals are completely independent beings. Meanwhile, Spinoza and Hegel have tried to bring together the Deist and Pantheist view of self. Spinoza's point of view will be analyzed further on. Hegel, who suggested that opposing views and theories should be unified, has called this approach "dialectic". According to Hegel, the synthesis to result from the unification of thesis and anti-thesis means the formation of absolute identity through philosophy. However, first Nietzsche, then Einstein have opposed to the Deist philosophers' concept of the absolute. Einstein theory of relativity has dealt the last blow to this concept and has opened the path for the Quantum theory. Scientific developments have shown us that Euclidean geometry and Newton physics can only be applied to the material events in our environment. There is a need for new laws in the astronomical and sub-atomic level. Matter loses its mass under certain conditions and transforms into energy. Or energy transforms into matter under certain conditions and gains mass. What we call matter is in fact a type of frozen energy. Then, not diversity, but completeness is in question.

The most leading characteristic of man is the fact that he can think. Thinking is an activity which is based on the brain's comparison and generalization mechanisms. In order to be able to do comparisons, at least two existences are required. Man is made up of the body and soul pair. However, the explanation of the concept of soul through rationality is very difficult. Since, dual rationality always compared two objects or concepts, it is distinction rationality. Since the soul is not placed anywhere in this rationality of distinction, it is not possible to comprehend it. Descartes claims that we need to trust pure rationality, mathematics and geometry which are independent from the senses. It is possible to see the same approach with Freud. Therefore, Freud's "soul" is a totally Deist soul. It is only a function of the brain. In positive sciences and technological development which followed that adopted this point of view, although great developments have been achieved, the human elements have completely been ignored. It is the Quantum theory which replaces man in science. Quantum has shown that the observer cannot be separated from the observed and material development which lacks the human element is not able to enlighten individuals. Mathematical theories and experimental methods are far from informing man about the existing things. Things which exist in the universe right t this moment are constantly affected from those which exist in other places. Those which exist here and now, form a whole with the ones which exist in a different place.

The propelling power behind all changes in the physical universe is energy. Energy is the most important characteristic energy has. Energy creates all the changes in the universe. Energy flows from one place and one object to another and constantly changes. According to Western science, the amount of universal energy is fixed. Although the amount of energy as a whole is fixed, it has not been distributed to all points of the universe equally. What causes the changes is the mobility caused as a result of equalizing this different distribution of energy. This mobility, which can also be defined as passing from chaos to order, takes place by itself. This change always takes place from different distribution of energy to equal distribution of energy. When energy distribution is equalized in the universe, changes will stop. Equalization of energy distribution by the universe also means the stopping of expansion. Some scientists suggest that this stopping means the end of the universe. Entropy is the amount of irregularity which is the opposite of order or which takes the shape of energy. Entropy expresses the order in energy distribution. According to the 3rd law of thermodynamics, all energy turns into absolute zero temperature (-273 C) turns into heat. This is the essence of Entropy. The 3rd law of thermodynamics states that as the temperature of a system starts falling down to absolute zero. That system's entropy will also get closer to zero. As entropy increases, the amount of preserved energy decreases and energy distribution is equalized. The more the energy is distributed equally, the higher the Entropy is. The equalization of energy at absolute zero is a sign of immobility and as a result death. The lower the Entropy, the more different energy distribution is. This point of view foresees that entropy will never decrease and that it will increase by time. However, the temperature is still -270 C and it is fixed at every point of the universe. The temperature staying fixed despite the expansion of the universe brings to the mind that a different development can also be possible. According to Esoteric point of view, man is the micro cosmos and the universe is the macro cosmos. If the universe and man are the same, then expansion will stop when energy is equalized. The stopping of universal expansion does not necessarily mean the death of the universe. Man grows until a certain point in accordance with the energy he gets, however his growth stops after some time. The stopping of growth is not death. It is well possible for the expansion of the universe to stop at a certain point and continue its existence for billions of years, preserving the same size.

The 2nd Law of Thermodynamics states that, matter which is left on its own devices will gradually reach the highest level of chaos or disorder. According to this claim, entropy constantly increases. If we take this explanation as true, then the concept of order which is the basis of mechanistic thought is artificial. Even if temporary order is achieved by force, this is opposed to the basic tendency in nature. Nature should stir towards absolute anarchy. This state of absolute anarchy is Chaos.

Quantum mechanics has proven that observing an event changes the nature of that event. There is no accuracy in quantum mechanics, there are only probabilities. The observer may arrive at different results using different observation methods. This reality has been disregarded for a long time. Scientists have rejected studies which have not been based on definite mathematical formulas as a series of linear relationships by being divided. Einstein has rejected the uncertainty aspect of Quantum mechanics by saying "God does not throw dice". God surely does not throw dice. There are rules for passing from chaos to order. However, these rules are not linear. Then, they must be non-linear.

The universe has begun at a Point of Singularity which cannot be explained. Prior to the big bang, which seems to be expressing a total chaos, first the sub-atomic particles and then the atoms have been formed. Atoms evolved into gas clouds, gas clouds evolved into stars, stars evolved into solar systems and solar systems evolved into galaxies. In the continuation of evolution, crystals, molecules and living organisms have appeared. It is seen that in our universe, being at a higher level are always developing. In nature, there is a continuous flow from chaos to order and not from order to chaos as Thermodynamics claims.

The 1st Law of thermodynamics states that energy can neither be created from scratch, nor be destroyed. According to this law, the amount of energy in a system is fixed and unchangeable. Energy can only change from one shape into another. Western science states just as in the case of amount of energy that, not a single atom has been lost or reproduced since the formation of the universe and every atom's age is the same as the universe's age. The same scientific sources also state that, some matter is sucked by black holes. A scientific explanation as to what happens to this matter which disappear in black holes has not been found yet. These sucked matters are said to be added once again to the material whole at another point of the universe. Some scientists argue that matter which is sucked by black holes in our universe may appear in another parallel universe. However, this prediction is completely opposed to Lavoisier's Law of Conservation of Matter, which anticipates that matter which exists in our universe cannot be destroyed, or new matter cannot be created. Lavoisier's law is a view put forward for the understanding of the fixed universe. However, the universe is not fixed. Science tells us that the universe expands. However, Entropy does not increase and the amount of dark matter at very point in the universe and the temperature remain fixed. Despite this expansion, the order not being destroyed brings to the mind the question whether there are some new additions from the points of the universe which we are not able to perceive right now. The Deist creation theory envisions that the universe has been created at the beginning and God has not made an addition to it later on. While the Esoteric discourse advocates the view that, emergence is infinite and it continues through returns to God and new emergences from God until eternity.

In 1789, Lavoisier has formulated the Law of Conservation of Matter, which asserts that matter which exists in the universe cannot be destroyed, or new matter cannot be created. This law is a view put forward for the understanding of the fixed universe. However, it has been discovered that the universe is not fixed, as it constantly expands. Contemporary science tells us that the universe expands. Despite this discovery, the view that Lavoisier's law is still valid is the general acknowledgement of the scientific circles. Thermodynamics laws are predictions which have been shaped in line with this point of view as well.

Within the framework of Lavoisier's law, 19th century science suggests in line with its own Deist approach that, the creation process has been completed with the big bang 14 billion years ago and all matter in the universe has been created during this event. After the big bang, not a single atom has been added to the universe. All matter and even energy are 14 billion years old and they only experience constant transformation among themselves. Lavoisier's law claims that not a single electron has been added later on. Then, how can we determine the age of an electron? In which laboratory and through which experiment has the age of an electron been identified? As determined scientifically, since the universe constantly expands, do the matter within the universe gradually het thinner? The thermodynamic laws claim this is so.

Getting thinner will cause entropy to increase and the result will be a great tear. However, this is not the case. No matter how much the universe expands, entropy remains fixed. In addition, it is a scientific assumption that there might be a continuous matter flow from the white holes which are thought to be located at the borders of the universe to galaxies which are newly being formed. Where do these new matter come from? Are the matter sucked by black holes transferred from there to new galaxies, or are new matter created?

Scotch thinker David Hume rejected the acceptance of some scientific claims put forward in the 18th century as unmistakable. According to the Cartesian point of view, a theory put forward can only be deserted if there is a scientific method of falsifying it and if an experiment to rule out this theory cannot be performed, then the theory remains valid. No matter how rational this new theory is, it is not valid, because it cannot be tested. It is not important at all that the generally accepted theory is tested or not. The best example to this point of view is the Lavoisier Law. According to his Deist point of view, all matter and energy in the universe have been created at that first moment of creation and it is out of question that a new addition be made to energy or matter from then on. After this theorem was put forward, it has been proven that matter transform into energy and even energy transforms into matter. In return, advocators of this theory stated that energy can change form, but its amount can never change. When the Lavoisier Law was put forward, while the belief that the created universe is fixed and deterministic, today it has been proven that the universe has expanded after big bang from a single point and continues to expand even now. There is not a single answer to how all matter and energy fit to a single point of a huge universe. Still, Lavoisier's law is valid today. Because it has been proven? No! Is there a method which can prove that no new matter or energy entered the universe? No! However, there is no method which can prove otherwise either. Therefore, this law which has been generally accepted is still valid.

Lavoisier claims that, no new matter increase takes place in the universe. According to the 1st Law of Thermodynamics, no matter which processes and experiences are lived in the universe, the total energy is preserved and it is fixed. As energy cannot be created from scratch, it cannot be destroyed either. It only changes from one form into another. For instance, a sun's dying does not mean that its energy is destroyed. This energy is spread to the universe under a different form. Then, would this inference be right? Is there a method or mechanism which can measure the total energy amount of the universe and determine that it does not change at all? If the Lavoisier law is valid, this means that the density of the universe which constantly expands is continuously decreasing. This in turn means that, the density of the universe will decrease, as celestial bodies increase their speed of escape in outer space. However, it is just the opposite. The density of the universe does not change at any point. The 1st law of thermodynamics states that just like energy, matter cannot be created from scratch or destroyed. According to this law, the amount of energy in a system is fixed and unchanging. However, black holes whose existence has been proven until now suck both matter and energy totally inside themselves. What happens to these matter and energy whose existence within the system ends definitely is not known. In the same manner, in quasars which are located at the expansion borders of the universe, it has been determined that matter and energy whose origins are not known are constantly emanated. The source of these matter and energy is not known either.

Entropy increases in accordance with mass. Therefore, the entropy of an object with bigger mass will be denser. Holographic principle has shown that entropy is related to the surface area surrounding the mass. If the information within the mass is measured with entropy, it means that the entropy increase is both affecting the mass gravitation and Quantum mechanics. In other words, the answer to the theory that everything may be found in the increase of entropy which both affects mass gravity and Quantum mechanics. According to Quantum mechanics, a system's entropy is finite. However, it is always possible to produce more entropy through randomness. Then, where does this entropy go? The answer is that entropy can only increase as long as the system's surface area expands. In that case, the mass gravity will also increase. The reality that Quantum entropy is proportional to area can be tested with the 2st law of thermodynamics, which claims that energy is protected and it can be observed whether the system's energy increases or not with the newly added information. IF the law loses its validity in case of mew information flow, it means that there will e a constant increase in energy along with an increase in information in the universe.

In order to measure information within a system, we need to look at the entropy of that system. Since the measurement of chaos in the system is entropy, then the more there is uncertainty, the greater the entropy is. For instance, water's entropy is greater that ice's entropy; because the water molecules in ice are lined with more order depending on their condition in water. Ice's entropy is less dense in comparison to water. Since disorder is caused by the increase of entropy, it means that the entropy of water vapor is greater than the entropy of water. The 2nd Law of Thermodynamics states that matter left on its own ascends to the highest level of chaos or disorder by time. Entropy (Chaos) constantly increases. According to this law, the concept of order is artificial. Even if temporary order periods are achieved by force, this is in opposition to the basic tendency in nature. Nature has to proceed towards absolute anarchy. This absolute anarchy state is Chaos. The least orderly energy is heat and one day, all energy will be heat and this means the end of the universe. This prediction may be valid for a closed system, however in nature, a flow from chaos to order is observed contrary to thermodynamics, which claims that the flow is from order to chaos. Even if it seems as if there is chaos within a system for some time, this period always ends with order.

Each system's entropy is proportionate with that system's surface area. This phenomenon is known as the Holographic Principle, because each electron constantly shares its information due to a requirement of the holographic structure. The total information of a system is determined by the calculation of mutual quantum information of electrons. As you can calculate the total number of bites in the universe by using this Holographic principle, you can also calculate the basic information processing capacity it has at the moment. In the light of this information, is it possible to produce a computer which has quantum memory? Even if it is possible in theory, it seems very difficult to produce a Quantum computer. The attempt to produce a Quantum computer is the struggle given against entropy. If we consider that entropy is the measurement which reflects the degree of uncertainty of entropy within a system, since the computer is a closed system, it means that entropy, or uncertainty will constantly increase within the framework of the 2nd Law of Thermodynamics. The problem is how the increase of entropy can be prevented within a closed system and most unwanted situation for a computer is the uncertainty of the results to be achieved. This problem seems solvable only through the quantum computer's open system, for instance the configuration of it over the Internet web. Maybe in this manner, whole humanity may have the chance to benefit from the opportunities of a super quantum computer and Access all kinds of information immediately.

The 2nd Law of Thermodynamics states that, all physical systems have the tendency to inevitably go towards their own maximum disorder and when a system reaches this maximum disorder, it arrives at its exhaustion as well. In other words, life, which is one of the strongest processes in the universe, will inevitably end and death will take place. According to this law, the universe is a system as well and sooner or later, thermal death is inevitable. On the other hand, life shows us that it can reproduce until eternity and the structures which seem dead are used to construct new structures. The use of the old and dead in the foundation of the new means a kind of rebirth. In this case, is the universe is going to die and be completely destroyed, or will a new one appear with the materials at hand? According to the 1st Law of Thermodynamics, if a total destruction is not possible, what is the answer?

In order to find this answer, we need to have a look at the thermal temperature of the system. The closest macro system which we can check whether its entropy, or thermal temperature constantly increases or not, is our own world. We know the stages our world has gone through almost from the date it has been formed. The technology we have has the capacity to measure the thermal temperature changes the world has gone through from millions of years ago. Periodic heating up or cooling of the world are in question, however there are no data that it has been continuously been heating up in accordance with the 2nd Law of Thermodynamics. The sphere has been extraordinarily not for the last 10 thousand years, but the reason is not the Thermodynamics Law, it is that the Flood, which has been a global disaster, which the science world does not ever accept. In the recent years, our world seems relatively to be heating up, however once again, the reason is not the world's own natural dynamics, us human's negative interferences to nature. Shortly, our world does not seem to fit the 2nd Law of Thermodynamics just like the other planets.

In line with the 2nd Law of Thermodynamics, if the increase of entropy is caused by an increase in knowledge, then the higher the entropy of the system, the more information it carries. A direct proportion has been determined between the entropy within a closed system and the system's size. If we apply this discovery to the universal dimension, then as information, or entropy increases in the universe, the universe expands and does not die by keeping its temperature fixed through this system. Therefore, entropy increases not in mass but as surface area and the evolution of the universe continues until eternity. Is it possible to prove the 2nd Law of Thermodynamics? Entropy is the 2nd Law's mathematical formula. Since entropy quantifies a system's randomness, it is never questioned in the world of science. Scientists say that a closed system's entropy will constantly increase. This seems right for closed systems of macroscopic scale which are carried out in laboratory experiments. However, is the universe a closed system? Since the universe expands continuously, how can it be stated that this system is closed? Moreover, the universe's entropy never increases and always remains the same. If each building block of the universe embodies all of the information within as the hologram theory shows, then the universe is made up of numerous quantum computers. If not for the 2nd Law of Thermodynamics, it is verified in the sense that information constantly increases. Each experience is recorded in the universal information storage as new acquisitions. Although we may not know whether we will know everything one day or not, this will never cause us to stand back from the attempt to learn what goes on which we may get to know through our current comprehension capacity.

On the other hand, the 2nd Law of Thermodynamics does not work in biology. The common characteristic of all living beings is about achieving the maximum benefit with the least possible energy. All living beings are evolved towards order, not disorder. Life spends effort in the name of producing order. Maybe it increases the entropy of its environment in this attempt; however it also spends constant effort to bring its entropy to the lowest level. According to the 2nd Law of Thermodynamics, it is not possible to create an order from chaos. The validity of this law has only been proven in closed macroscopic systems which cannot interact with other systems. However, no being is a closed system. Every being definitely has interaction with its surroundings. They exchange energy and matter. The world, which constantly takes energy from the sun and the rest of the universe, is not a closed system either. Order is always in the foreground in living systems. While order is being formed, chaos is always reduced to minimum. In other words, Chaos (entropy) is excluded. Both energy and information is needed for order. Lehninger has calculated that to be able to reduce chaos in the 1 kcal/mole scale, information as much as a 23 zero digit number is required. Thus, it has been shown that energy and information may transform into each other. Then, the building blocks of the universe are information besides mater and energy. Natural selection always works on the side of organisms which minimize their entropy. Those who cannot do this die. Therefore, in living systems, the 2nd Law of Thermodynamics is not valid. An evolutionary system, which is based on order, is the single theory we may explain for the chaos of life around us.

German thinker Frederich Nietzsche has based all of his philosophy on the 2nd Law of Thermodynamics, on the understanding that everything will gradually turn into chaos. Life is meaningless and is bound to be destroyed sooner or later. Life's evolutionary process is only an illusion. Nietzsche, who has not been able to tolerate his own theory which is totally a product of materialism, has spent the last 11 years of his life in a mental hospital, in resentment and loneliness. However, life shows us that, when a system's inner order increases, beauty emerges within balance and harmony. Balance, harmony and secret symmetry are the indispensable requirements of beauty. Beauty shows that knowledge exists in everything in nature either in a hidden, or an open manner. The cyclical mobility in all levels in the universe allows the preservation of energy and linear momentum. The repeated motions are directly related with the objects' inner symmetry and balance. In all systems which contain symmetry and order, both knowledge and beauty are found together. In orderly formation, there is the rational mind, intuition and emotion in beauty. According to the "Chaos Theory" put forward by Edward Lorenz, the chaos in the universe is actually the expression of a certain order. A permanent chaos or a permanent order is not in question. There is chaos in each moment, a secret order in all disorder and a fixed law in all variables. Unity is achieved when chaos reached balance. In Chaos Theory, it is stated that even the smallest changes in a system's beginning will trigger each other and this will give way to great and unpredictable results. This discourse is defined as the "Butterfly Effect".

According to the 3rd Law of Thermodynamics, all energy turns into heat in absolute zero temperature (-273 C). This is the fundamental aspect of entropy. The 3rd of Law of Thermodynamics says that as the temperature of a system decreases towards absolute zero, that system's entropy will also come closer to zero. The equalization of energy in absolute zero is an indication of inaction and as a result, death. This point of view envisions that entropy (disarray) will never cease and that it is always increase by time. The lower entropy is the more different the distribution of energy will be. However, Entropy does not increase and the amount of dark matter in every point of the universe, as well as the temperature, remains fixed. The temperature in all the space is currently -270 C and is fixed in every point of the universe. While – 273 means the stopping of all movement and absolute death of the universe, -270 C means the sustainment of the existence of the most ideal conditions for existence to continue. Then, why doesn't the entropy of the universe increase? Is there a mechanism to lower, or at least keep entropy stable? What is the factor which decreases the tendency of disarray?

The laws of thermodynamics say that the multiplication of a system's entropy with the system's temperature indicates the total amount of energy in that system. Since the temperature of the universe remains fixed, we may say that the energy of the system remains fixed as well. However, if the increasing of the volume of information means the increasing of entropy, it means that the continuous growth of the universe, as a result of the multiplication of the increasing information (entropy) with the fixed temperature will indicate the amount of energy of the universe. In that case, as a result of the growth of the universe, the total amount of energy is continuously increasing. This continuous increase of energy is only possible with the sustenance of new energy from the source. This hypothesis is in line with the claims of Esoteric, which advocated that Godly emanation (outburst) continues eternally.

The galaxy groups continuously getting removed from each other in the universe shows that universal expansion is in fact the expansion of the space vacuum between these galaxy clusters. In 1965, Penzias and Wilson have determined that the wave temperature of the microwave radiation of space vacuum is 2.7 Kelvin, or 270.3 C. This temperature is fixed for all space vacuum and = Kelvin, which means absolute temperature and death, is 2.7 C hotter than – 273 C. All motion in the universe is possible due to this 2.7 C degree heat. The temperature at no point in the universe falling down to the absolute 0 value, which means absolute death, is another proof of the existence of a magnificent plan.

Lavoisier's laws and the Laws of Thermodynamics are the products of a period during which the Deist thought hit the ceiling and they are completely constructed to support the Deist discourse. The same understanding is still being defended by a majority of scientific circles in the West. What is the Deist discourse? "There is a Creator. During creation (Big Bang), all its functioning has been arranged, its conditions and environment been prepared, its laws laid down and drawn aside. It under no condition interferes with the operation". There is no answer to the question, what has happened to this God after the act of creation? In the same manner, there is no answer to the question, whether this creation has been made out of nothing, or whether God's unique material has been used. The Lavoisier Law says that "Existing matter and energy are not destroyed. They only change shape. Addition of new matter or energy is not in question." Deism says "All matter and energy has been created at the beginning. In the coming process, the addition of new matter or energy is not in question." The adoption of this world view by the enlightened scientists who are opposed to Theism is a natural process. However, there is no difference between their putting their shoulder this belief and the point of view of those who defend Theism. How can it be scientifically proven that new matter or energy is never added to the universe, or that extinction is not possible? If there is no addition, how can entropy's fixedness be explained despite the magnificent universal expansion? Is it not true that quantum physics has been discerningly rejected by the scientific circles because it points out to the possibility of the existence of a supreme being? Aren't there still hundreds of scientists spending effort to reverse the realities of Quantum science? Don't they hide behind the discourse "It is not possible to understand the functioning of Quantum" as much as they cannot succeed? According to Esoteric (Pantheism), emanation (outburst) is a process which will continue until eternity. Both in the material (physical) dimension and the spiritual (metaphysical) dimension, emanation still continues. The emanation in the white holes whose existence has been determined on the universe's expansion boundaries verifies this point of view.

Shortly, all these laws which are based on the scientific results of 150 years ago need to be reviewed in the light of current scientific data. Blindly being stuck with "Scientific Laws" which have had general recognition even if they do not overlap with new scientific findings is not different from being stuck in religious dogma. This approach is not "Scientific", but "Scientism".

Energy shows an object's skill in performing an action. Heat, movement, light, sound, electricity, magnetism, radioactivity, chemical changes and similar things are all different forms of energy. A type of energy can turn into another type of energy. The total amount of energy within the closed system envisioned by Western science is fixed. This is called the Law of Conservation of Energy. While some objects gain energy, some other may lose energy. It is assumed that the amount of energy in the universe will always remain the same, due to the idea that the universe is a closed system. However, the continuous growth of the universe indicated that the system is not closed and that it is an open one. Energy has been created with the Big Bang. Matter turns into energy and energy turns into matter, however according to the laws of conservation of energy, the amount is fixed. Any kind of Godly emanation or increase in matter or energy in the universe after the Big Ban is not in question. While this can be accepted only for the material world, or physical universe, it is not valid for the immaterial world, or the spiritual universe. Emanation or spiritual outburst in the metaphysical world continues endlessly.

The continuous interaction of speed and forces transforms into an infinite motion. Motion is an expression of universal life. In action means the end of interaction and death. Matter is in a continuous state of interaction and change. This interaction points out to the continuity of material life. When man dies, his body changes, but life does not end. Both in physical and spiritual terms death is not in question. The purpose of both the material and the spiritual world is to increase divine knowledge. This continuous change besides immortality creates the most ideal environment for knowledge to increase. Universal balance, the constancy of divine laws, the responsibilities brought by these laws on humankind is the mission to search for reality. Both in the world and the universe, all kinds of action create adverse reaction. Action and adverse reaction create motion and harmony in return. Balance is a part of the soul, as much as it is a part of the material world. The force which pushes a planet away from the Sun and pulls it are the same.

God creates everything by predicating them on a reason. Achieving universal balance is only possible with the creation of everything with their opposites. In the beginning, matter and antimatter appeared and the universal momentum has been created through the collision of two opposing forces. If our universe is made up of matter right now, then where has antimatter gone? Where is the antimatter of the universe? Is an anti-universe in question? The argument that there might be an anti-universe has gained strength with the discovery of the antimatter. The material universe may be considered to continue its existence in balance as a result of this. The dialectical law says that things do not transform into each other but their opposites and evolve in this manner. If an evolution is in question, then it is because everything embodies its opposite within itself. According to dialectics, everything is a union of opposites. Even the existence of evil is necessary for good to be able to emerge.

Everything in the universe is based on a balance of the opposites. If there is no opposition, there is no existence, motion and continuum. If there are no opposites, there is no life or death either. Everything has been created in pairs and as opposites. However, these oppositions do not exist for conflict, fights and chaos, but to complete each other and define itself in accordance with its other. All objects, facts, concepts and events consist of two opposing sides without fail in nature, society and human consciousness. Oppositions are the requirement for each other to exist. One of the oppositions cannot exist single on its own without its other. They can only exist together. Therefore, oppositions require each other. There is an inextricable dependency between then. Each of the oppositions attempt to establish superiority on the other. As a result of this struggle, it is possible to talk about a continuous evolvement for the sides. The oppositions remove each other's imperfections, smooth away extremeness within this discipline and enter a supplementary harmony and discipline of balance. Shortly, we may say that God is a being who embodies, reconciles all oppositions inside and transforms these oppositions into a great harmony.

The most universal symbol of oppositions is Yin-Yang. Water and fire are its symbols. Water and fire are the first two of the four basic elements which emerged as a result of the Big Bang. Therefore, the existence of oppositions has been in question even right at the beginning of the universe. The four main forces will be dealt with in detail in the coming chapters. The Yin-Yang theory claims that everything has two opposing characteristics called yin and yang. In addition, there is yang in each yin and yin in each yang. Yin and yang reflect the opposites' ability to keep each other under control. It is not possible for one of them to sustain its existence without the other. The two of them form a perfect circle together. There is a unity and wholeness within all changes and oppositions in nature.

All objects observed in nature have been sustaining a never deviating order for billions of years through the orbits they follow, force of gravity, their revolving around themselves, births, death and rebirths. The materialist thought, which claims that this order does not continue due to a universal intelligence and that events develop as a result of coincidences, is left helpless in explaining the infallible and unchanging conditions of billions of years of order. Intelligence constantly puts itself forward both in the macro and the micro level through the same, unchanging conditions.

THE BIG BANG – QUANTUM RELATIONSHIP

Before we start analyzing the universe, we need to scrutinize the historical process of scientific developments until the big bang theory which explains the creation of the universe. The Ancient Cosmology notion that the universe is made up of 7 layers with the world in its center has been questioned for the first time by Copernicus after 2 thousand years. Copernicus and ten Galilee have been the first scientists who expressed that the world is not the center of the universe. German philosopher Kant claimed that questions such as "How is the geometry of the universe?", "Does the universe have a beginning and an end?" are metaphysical questions which can never be answered and that human intelligence needs to give up trying to answer these. However, with the beginning of the Enlightenment Period, in the light of observation, experiment and accumulation of knowledge, there arose the need to reinterpret the laws of the earth and the heavens.

Including Newton, through the philosophers and scientists of the Enlightenment Period, dogmas began to leave their place more and more into scientific facts. Until that period, while religion did not object to interfering with problems only science can solve, with the beginning of the Enlightenment Period, science laid its hands on areas which religion monopolized and changed the history of humanity dramatically. The power of science comes from the fact that it has the capacity to continuously develop by constantly creating problems and attempting to solve these. Otherwise it would not be any different from religious beliefs which do not evolve at all, which contain frozen and rigid rules.

Newton discovered Gravitation, founded optics, discovered the laws of optics and motion and made science a part of mathematics. Newton, who proved that all objects pull each other, has shown the mathematical proofs of theories and created the classical science of physics. Newton, who is the first person ever to suggest the theory of gravitation, believed that gravity and centrifugal force balance each other. Laws are valid both on earth and in the heavens. Newton has carried the concept of infinite space from the metaphysical plane to the scientific plane with the publication of his work titled *"The Principia: Mathematical Principles of Natural Philosophy*, in 1687.

In the 19th century, giant steps have been taken in industry and science. The term energy has first been used by Young, in 1807. Light's travelling in waves is known since the experiments Young has done in 1803. However, it was Einstein who proved that light also travels in the form of photon particles a century later. In 1864, Maxwell combined magnetic force and electrical force and proved that electrical waves travel with the speed of light and that light is actually an electromagnetic wave. In 1888, Hertz discovered radio waves and that these travel with the speed of light.

The 20th century is the century of geniuses. Together with Einstein, the classical Newton physics which had been valid in the worldly dimensions left it place to the Einstein physics, valid in the universal dimension. Within the framework of the Newton paradigm, reaching the speed of light, or even exceeding it is possible theoretically. In Newton physics, space and time are two absolute concepts which are independent of each other. Einstein is the person who has questioned Newton physics. The Theory of Relativity developed by Einstein has put into place a 4 dimensional space-time concept, three being space and one being tine, instead of these two independent concepts. While the weight of mass is fixed in classical physics, it has been shown by the Theory of Relativity that the weight of mass increases with speed. All matter has a mass. On object can never be without mass. Mass is fixed and cannot change with the force of gravity. There are only two things which have zero mass: Photons and Gravitons.

Einstein's famous correlation formula which shows that energy is equal to mass is $E = mc2$. The formula is Energy = mass X speed of light square. As an object comes closer to the speed of light, its mass comes closer to an infinity which can never be calculated. The meaning of this in physics is that, an object can never reach the speed of light. Through this Formula, it has been determined that the energy of 1 gram of mass is 21,5 billion kcal. In other words, if it were possible to transform the mass of 1 gram of matter into pure energy, the whole world's energy need can be met for 24 thousand years. These kinds of energy transformations are not possible with the current technology and are bound to remain only in theory. With the Theory of General Relativity, a new dimension has also been brought to the concept of force of gravity that is effective from afar in Newton's theory. In classical physics, there are two definitions of mass: gravitational mass and inertial mass. With Einstein, these two different definitions of mass have been removed and it has become possible for mass to be reduced to a single definition. Einstein with his $E = mc2$ formula has shown theoretically that mass and energy can be turned into each other.

In the same period, the understanding of the nature of light, or the knowledge of light through Planck, has resulted in the unfolding of the Quantum Theory. It seems as if Planck started out his studies in an effort to reveal a delusion about Radiation Theory, which is one of physics' most believed in subjects. This principle put forward by Planck shows that the energy exchange between objects and radiation is not continuous and that it is in the form of packages, or determined amounts. Quantum is the name given to these basic packages. Each quantum has energy proportional to the frequency of radiation. The plural of Quantum is "Quanta" and Einstein has given the name "Photon" to quantum energy. Photon energy is determined by the multiplication of frequency with the Planck constant. In short, Einstein has also approved that light is made up of broken energy quanta. According to Einstein, light is made up of infinite particles which carry quantum energy. While Planck assumed that light sources exchange energy which has gone through quantization, Einstein has shown that light goes through quantization itself and it is made up of particles which he calls "photons". Light is a broken structure. It is made up of energy particles (photons".

Einstein has proven that light both travels as waves and particles. It has been proven that all the particles of atom, including light photons have both particle and wave characteristic. However, despite this discovery, Einstein is not the person who has put forward the Quantum Theory as a whole. Einstein is a scientist, a physicist raised up with the Deist understanding of science. Despite his great genius, his world view has been conditioned and limited with Deist philosophy. Einstein has not been able to internalize the Pantheist point of view adequately.

The direction taken by Pantheism, which is the philosophical expression of Esoteric, after Ancient Greek has been through Pythagoras, Plato and New Platonism in the Western world. New Platonism has evolved into Gnosticism after the emergence of Christianity and the Gnostic view has continuously been blamed with perversion by Orthodox Christianity and attempted to be destroyed. Deism has been developed by 18th century philosophers as a reaction against Theism which is an Orthodox Christian discourse and gradually became a world view adopted by the majority of the advocators of enlightenment as Theism's belief of God. The most known advocator of Pantheism in the Western world is Spinoza. Spinoza seems as if he has borrowed the Pantheist point of view from Arabi, Ibni Rust and Maimonides, who are Andalusian philosophers. However, Spinoza has tried to reconcile the Pantheist discourse with the Deist discourse under the influence of the powerful philosopher of the period Deist Descartes and a hybrid discipline thus came into the Picture.

Spinoza asserts that God is identical to the universe and that each being in the universe is actually a part of God. This is a totally Pantheist discourse. However, according to Spinoza "There are unchanging rules which determined how everything should exist and behave and all these beings act in accordance with these unchanging laws. There is a reason for everything. Certain events always cause definite and unchanging results". Spinoza stated using the science of geometry that all the geometrical shapes in space are in fact manifestations of God. "The relationships between them are always subject to certain laws. The universe is a system of obligations. It is a mandatory chain of relationships. A reason for something's existence is another thing. These reasons are the chains and they sooner or later reach God. The beings of objects can only be understood by understanding God". This is a totally Deist discourse as well. "Laws of nature have been brought into existence have been derived by God and He is subject to the same laws as well. All kinds of knowledge are derived from God. God has derived all existing things, to which he has given a specific order from his own essence". Spinoza's discourse is an effort to reconcile both of the world views.

Einstein is a great follower of Spinoza. He has stated "It seems as if there is someone who knows what is going on behind the universe" and expressed his point of view about God *and religions as follows: "I* believe in Spinoza's God, who reveals himself in the orderly harmony of what exists, not in a God who concerns himself with the fates and actions of human beings. The human mind, no matter how highly trained, cannot grasp the universe. Behind all the discernible concatenations, there remains something subtle, intangible and inexplicable. Veneration for this force is my religion. To that extent, I am in point of fact, religious. My religiosity consists of a humble admiration of the infinitely superior spirit... That superior reasoning power forms my idea of God. This firm belief in a superior mind that reveals itself in the world of experience represents my conception of God. As a result of the studies I have carried on space, I have arrived at faith easily in terms of science. Understanding the structure of the universe scientifically and intellectually gives a person the deepest sense of faith. Kepler and Newton had arrived at the same conclusion".

Einstein who stated "We see a universe marvelously arranged, obeying certain laws, but we understand the laws only dimly. Our limited minds cannot grasp the mysterious force that sways the constellations. That, it seems to me, is the attitude of the human mind, even the greatest and most cultured, toward God," answered the question "Do scientists pray?" as follows: "Scientific research is based on the idea that everything that takes place is determined by laws of nature and therefore this holds for the action of people. For this reason, a research scientist will hardly be inclined to believe that events could be influenced by a prayer, i.e. by a wish addressed to a Supernatural Being. But also, everyone who is seriously involved in the pursuit of science becomes convinced that some spirit is manifest in the laws of the universe, one that is vastly superior to that of man."   This is definitely a Deist expression.

Einstein who expressed "The real belief in God can only emerge through positive sciences," defines God as "Supreme Intelligence". His statements are very much in line with Spinoza's reconciling attitude. He is not an Atheist. He has adopted Pantheism which advocated the sameness of the universe, man and God, because Pantheism is not deterministic. Determinism is the name given to the teaching which asserts that all objects and events take place through the influence of certain laws or powers, which force them to be the way they are and predetermine the way they are. Shortly, it is the philosophical thought which regards that all events are the mandatory result of certain material or spiritual reasons. While Determinism, which is a discourse of Deism, claims that everything depends on unchanging conditions and results, Pantheism defends development and evolution. Spinoza's laws of stableness and Pantheism's laws of evolvement do not overlap. That is the reason why Einstein has stated "I am not an Atheist. I cannot call myself Pantheist either". Einstein is definitely an advocator of Spinoza. In one of his letters, he has written that, since he is sure that a deterministic theory will replace the basics of Quantum Mechanics, he will remain determinist. The lack of determinism observed in Quantum Mechanics for Einstein is an unacceptable notion, due to the rationale that "it is related to an area, where rationality subject to a law does not exist".

In terms of fate, Einstein stated "If this being (God) is omnipotent, it means that all thoughts of mankind are his creations as well. Then, can how man be held responsible for his actions and thoughts before a being who is omnipotent? It means that, God judges himself up to a certain extent through giving punishments and rewards. Today, the most basic source of conflict between religion and science is found in this personal God concept". This point of view is accurate in terms of denying the Theist discourse, however it does not embody Pantheism's point of view about fate. According to Pantheism, fate is only valid as an assumed duty and except for that, all beings are free. Besides Spinoza, Einstein is also a fan of Kepler and Newton who worked on laws of nature which are dictated to be unchanging. Although he has razed Newton physics to the ground, his single aim was to discover 'a single formula' which is unchanging and is able to explain the formation of the universe. He expresses this expectation as follows: "My goal is to discover a formula which explains the transmission of light and radio waves and the formation of the stars and matter". He has never been able to discover this 'single formula'; however he has not stopped believing it until the last day of his life.

Einstein opposed Planck's Quantum Mechanics which is not deterministic with the same point of view. Einstein's point of view about Quantum Theory is expressed in the following manner in his own words: "Quantum mechanics is very worthy of regard. But an inner voice tells me that this not yet the right track. The theory yields much, but it hardly brings us closer to the Old One's (God's) secrets. I, in any case, am convinced that *He* does not play dice". Einstein stated "God does not play dice with the universe" about quantum mechanics and has never accepted that this theory is the most competent voice in terms of explaining the universe; because, this theory requires a universe which is not static and constantly expands. This claim is in opposition with Spinoza's "God or God's attributions do not change," thesis. An expanding universe is in contrast with Einstein's beliefs. Motivated by this belief, Einstein has spent effort to change the field equations and formulas he has discovered in the name of achieving a static and unchanging universe. Perhaps, by doing so, he has missed the chance to announce to the world of science the most important discovery of his General Theory of Relativity which he announced in 1917: the fact that universe is expanding. The honor to announce this fell to Hubble in 1920, three years after Einstein announced his General Theory of Relativity. Hubble announced that the universe has expanded tremendously through his own observations. This finding has been verified afterwards though the telescope which was given his name.

Einstein has drawn attention to the fact that, in order to be able to understand a system of motion, we need to have an environment of immobility to compare it with. Not knowing is as real of knowing. For man to understand the existence of knowledge, he needs to find an obscurity to compare it with. This obscurity is the infiniteness of the universe. Science giving names to the things it does not know about and does not understand does not mean that the reality of these unknown things has been reached. Science needs to be removed from an area which only involves positive and material experiments and should be transformed into an understanding as to cover experiments conducted on psychic and spiritual as well. The reality can only be revealed by using mental means as well as intuitional and spiritual means. We may talk about the freedom of science only as a consequence of studying the reality without being obsessed about anything.

Einstein believed that the universe is in a state of static balance. When the field equations of the General Theory of Relativity are applied to the universe as a whole, Einstein realized that he came up with a universe which is not in a state of decisive balance and had to add a term he named "Cosmic Constant to his equations, in order to achieve a universe which is in a state of static balance. Einstein, who insisted on the static universe model, developed a new model in 1932. The constant of this model which had critical density is zero. The model's space in flat; therefore, it is a Euclidean space. However, the development and theoretical studies in observational astronomy have caused science to leave the static universe model: The space is not flat, it is spherical.

According to Einstein, the laws of nature at every point of the universe are the same. An event's different manifestation in comparison to another is only relativity. The laws are fixed and the events are relative. The Theory of Relativity, which proved that as speed increases, time slows down, is not valid for speeds which are close to the speed of light. Einstein's theory can only be analyzed and tested in great speeds. Time is an inseparable part of the universe. A timeless space cannot be described. Einstein has discovered that as speed increases, the passing time decreases. Theoretically, when the speed of light is reached, time completely stops. However, since no object with mass can reach the speed of light, it is not possible for time to stop for any being with mass. We cannot talk about relativity in limited speeds, because the differences are so small that they cannot be detected. Since the differences envisioned by Einstein which are related to the transformation of matter into energy are very small in limited speeds, their detection is nearly impossible. For speeds which are much lower than the speed of light, the equations of Classical Newton physics are valid.

Einstein with his Theory of Relativity has proven by descending to the sub-atomic universe that matter is in fact a form of energy. Einstein, who made it possible for the sub-atomic world seem the same with the macro universe, has in a way proven that there are no separate objects in the universe. This is exactly the reality shown by Quantum physics. There are no independent and separate objects in the universe. Everything is connected and the identical. The universe is a Quantum unity. Everything in the universe is caused by the vibrations of a single being, or consists of the effects of this vibration on different frequencies. Hearing, sight and heat waves are the same vibrations in terms of quality. They cause different perceptions only because of their different frequencies. Even though point out to a single being. Einstein has proven that all forms of energy spread as quantum particles in space. The more distance there is from the source of energy, the less number of particles, however their speed remains the same. If the photon's frequency is high, it means that the particle is charged with more energy.

The mind forms connections between information and uses these. Through the scientific point of view, science is information which is achieved through a specific method and is verified with practice. According to Einstein, science is the effort of achieving relevance and finding laws between data which lack all kinds of order and rationally orderly thought. Scientific point of view demands that all kinds of explanations about the universe be left to the scientists. Meanwhile, philosophy suggests that, to be able to reveal the structure and quality of all objects, the mind and intuition are not necessary and that there is no need to be a scientist to make explanations about the universe. It is apparent that merely science and the mind are insufficient in man's search for reality. For instance, through the mind and science, it has been possible to explain that matters attract each other; however the question why matters attract each other has remained outside the domination area of science and the mind. The answer to the question is intuition. Our intuition tells us that the force of attraction is Divine and everything is drawn towards it.

The most basic building block of life is water. Science explains that two hydrogen and one oxygen atom come together and form the water molecule. However, science cannot answer why these two hydrogen and one oxygen atom come together. But the answer is quite simple. It is not even scientific. The existence of water for the continuation of life is a necessity. The reason behind the coming together of these two elements right in the beginning, at a relatively short time after the Big Bang and spreading to the universe is the Divine necessity. Man has found the answer to all kinds of How questions through the mind and science and will continue to do so. However, his mind which he trusts too much does not have an answer to the Why question. The mind is hopeless on the face of the Why question. As Einstein has stated, only the mind is not sufficient to feel the basic and end purposes. The answer to the Why question is always intuitional. Einstein has understood intuitively that space and time form an integral structure.

Einstein has proven that the speed of light is the maximum speed and that anything with mass cannot even reach the speed of light. The maximum distance light travels per second is 300 thousand kilometers. This shows that there is a limit to the speed of light and nothing with mass can exceed this speed. As long as mass does not transform into energy, it cannot reach the speed of light. However, in the recent years the existences of physical effects which are faster than the speed of light have been proven. These particles which are considered to belong to the metaphysical world are called Tachyons. These particles which come from the metaphysical world and are faster than the speed of light affect the physical world. A physical effect which comes from the metaphysical world in infinite speed on humans is called "perception outside of the senses", or "intuition". It is not possible for man to reach reality through his 5 senses. Reality exists in our personal level of perception beyond the five senses, where our mental abilities mix with our intuitions.

The scientific thought which lies beneath the reality that the universe came into with the Big Bang is the Quantum Theory. Therefore, The Quantum Theory has become the branch of science which verifies the Theory of Emergence, which has been argued by esoteric for thousands of years. In 1922, Russian mathematician Friedmann used the same field equations in Einstein's General Theory of Relativity and became the first scientist to say that the university is not in fact in a state of static balance; it is in a state of change and goes through evolution. Friedmann, who can be regarded as the precursor of the Big Bang Theory, has calculated the age of the universe as 10 billion years as a result of the theoretical calculations of the expansion-collapse assumption. Lemaitre has opposed to the idea of 2 thousand years old fixed universe persistently defended by Einstein as well, by working on Friedmann's model of the expanding universe. He is the first scientist to bring together the Quantum Theory and the Theory of Relativity. Lemaitre, who was influenced by the Quantum Theory which was newly developing in the late 1920's, has stated that the universe emerged from a primitive quantum. In the Lemaitre model published in 1927, the universe does not have a beginning, thus an age. Lemaitre has argued that the universe started expanding through a degradation of a single quantum, which he calls 'primitive atom'. Materialist scientists reject this "Single Beginning" concept discerningly. This discourse is criticized as Lemaitre's effort to identify Science with Creation as a Catholic. Lemaitre found the concept that nature's order today has a beginning philosophically repellant. He has spent great effort to undermine the idea that there is a Creator God. Despite all these great efforts, Lemaitre has brought together the Quantum Theory and the Theory of Relativity in 1931 and persisted in his wish to form a connection between the universe's great scale of structure and quantum physics. Thus, the foundation for the science branch known today as "Quantic Cosmology" is laid.

Contrary to the view of the scientific circles, Hubble has proved that the universe is expanding through his observations. As a result of his observations, he has conclusively proven that the Andromeda galaxy is located much further beyond the dimensions of the Milky Way in 1923. In addition, Hubble discovered that many galaxies get far away from the Milky Way with great speed and that there is a direction connection between the distance between the galaxies and us and their speed. All of the galaxies get further away from us with great speed. It has been discovered through these observations that, the universal expansion is the same at every point in the universe and it does not a specific center. According to the Doppler laws, if objects sending light to the world are getting further away, the length of the light it sends extend, thus it steers towards the color red in the color spectrum. If the light is getting near, the wave length gets shorter and the color steers towards the color purple. The ratio of the amount of extension or shortening in wave length is equal to the ratio of the speed of light of that object's speed of becoming distant or coming closer. The method of calculation between the galaxies' speed of getting distant and their distance is called the Hubble Law.

The scientific circles have not leaned towards the concept of a dynamic universe which is in a state of evolution due to the same materialist concerns for long years. Although the acceptance of universal evolution is not Theist, it at least means the acceptance of the existence of a Pantheist God. Newton cosmology's concept of "infinite universe with an infinite past" which it took over from Aristotle has been acknowledged as such an indisputable reality that, the concept of a universe with a finite past has not been acknowledged very easily.

In 1924, French De Broglie has proven that electrons which are each particles behave like waves while spinning in their orbit around the atomic nucleus. Just as a photon which is a particle of light has both particle and wave characteristics, electrons and even sub-atomic particles which have been discovered in the recent past behave in the same manner. De Broglie has discovered that just as photons are particles, particles are each energy packages and these packages which are paired in wave length from "wave packages". If electrons can cause interferences, this shows that they behave like waves as well. Each particle, each mass is paired with a wave. In the macro level, the save length paired with objects is very small and since the wave appearance of the motion of matter has immeasurable small values, it has not been discovered for centuries. There is no more wave, or particle. Electrons are now accepted as waves. This means that, matter and energy are not separate structures as in the determinist universe, but they from a whole. Shortly, instead of talking about separate matters, it has become obligatory to talk about an area of unity. The reflection if this on the micro universe is seen in the structure of the atom. In the classical definition of the atom, while the nucleus is described as being surrounded by electrons which have fixed orbits, today it has been understood that it is not possible to determine on which orbit or even where they are and that they only surround the nucleus as a cloud.

In 1926, Schroedinger has formulated the wave equations of particles. Since the wave equation Formula which shows the behavior of matter particles of Australian physicist Shroedinger, electrons are not regarded as objects, but as electrical vibrations which spread around the nucleus. In 1927, Danish physicist Bohr has drawn the line in the sand in terms of the wave-particle duality. According to Bohr's "Principle of Complimentary". According to this principle, there is a single physical being and this physical being sometimes appears to us as particle and sometimes in wave form. Niels Bohr has proven that the same reality created by particles and wave structures which complement each other has two different reflections.

In 1927, German physicist Heisenberg has put forward his theory named the "Uncertainty Principle". Heisenberg has developed a matrix mechanics, saying that the only thing known about atoms is their frequency and the density of the light they emit. It does not seem possible to attribute a definite location or speed to a particle at a given time. This is called the "uncertainty principle". According to this principle, when electrons behave like waves, their particle appearance also disappears; when they behave like particles, their wave appearance disappears. The wave and particle appearances can never exist at the same time and only one of these appearances can be seen within a given amount of time. According to Heisenberg, during a particle's movement, both its location and its speed can never be known at a given time. Within that time, only one of these can be seen and the other remains uncertain. When the particle's position is found, its speed becomes affected and becomes uncertain. When the speed of the particle is measured, its place changes. The most apparent conclusion of Heisenberg's uncertainty principle is that, we need to quit our habit of seeing our universe in the universe of the atom. The analysis of a particle is only possible through sending a photon on it. The shock which the particle will be subject to will change its behavior and will allow it to be measured. Shortly, all measurements to be done in the micro level are only possible s a result of the breakdown of the system and this can cause in constantly changing results.

Upon Heisenberg's discovery, Schroedinger has claimed that this uncertainty embodies a paradox. According to this paradox, quantic structures having different characteristics will create an infinite number of possibilities. Schroedinger has explained this with his famous "Cat Paradox". Schroedinger's Cat Paradox is directly related to the problem of the existence of thought and/or matter. In this paradox, a car is put in a box. There is also a glass bottle with a volatile poison in it with a closed cap. A hammer is hung on the bottle and it is tied to a circuit device which will be activated by a proton particle. It is necessary for the device to function and break the hung bottle and as a result for the cat to die, the proton to do the spin motion as a particle. However, according to quantum physics, the proton cannot do a spin only as a particle. It has to do a spin as energy, or photon. In that case, the device will not function, the bottle will not be broken and the cat will not die. It looks like a quantic paradox which result should be achieved. Each particle's action necessitates for two different universes, one being negative, and the other being positive. This experiment shows that, each different action each particle will carry out will cause different result to come into the Picture. The Materialist scientists who developed this idea have claimed that, there should be the same number of that is, infinite parallel universes as the infinite number of possibilities which will emerge.

This paradox is a completely presumptive paradox created by human intelligence, because it is impossible for such a device to be built. In fact, Schroedinger has never given thought to whether the experiment can be carried out for real. The claim that the proton spin will create two universes, one being positive and the other being negative, is nothing but a crazy materialist concept. In the real universe, it does not seem possible for such a separation to take place. The purpose is to find a predicament of quantum science and question its philosophy and even its existence. It is not possible for a proton spin which emerges in the micro cosmos to influence a structure (the device) in the macro cosmos due to the Decoherer Effect. Whether the spin's direction is negative or positive, as long as there is no interference from the outside, Schroedinger's cat will never be poisoned and die.

The concept of multiple universes is never a plausible one. According to this theory, each atom's quantum behavior will renew the whole universe and the possible consequence so this behavior will create parallel universes as an alternative. We know that there are billions and billions of atoms in a single human body. There billions of people on earth and billions of planets in the universe. Each of the atoms they have carry out quantum passages each moment. Imagine that there are immeasurable parallel universes even for a single person and multiply this with other universal beings which are again immeasurable. This means an infinite number of parallel universes. However, the story should not end here, because this assumption means that each of this infinite number of universes will create another infinite number of new universes and it goes on like that. This approach is silly. Multiple universes do not go beyond the claims of materialist scientists who wish to reduce humans to aimless beings and attempt to negate the role of the Upper Conscience in the creation of the universe and rebut the esoteric interpretation of Quantum science.

Quantum physics is fictionalized over the indecision of things (matter or energy). This expression defines the notion that an object can have more than one state simultaneously. This is called Quantum Super Position. However, it is interesting that in all experiments carried out on photons, only one result has been attained. Other possibilities do not ever exist. Photon truly has the capacity to exist in two spatial places at the same time. In the experiments conducted, it seems that the proofs achieved show that an object can exist in two different places in the universe at the same time. However, such a situation never occurs within the macro cosmos. In fact, the moment matter which is applied quantum interacts with its environment, quantum immediately collapses and matter remains in its fixed state. No matter can be free of its environment and at this point, the determinist physics sustains the validity of its rules. Matter's being in quantum interaction is only valid in the micro cosmos scale. However, quantum indeterminism, or the object's being in two different places at the same is possible in the microscopic scale.

What aren't quantum laws valid in the macro cosmos? It should be known very well that quantum behavior change immediately when any kind of observation or measurement is done. The moment information is shared in the macro level, the macro system as a whole changes. Since this new change occurs within the moment, it causes different macro factors to take a position against each other; that is, to function as a measurement mechanism against each other. In this case, the effects of Quantum Laws on the macro systems are cancelled out. As soon as information leaks outside, the super position of the atoms are also cancelled out. In technical language, this is called Decoherer (not being coherent). The more the number of atoms which are in super position, the more impossible it becomes to prevent their Decoherer state with their environment. It has not been determined at which level the Decoherer Effect begins. It is this Decoherer phenomenon which lies beneath billions times billions of atoms not displaying quantic behavior. Another reason why quantic behavior does not continue at this level is the existence of microscopic waves. These microscopic waves inactivate formations which cause quantic behavior patterns. In Schroedinger's assumption, the reason for the device not functioning and the cat still living is the same. The highness of the number of photons is another factor in the emergence of the Decoherer effect. In addition, the magnitude of the measurement device creates a similar effect. It is assumed that the greatest reason why Decoherer effect emerges is that, the quantic interaction electrons from with the rest of the universe causes this phenomenon. Thus, the communication between the part and the whole removes the dual structure of quantum and acts as either matter, or energy in accordance with the information received from the universe. Shortly, the Decoherer effect regardless of the reason is the sole reason why Quantum Laws are not effective in the macro cosmos. For the same reason, there are no infinite parallel universes which emerge as a result of different behavior.

Heisenberg stated "It is not even possible to know a moment even in principle. All of our observations are choices made from the rich range of opportunities. Each choice is a limitation as to what will happen in the future"; however, this choice is one that can only affect the future. The Heisenberg principle suggested that there are an infinite number of possible futures before each individual and that individuals may form one of these futures with their choice. Again, Heisenberg's principle shows us another method of proving the validity of the Esoteric Discourse. According to the Uncertainty Law, no quantum object can completely reach the point of stagnation. Each quantum object has an oscillation. In other words, there are electronic oscillations in each possible frequency. When all these oscillations are accumulated, a sea of light is achieved where the total energy is enormous. This sea of light is called the Electromagnetic Zero Point Field. The zero point field is also the lowest energy state which makes it unobservable. The zero point field creates light blinding. The zero point field is everywhere. Inside, outside and around us. Although it has penetrated in every atom in our body, it can never be observed since it blinds us with its existence. However, He is still closer to us than our carotid artery. The Heisenberg Uncertainty Principle tells us that in each point in the universe there is light energy. This principle has no doubt that the light energy has taken the whole stretch under its influence. God is everywhere.

The principles put forward both by Heisenberg and Bohr overlap one to one with the thousands of years of the Unity of Existence discourse of esoteric. The operational quantum theoreticians, who are a part of the Copenhagen School which Bohr and Heisenberg also belong to, claim that matter and the mind as only two aspects which complete each other and that there is a deeper reality. According to this point of view, quantum physics does not depend on definite realities, but our state of awareness related to realities. This awareness depends on our level of knowledge. Knowledge is an expression of wave function. In other words, our level of knowledge of reality itself is variable in accordance to our level of knowledge. The discourses of the Copenhagen school totally overlap with the foresight of this book. The Principle of Communication put forward by Bohr shows that, when the number of particles reach a certain threshold, Quantum physics and classical physics begin to give the same results. This does not mean that, classical physics has won a victory over quantum physics on the macro level. The laws of quantum physics provide suitable expansions in many areas in the macro level; however they are sufficient to explain each macro notion. Even matter which is expressed through macro numbers such as super fluids and supra conductors behave in accordance with the quantum laws.

The basic foundations of Quantum Physics can be stated to be Heisenberg's matrixes and the uncertainty principle, de Broglie's and Schroedinger's waves and Bohr's communication principle and complementariness principle. However, the adoption of quantum as a science took place through many hardships. After these developments, in the 1950's, physicists Gamow, Alpher and Herman brought together the Quantum theory and nuclear physics studies and conducted studies on the evolution of stars. This trio consists of scientists who formulated the Big Bang theory. These three scientists, who stated that the expansion of the universe right now would necessitate a starting point as we go back in time and have shown that time and space have a beginning through their studies. Gamow, Alpher and Herman have opened their thesis to argument before a scientific committee in 1956. According to this theory, the universe in the beginning is point of light. When a big explosion took place, space and time were created and sub-atomic particles came into being. Electrons and protons from these particles came together and Hydrogen which is the first atom of the creation appeared. Gamow and friends claim that the great pressure and density which took place in the beginning of the universe is a result of a previous collapse. When the density in this collapse reached the maximum value, a new expansion process began and this process continues today as well. The Big Bang is a result of the transformation of the forces of attraction into propulsive from attraction. This transformation entered the picture on its own as a natural consequence of the anatomical structure of space-time. The universe model, which is in a state of expansion-collapse, has been named the "Phoenix Universe" in referral to the legendary bird who was reborn from its own ashes after every death. Gamow and his friends' study has not been accepted and rejected for 17 years by the scientific circles. However, time and astronomical observations have shown that they were right. Therefore, although not voiced very openly, the ideas put forward by esoteric has been accepted by the world of science.

For the universe to collapse on itself, the average density needs to be over a certain value. If the average density is equal to critical value or smaller than that, it is assumed that the expansion of the universe will continue until eternity. In total density calculations of the universe, material density and radiation density are taken as basis. Is the universe going to expand until eternity and separate due to a great tearing, or is the expansion going to be reversed after some time and is a great collapse going to take place? Will the universe continue to expand? These questions point out to a problem which needs to be answered. When the total universal mass is calculated today, it is seen that the density of the universe is smaller than the critical density. The masses taken as basis for the calculated universal density are celestial bodies which emit light or solid matter. However, it is understood that there is an invisible matter as well besides the visible matter in space. This invisible matter is called Dark Matter. Astronomer Zwicky has discovered that the movements of galaxies are very fast in accordance with the observed matter in clusters in comparison to its visible mass. According to Zwicky, these over drive speeds of the galaxies can only be explained by the existence of an invisible matter 9 times the visible matter within the cluster. Another astronomer Peebles stated that, there should be another invisible matter of great amount within the discs of spiral galaxies, other than the visible light emitting matter; otherwise, the galaxies would have to fall to pieces. Scientists studying this area assume that Dark Matter consists of weakly interacting mass particles. Although the existence of these particles has not been identified yet, the theoretical reasons corroborate their existence. Through theoretical mathematics, it is calculated that the critical density of the total amount of matter is around 30%. It has been determined that only 5% of this is visible matter. Therefore, the remaining 25% is most probably Dark Matter.

In 1998, the claims that the expansion rate of the universe has been accelerating. The basis of this calculation is formed by the assumption that as space expands the density of matter and the force of attraction decreases. Since the density of energy does not change, the force of attraction will decrease and the rate of expansion will gradually increase. However, the density of dark matter is not included in this calculation. Quantum physics shows it is not possible for the expansion to continue until eternity. According to quantum physics, emptiness is not nothingness. Emptiness is an energy area where there are continuous Quantic fluctuations. Contrary to matter, the energy of emptiness is not clustered in certain places. Energy has spread to all parts of the space in an orderly and relatively equal density. In longer instances, this energy is very active. Therefore, the expansion which continues today will not last until eternity and will stop at a certain point. In science, it is not possible to say that any rule is definite and cannot be changed. For the last 2 thousand years, it was thought that we were living within a universe which was static, constant and where no major changes took place. Biological evolution, which is a notion of 19th century, has been evaluated as a singular event unique only to living beings. However, today we know that we live in a universe which is in a state of evolution as a whole. Biological evolution has thus taken a more meaningful place as the last link of the chemical evolution process today. Evolution, or as Esoteric discourse expresses evolvement, is spread to the whole universe. Today's science studies on a "Quantic Gravitation" theory which will reconcile the general theory of relativity and quantum physics. Although promising developments have been achieved, sufficient experimental and observational proofs of this theory have still not been put forward. There is no Quantic Gravitation theory which has gained the approval of the majority of the science today yet.

Quantum fluctuations are a key component as to how our universe expands. The Quantum Theory shows that intelligence with infinite consciousness has designed the universe beforehand. It is understood that the reason behind it is to transform its own latent power into experiment. In 1930, astrophysicist James Jean stated "Universe resembles a great thought rather than a great machine. Einstein with his E=MC2 formula has shown that we are each a condensed package of energy. This Formula is the universal Formula of existence. It is its expression in mathematical language. All laws valid in the universe are formulated through mathematics. Mathematics is the communication language of the universe. There are coincidences in mathematics. It is not formed with coincidences. Each randomness brings along the explanation of a new Formula. For instance, it has been shown through the collision of energy particles with the speed of light in CERN that if we condense energy enough, we will achieve mass. Therefore, matter has not been formed as a result of coincidence. There is a mathematical formula for the formation of matter as well. All this mathematical language points out to the existence of a supreme consciousness. Where there is consciousness, coincidental existence is out of question.

The world of science has argued for the principle of "the unity of mathematics" until the middle of 20th century. According to this, there is no problem which cannot be solved through mathematics. Either the mathematical thesis is wrong and it is refuted, or it is correct and it is proven. However, the principle of the Unity of Mathematics is never a result which has been proven by being tested like the Lavoisier Law; it is a presupposition. In 1940, the Austrian mathematician Kurt Gödel has used mathematical methods accepted as proofs by the world of science and he has proven that thesis in some systems can neither be falsified, not proven. Due to the Unity of Mathematics being a principle which has been accepted as natural, Gödel's theorem has left the world of science in great shock. Through Gödel, the point of view of scientists has changed in many areas, primarily physics and not only in the area of mathematics. In fact, science regards mathematics as its own language. If it is accepted that there is a lack within mathematics, its reflections will be regarded as natural in other scientific branches as well.

Atom has been regarded as the smallest basic structure which cannot be divided for a long time. The word atom is formed by adding the negation particle A to the word "Tomon" in Greek, which means "part". According to the Ancient Greek science, A-Tom is the smallest, indivisible part. The idea that atom is not the smallest structure and that it can be divided goes back to German writer Herbert George Wells, who wrote a science-fiction story in 1913. Hungarian physicist Szilard who was very much influenced by the story began studying a chain reaction and these studies resulted in the breaking up of the atom's nucleus. Humankind who has broken up atom has seen that a broken up atom influences other atoms nearby. Thus, the idea of building the Atom bomb came into the Picture. Atom's spreading photons is its state where it is a lower level quantum. Its state as a low level quantum has influenced other atoms and chain reaction thus emerged.

Since Einstein, it is known that matter is the dense state of energy. The best example of matter transforming into energy is the Atom Bomb. Through the reaction in this bomb, the Uranium Matter transforms into a tremendous energy with the breaking up of the atoms as a result of the chain reaction. The Atom Bomb is a quantum invention. Only uranium 235 and Plutonium 239 are used in Atom Bombs. The chain reaction of both is only possible due to some quantic phenomenon. The more a neutron is slow, the more chance it has of spreading through place and being caught by a nucleus. The result of being caught is the breaking of an inconsistent nucleus. The interaction of the inconsistent nucleus with a neuron that is idle results from the neuron's behaving like a wave rather than a particle. The Atom Bomb can reach an enormous explosive power as a consequence of the quantic effects of neurons wave structure); relative effects (matter transforming into energy) and the use of the calculation methods of classical physics.

Beside the Atom Bomb, many of the predictions in the 1970' science-fiction series Star Trek have become real due to quantum science. Then, why has it not been possible for the same quantum knowledge to find a method for the prediction called teleportation which allows the transportation a body or an object from one place to another? The answer is the Decoherer effect. Within the framework of quantum laws, each atom in accordance with its nature can be teleported from one point to another. However, if the human body as a macro structure or another macro being is processed in the same manner as a whole, whether it can preserve its structural unity and function is not known. The problem is once again to be found in the fact that, we do not know the method of using micro cosmic laws in the macro cosmos. The formula which will solve teleportation can bring everything's law (if there is such a thing) out in the open.

The experiments carried out by French physicist Alain Aspect in Orsay university between 1979-1982 have shown that between electrons, atoms and molecules, communication is established in some way regardless of the distance separating them. This experiment has deeply shaken the space and distance perceptions of determinism. However, the advocators of intellectual traditions borrowed from the science of the 19th century try to prove vehemently that determinism is still valid and go far as to ignore many scientific developments for this cause. What is interesting is that, the old perceptions are being persistently tried to be continued in particular in the areas of biology and neurobiology. The main concepts of these areas still come from molecular biology which is a product of 19th century science. For instance, in the science of psychology, the manner of perception about the essence of consciousness is still being explained through Freud's Cartesian perceptions.

In the experiment carried out by Aspect, when the direction of one of the two particles subject to test was changed, it has observed that the other particle directed itself at the same time to the same orbit. Even if it is not important what the distance between these particles are and even if there is a distance the speed of light can travel for billions of years, it has been observed that a change in the motion of one particle is immediately reflected on the other. This interaction is not only valid in terms of the particles' change in direction, but also for the spin motions. In other words, an electron is able to send the knowledge it contains to billions of light years in an instant. In short, each point in the universe gets to learn about the changes which take place at another point in the universe immediately no matter where that point is. The Aspect experiment seems to show the existence of a mysterious, telepathic bond between the particulars. How do the electrons transmit their experiences to each other? How do they receive these mysterious signals and carry out what is needed with an infallible accuracy? Science tells us that no signal can go faster than the speed of light. In each experiment carried out which is related to photons, photons can only advance in the speed of light. Then, how does the communication between the electrons takes place much faster than light?

Aspect's Young's Interference experiment has shown that photons (electrons) somehow know which direction they should go and make preferences. If one of the interferences closes, all electrons immediately stir towards the one that is open. Science does not have an answer to the source of this mysterious information. Aspect has shown through his experiment that, particles have knowledge and that the communication between them is not interrupted in any way. This information which has been named Quantic potential is carried no matter what happens, particles remain connected at all times and a measurement performed on one particle immediately causes another's position to change. Quantic differentiation does not contain potential energy. What is transmitted is information and not energy and the change is not limited with the speed of light; it is infinite. The change almost takes place with the speed of thought. Scientist says that the two basic particles interact by exchanging a particle which transmits the quantum area; however they cannot explain where these particles come from or how they move. One of the claims is that, the emptiness in the universe is full of sub-quantic particles and these particles transmit information to each other within the moment.

Light and sound may be expressed as the differences in the magnetic spectrum of an environment. Light is energy and sound is material vibrations. Although light and sound are each a source of primary energy in themselves and transform among themselves continuously, in order for one of them to appear for the first time, it is necessary for it to have an initiating source. There is a third source of energy beyond these two sources of energy. It is power of thought. Thought is the creative source of the self. Pure creative power, the beginning of everything is thought. It seems as if the universe has first been thought about and then came into existence. Without a creative and conscious thought, it does not seem possible to provide an explanation for the perfect order of the universe. It has been proven by the Aspect experiment that thought, or knowledge travels much faster than light. Thought seems to be prioritized. Thought is the form of which make it possible for the individual to act. IT has no limits and an end. Civilizations are products of actions which have been put into application as a result of thoughts as a whole. While the Aspect experiment has been performed only with electrons, similar experiments are being conducted on humans. In many experiments, there are many findings about subjects transmitting their thoughts in an instant to other individuals who are far away. The existence of Telepathy, which is gradually regarded as a branch of science is constantly being proven through such experiments. The greatest aspect of telepathy is that, regardless of the distance, the thing being thought about appears in the brain of another individual at that same instant. In other words, it seems that there is no speed limit for thought.

The speed of light and the speed of light which the light emits may relatively be different. For a particle which travels in the speed of light, all distances will shrivel into zero and all times will go towards nothingness according to the special relativity theory. Therefore, each single photon in your eyes means that it appears within the moment and has been created as a result of a single leap which does not take any time. Although the photon moves in space for two million light years, from your point of view, it leaps here from the point it has been created within the moment. After Aspect, Maxwell and Dirac have also shown in their studies on Quantum physics and Quantum mechanics that, particles communicate with each in an instant and faster than light among themselves and as a result, particles which move synchronously appear. This synchronized competence to move takes place regardless of directing two photons to two opposite directions, polarized in the same direction or vibrates with the pendulum motion.

English physicist Bohm, in his work titled "Wholeness and the Implicate Order" published in 1980, argues that a space/place area contains information on the implicate order of the wholeness of the universe, no matter how small it is. Bohm, in the section titled Matter, Consciousness and Their Common Foundations of his book states that deep reality is not spirit or matter, but a reality with a greater dimension which is their common foundation. Some scientists who had difficulty in understanding the real structure of quantum physics and attempted to explain the realities of quantum through the teachings of the previous centuries evaluate Bohm's claims as "an attempt to turn physics upside down". These "scientists" who state that the subject of Bohm's theories is not quantum physics but philosophy seem persistent in not seeing the reality that in fact these two areas of science are one and whole. Their demand is for the science of physics to be made the subject of discussion and the interpretation of quantum physics to be done through indeterminable variables. However, what these indeterminable variables are remains a mystery.

After the quantum realities came into light, scientists have tried to explain the findings by attributing them to idealism, or materialism, however, they have not been successful in that. In fact, the structure of quantum can philosophically only be explained by Pantheism. At the end of 19th century, scientists had the idea that the last word has been said in the area of physics. Everything from the movements of the planets to electromagnetic waves could be explained with Newton's and Maxwell's laws. Almost all physics phenomenon resulted from two types of explanations: Either their magnetic effects, Maxwell's Electromagnetism Theory which explained light interference and similar things, or Newton's Universal Law of Gravitation which formed the basis of mechanics and in particular astronomy. These two theories created the concepts of wave and particle and distributed these to the different areas of physics. The particle concept allowed the calculation of mass by considering the amount of accumulated matter. Wave was not matter, but energy. However, Planck's hypothesis at the beginning of 20th century, which showed that wave and particle are in fact the same things, resulted in the immediate collapse of this strong foundation. Quantum physics first allowed the production of the Atom Bomb, then took a place right in the center of the world of technology with transistors, semi conductors and gradually supra conductors.

Quantum calculations are an area of research which is extremely exciting and fast developing. From physics to computer sciences and knowledge theory, mathematics to physics, the number of researchers who have different backgrounds and work in various disciplines is increasing. All these thinkers and scientists still rack their brains over the characteristics of quantum laws. For instance, the science of cryptography (deciphering, enciphering) which is used to make communication safer or to cut communication has become one of the most plain and effective application areas of quantum science.

Quantum physics also accepts that the space vacuum is covered with invisible particles. Since this discourse has first been put forward by physicist Peter Higgs, the name of this invisible particle is Higgs Particle, or Higgs Boson. Particles which carry force are called Bosons. The photon is a type of Boson. The theory suggests that space-time is full of Higgs particles. These Higgs particles are basic particles which allow other basic particles to gain mass. In other words, the smallest force carrying particle, which transforms the energy which merged with the Big Bang to basic particles, or transform them into matter is called the Higgs Boson. The CERN experiment has proven the existence of the Higgs particle and that it is still active. Through this particle which has been named "God Particle" by Leon Lederman, it has been proven inside the Hadron Collider that energy can gain mass. While it has been proven in the $E=M.C2$ equation that all kinds of mass is made up of energy and mass transform into energy under the required conditions, this time it has been proven that $M=E/C2$; in other words, all kinds of energy mean matter at the same time and that energy can gain mass under the required conditions. Thus, modern physics has reached the point that matter and energy are the same things and that they are different manifestations of God and the point of proving and verifying the ancient Esoteric discourse. The fact that the particles which make this possible being given names such as "God Particle", or "Tau" shows that the Esoteric discourse is an accumulation of knowledge which belongs to the whole that already exists within human genes.

When looked from the point of view of a beam, all distances fall to zero for light. The zero point field shows that matter, or mass which is a derivative of inaction, is created with light. Einstein has proven to us that energy is created through the collision of mass with the speed of light. The, mass is also created through the division of energy into speed of light. Higss particle which has been discovered as a result of the experiments conducted in CERN, the notion of energy turning into matter has been proven. Quantum Fluctuation in fact seems as tools of creating fixed matter at the zero point. On the other hand, even in the experiments carried out in CERN, it has not been determined what the conditions are in the first millisecond of the creation of the universe. The experiences which took place in this process called Planck Time are still not known. There is no strong matter which has reached the present time without going under any change from that moment on. However, the calculations show that a slope is formed in space and time and time moves forward instead of going backwards to zero point in Planck Time. In other words, the beginning of time's travel is Planck Time. There is no other direction. Therefore, in the light of quantum laws, there has not been a definite zero time in the history of the universe. That is the reason why there is time prior to zero. This discourse shows that there has never been a time in which the universe did not exist. Perhaps, the prior universe had gone back all the way to Planck Time and began to proceed onwards with the Big Bang. This theory seems like the simplest way of proving that the universe has always existed and it totally overlaps with the Esoteric discourse. The Universe, that is, God is unprecedented. He has not created the universe and left it aside. God is not an observer, or the keeper of the universe. God supports and carries the universe at each moment; in fact, God is universe itself. The universe is in a state of constant change. Creation is always and there and will continue to be so.

According to another claim, God is an upper dimensional concept. The universe being connected with the Upper Dimension theory is called the Kaluza-Klein theory. According to this, light can travel in the 5th, or upper dimension and what makes this possible are the super strings. The Super String Theory claims that matter is made up of small vibrant filaments. These small filaments which are hundreds of millions of times smaller than the proton vibrate each in different tones and harmonies. According to scientists, in order for this theory to be functional, we need to accept the existence of dimensions other than the 4th dimension we know. Physicist Paul Davis who put forward the Unified Field Theory argues that the amazing order of sub-atomic particles, the forces which are observed to move between deep connections should have dimensions other than the dimensions of the universe we know. According to Davis, all sub-atomic particles have penetrated to the universe as a whole and connected to each other with an invisible "Super Power". This discourse overlaps totally with esoteric expression that everything is one and a whole.

According to physicist Donald Hatch, today we are discovering that all matter is in a state of vibration and that the universe is not made up of matter but music. This narrative corresponds totally with the super string theory. If this theory is taken into consideration, the unique vibrations created by each vibrating sub-atomic is a music note and the harmony they produce together create mathematically compatible and living material forms. All matter in the universe are Divine musical works which created different shapes and models by coming together and taking shape. The whole universe performs a single magnificent work like a great orchestra, in accordance with the rhythm law of the universe. The rhythm law is the law of balance and is hidden in the entirety of nature. Each being needs to continue its life in accordance with this law. There is no movement without sound and rhythm. At this moment, a magnificent symphony is playing both in the universe and inside each one of us. We are all owners of our own compositions with our individual vibrations. Physicist and mathematician Brian Gene says the following about this issue: "With the discovery of the super string theory, musical metaphors have gained a surprising reality. It can easily be said that the vibrational order of small filaments are constantly composing new works for the evolution of the universe".

THE UNIVERSE

The word Universe is derived from Uni-Verso in Latin. It is means individual (unique) and indivisible (verso) in Latin. Man is an indivisible whole. The Universe and the Individual are both a whole and in an effort to reach oneness, that is, God. God, the Universe and Man are the same. Mankind has been newly developing his knowledge about the universe. A majority of what we know about the universe has appeared in the 20th century and in particular in the last quarter of the century. About 450 years ago, mankind thought that earth was the center of the universe until Copernicus. Through Copernicus new knowledge about earth which was regarded to be swimming in an infinite sea. The Earth was not the reason of existence for the universe. It was not at the center of the universe either. The Sun was not spinning around it; on the contrary, Earth was spinning around it. However, Copernicus had placed the Sun at the center of the universe this time. This faulty theory remained as the "truth" whole mankind adopted until the strong telescopes enter the picture in the 20th century. We have been able to understand only in the last century that our world, our sun, even our galaxy is not at the center of the universe. The knowledge about the universe is increasing day by day. Only since the beginning of the 2nd Millennium, the findings are higher in comparison to the total findings achieved in the 20th century. Still, what we know remain very small compared to what we do not know.

Astronomer Hubble claimed that the age of the universe is about 2 billion years. In 1956, another astronomer Sandage changed the Hubble parameters as a result of his observations and announced that the age of the universe is between 10 to 20 billion years. In line with the accepted calculations, the age of the universe is calculated as 14 billion years. When the speed of the farthest galaxies is calculated back in time, they reveal that all of the galaxies had come together at a center about 14 billion years ago. The universe appeared 14 billion years ago, the Milky Way 10 billion years ago and our Sun and the Earth 5 billion years ago. Today's universe was created 14 billion years ago with the Big Bang and it is foreseen that it will go on living at least for 66 billion years. It is predicted that the life span of the universe will be 80 billion years. The world of science believes that in the first second of the creation all basic matter of the universe which will live for 80 billion years was created. This is nothing but a postulate. On the other hand, emergence continues in the infinite process in metaphysical terms. There is no barrier for the same process to continue in the physical plane.

The beginning moment for universe models based on the theory of relativity, it is at a singular point which is infinite in terms of magnitudes such as pressure, density and heat. Hawking and Penrose have shown theoretically that it is inevitable for a singularity to be formed in the universe models developed within the framework of the general theory of relativity. The universe seems as if it has erupted from a single point. In terms of quantum physics, since there is no physical narration for a time beyond Planck time, it is believed that the Big Bang began in Planck time. In Planck time, the heat is so great that it cannot be measured. It is not possible for any nucleus to exist in such a temperature. According to quantum physics, the universe at the first moment of the Big Bang is a mixture made up of quarks-anti-quarks, leptons-anti-leptons and photons. When the temperature falls down to one billion degrees, protons begin to catch neutrons and the first nucleus formations are observed. As the universe begins to expand, the density decreases and as a result of cooling, the thermonuclear reactions end. This process has taken place in a matter of about 3 minutes. The universe, which is created at the end of this 3 minute process, is made up of 27% Helium and 73% Hydrogen. Besides these, there is certain amount of free electrons left over from the electron-positron annihilation period in the universe. Other elements, which make up about only 2% of the total chemical elements today, have been formed later on in the stars and spread to space through supernova explosions. From the first moment of Big Bang, it seems that the universal program has become active.

The universe is a large body. The galaxies are the cells of the universe, whereas star systems and planets are the cells of galaxies. Man makes up the cells of the Earth along with all the other existences. The cells are human' building blocks and atoms are the cells' building blocks. In the hierarchical level, an endless and infallible order continues its existence until eternity. Each universal law affects all existences at each level of this infallible order. All existence from the largest to the smallest are subject to this infallible order and laws. Within this framework, each existence is in a state of communication with one another. Including man, all beings are made up of the mix of various atoms in the universe. Each atomic energy contains God's energy. The Spirit is the Divine particle bestowed upon all these existences. Matter and Spirit unite and create life. Life is the essence of the universe. Spirit is not only unique to humans and as it embodies all beings, it is not a formation unique only to the world. It is spread to the whole universe.

The basic foundation of the universe consists of Life energy. The continuity and evolvement of the universe is possible through life energy. The universe which we think is solid and dead is on the contrary a live and fresh energy. The spirit of God is found in every particle. The essence of each existence is the same. It consists of matter and spirit. The difference between them exists only in the vibrational dimension. Being which vibrate in different energy dimensions appear to us as types which are different from each other. The energy vibration of matter like Stone which we define as solid is at the lowest level, while the energy vibration of beings which we define as living gradually increases. Man is a being which vibrates in the highest level known.

It is impossible to differentiate forces which form matter and energy at the moment of the creation of the universe. As the universe expands and cools down, matter and energy have separated from each other. The whole universe and all other being in the universe are made up of different mixes of this matter and energy. In the universe, there are an infinite number of galaxies and an infinite number of stars and planets in those galaxies. Each of these acts in accordance with the laws of the divine being. Vitality is a law spread to the whole universe. The continuity of life and the universality of evolvement depend on this vitality. The Ore which has emerged from the perfect Essence is spreading to the whole universe, increasing and reproducing. Vitality continues its existence everywhere, without breaking away from the absolute principles and the infallible order. Just like life, knowledge is also everywhere. The whole universe is equipped with knowledge. The total knowledge and the knowledge in one speck are the same. Knowledge is the same in essence. However, it may cause different perceptions in multitude, variety and in appearance. Yet all knowledge is whole and One. The whole universe in its essence carries the knowledge of reality within. Man who embodies the knowledge of reality can only reach this reality by knowing himself. The knowledge of the final purpose of existence is hidden in human soul. Evolvement is the only method which allows for the increase in knowledge.

Even at that first moment of the universe, it seems that the types and amount of particles have been arranged. The number of protons and electrons are equal to each other and thus, the balance of electrical charge has been attained in the universe. An adverse situation would not allow the universe to form its own order and chaos would take place. In the first second of the creation, less number of neutrons has been created in comparison to the number of protons and electrons. If it were not so, the nucleons would always create the Helium atom in the formation of atoms and there would be no Hydrogen nucleus. Hydrogen is the basic fuel of the universe. Without hydrogen, the stars and our Sun would not be formed and our universe would be stillborn. In the first three minutes, one fourth of helium and three fourths of hydrogen has been created and creation has been stopped. If not, it would be inevitable for heavy elements with more nucleons to be formed in the universe. That would once again mean the lessening of hydrogen and fuel deficiency. If the creation had not been stopped in those first minutes, the universe would in a way commit suicide. The heavy elements were formed much later on, as a result of star explosions.

Matter and anti-matter which emerged after the Big Bang destroyed each other and produced the required energy to spread to the universe. As a consequence of electrons and anti-electrons cancelling each other out, a tremendous energy has been born. In the first seconds of the Big Bang stage, all electrons with the exception of electrons needed to balance the charge of the protons and the opposite charged positrons destroy each other and created the energy fuel required for expansion. All this program of existence seems to be placed on this tremendous energy and all particles through millions of centigrade degrees of heat. As the universe expands and cools down, the speed of electrons and anti-electron particles' destroying each other falls below the speed of formation. Since the number of produced electrons is more than anti-electrons, the universe has been built on the remaining electrons. As temperature falls, the electromagnetic power atoms were formed. Through strong nucleus power and weak nucleus power, different elements were formed and these elements came together through the force of attraction and formed galaxies and stars. Mass attraction allowed the expansion of the universe. In order to be able to understand how the universe began, we need to understand how mass attraction and quantum mechanics unite.

Kiti Ferguson argues that the empty space is full of particles and anti-particles and their sum will reach great amounts of an infinite energy. It is true that the collision of matter and anti-matter will produce a tremendous amount of energy. Perhaps, the weapons of the future will be based on anti-matter (or it has been that way in the past. An anti-matter weapon used on the Ancient continent of Mu could be the explanation why there are no remains of this continent). However, anti-matter can be produced in very small amounts today in laboratory environments. There is no sign that anti-matter exists in nature. As far as it is known, the existence of anti-matter in any point of the universe is not in question. An adverse situation will cause the collision of matter and anti-matter and produce an extraordinary chaos environment.

As Ferguson claims, it seems that it is not possible for anti-matter particles to exist in empty space. The opposite would be the turning of the space vacuum into hell as a whole, but such a situation is not in question. In the universal level, with the exception of only certain chaotic situation which we may cal local, space has a quiet calm and orderly structure. Anti-matter is a building block which is necessary in the first stages of the Big Bang. The energy required for Big Bang to take place, the expansion of the universe and the creation of matter, has been understood to be the result of the collision of the two opposite poles of the first essence, the positive and negative primary matter. In this first planning stage, positive force won over negative force and thus, it has become possible for the material universe to be created. Since the equality of the two forces would mean nothingness and due to the universe enveloping us, it is understood that the positive force has appeared more densely in that first moment of emergence. Therefore, it does not seem possible for our anti-matter to exist in the inner parts of our universe. In fact, even the smallest of negative particle would react with the positive matter particle within the moment and be destroyed.

Anti-matter existing only in the expansion boundaries of the universe where emanation still continues seems rationally possible and likely. In fact, there may be a need for continuous energy to keep expansion go on and energy may be transforming into matter and matter into energy. It is possible to say that a planned chaos is sustained and existence or emanation still exists in the universe only here. The law of Entropy proves this as well.

All objects in the universe are finite, or mortal. The only thing infinite or immortal in the material world is electrons which emerge with the fragmentation of atoms. All particles with the exception of electrons transform into energy. Then, the same electrons are used from the same energy and new matter is formed. According to the Law of Conservation of Matter, electrons have emerged with the Big Bang. Nuclear force, electromagnetic force, weak force and force of attraction which were together at the beginning within a cosmic egg separated from each other with the Big Bang and began their activities to take the universe from chaos to order. The universe does not consist of structures which are disconnected. Each object is an energy ball as well. Objects are not disconnected and independent of each other due to their wave structures; they are pieces of a whole. We cannot talk about independent objects. The universe consists of a holistic web of energy. Each electron which belongs to the different structures in this area has a relationship with all the other electrons and communicates with them. Objects are the local density differences which are formed within this infinite and holistic web of energy. In this framework, we cannot talk about locality either. Objects at each point have knowledge about an object which is at any other point no matter what the distance is. The Quantum Theory invalidates the concept of solid object. Each object is an energy ball which moves in the infinite and holistic energy area and communicates with the others. Since there was no universe prior to the Big Bang, it does not seem possible for the laws that we are familiar with to exist. Since the universe is a structure which comes into existence from a single point, it would not be wrong to say that prior to it was a whole with a single structure as well. Nothing else can be said about the condition prior to the universe but to express that it is a Single Whole. This expression overlaps with the single being mankind has been feeling in its heart since the day he existed: God.

On the other hand, a majority of scientists claim that there is no background energy through which existence is possible, there is nothing but the universe itself, the universe contains all the energy which existed until now and the universe exploded and has begun to inflate as a result of the explosion of the energy which is stuck with an infinite amount of density at a mathematical point. According to this point of view, every event in the universe is a consequence of a chain of coincidences. However, the universe is neither a supreme structure it is today due to obligations which began as a result of coincidences and evolution which depended on coincidences, nor a structure which has been created out of nothing by a Creator in its present state. On the contrary, it seems as if everything has been created by a Supreme Consciousness through a definite plan. It is not mandatory that nothing has been created out of nothing. The Big Bang process that everything has been born from a single point and went through evolution. The Big Bang being not an act of creating out of nothing, but an act of exposing itself is a rational consequence all scientific data has reached. On the other hand, those who argue for randomness have no answer for Life Energy, in particular the knowledge accumulation found in DNA. In the same manner, they do not have a satisfactory answer to the continuation of universal laws and a specific order from the beginning until today. The universe acts as if it has its own DNA and continues growing in accordance to certain rules. The universe's continuing its activity in line with certain knowledge and planning, takes us to the conclusion that there must be a universal code which dictates how the universe should be built and the Universal DNA to be written by a Supreme Consciousness. The extraordinary order of the universe shows that this DNA coding embodies the whole universe and the matter it contains.

A specific number of protons, neutrons and electrons coming together produce a certain atom structure, certain atoms constantly unite with each other and the same molecules are formed each time. It is as if an atom chooses the other atom it will unite with. For instance, 11 protons + 12 neutrons + 11 electrons always produce the sodium atom and sodium always prefers chlorine to unite with. It cannot unite with potassium, because their structures are not suitable for each other. Choices can only be made through the existence of knowledge. This knowledge is unique to the object. It is the knowledge inherent in its structure.

The Big Bang and the process of evolution which continued afterwards shows us that a primary energy already existed and everything consists of the different manifestations of this primary energy. Therefore, the supreme consciousness which embodies this primary energy in fact means the universe as a whole. All created structures and living being going under evolution is due to the necessity of the existence of a primary structure. Within the framework of laws of evolution, there is place to both randomness and mutations and evolvement in accordance to a specific plan. Each living being is born in accordance with a pre-determined plan and continues its existence by constantly developing if it is compatible with its environment. In accordance with certain laws, the future of these living being are determined only through certain events or changes which take place in random. The existence of these coincidences never shows that there is not a general evolvement plan. On the contrary, it is a universal obligation that these types of coincidences take place in order for different experiences to be lived.

The universe has gradually evolved after the Big Bang and reached the shape and dimension it has today. It is a common view that at the beginning of the universe, an environment of chaos was in question. Yes, it seems as if there was an extraordinary chaos and havoc dominant in the beginning. However, this chaos is not evident of an irregularity. The process of evolution has shown us that, each environment of chaos is created in an absolute manner in accordance with the universal laws and definitely serves for a purpose. Therefore, it is not possible to speak of a chaos at the beginning. This chaos most definitely embodies an order which depends on the infallible functioning of physical laws in the environment and all forces are active within the framework of their own laws. That is the reason why an environment which seems chaotic has left its place to total order after some time. In the universe, an event which can continue its existence as chaos has never taken place. The four basic forces always transform chaos into order. For instance, it is due to the force of gravity in its existence stage being active that it does not spread to the growing universe and continue to grow within a certain amount of time. The universe has been filled up with the energy it was formed in and thus, the continuation of the existence of the physical universe has been made possible. All forces are continuously in charge.

Then, how accurate are the claims of Esoteric that the universe is without a precedent and infinite? If the universe is still expanding, it is not possible to claim that the universe is infinite. Everything that expands is finite. It is apparent that the universe is not without a precedent since it came into being with an explosion. On the other hand, it can be proven that the universe has an end through mathematical calculations. In fact, even with the most advanced telescopes the furthest boundaries of the universe cannot be observed. It is not possible to observe boundaries which already exist, because it is not possible for us to observe the light of the newly emerged celestial globes or formation since they their light does not reach us. However, since the universe is still expanding and therefore not infinite, being without a precedent and infinity can only be possible within a space-time which is without a precedent and infinite (which we have not been able to define yet and perhaps will never be able to). Not having a precedent and infinity can only be mentioned for an environment which embodies universes which are side by side, or which are consecutive (maybe both).

The existence of two opposite energies, which create the Big Bang that created the universe from within an essence that has no precedent and is infinite, seems mandatory. Only when two different forces which have positive and negative charge react with each other energy is created and it is understood that, in order for the material universe to exist, it has been planned for the positive charge to be higher proportionately. While the physical universe is created as a result of energy turning into matter, the metaphysical universe might have been created under the density of the negative charge in accordance with the principle that everything should be balanced. Where this energy comes from is as meaningless a question as the universe not having a precedent and being infinite. The force which does not have a precedent and is infinite is there because it always exists at least for us even if not for itself. The zero time of our universe is the zero time of a new formation which emerges in an environment that is without a precedent and exists within a timeless infinity.

Physicist Andrei Linde from Stanford University states that the existence of the universe will continue in an infinite process. According to Linde, the universe has begun its life in the manner which can be explained today and although it is not definite yet, the life of the universe will end in some way. However, since these birth and death processes continue in a manner that is without a precedent and infinitely, we may talk about the infinity of the universe's duration of existence. Linde defines this infinite process as an unconscious process which has no purpose. On the other hand, Esoteric suggests that, there is a range of universes without a precedent and which are infinite in space and time, which exist through an infinite intelligence that continuously lives experiences and goes through evolution due to finite diversity.

The basic matter of the universe is the most basic element Hydrogen. Atoms which have come together as a result of hydrogen spreading to the space have formed great masses and as a result of the fusion which took place, Helium was created through hydrogen. At centers such as supernovas, where the temperature reaches 10 Millions of degrees and where heating and radiant energies are formed, heavier elements have been created during this process and this resulted in 92 different elements. Hydrogen clouds which have not gone through fusion have spread to the whole universe and created the space vacuum. This process has been going on for 14 billion years. Today, the basis for all these formations is the balance between the atomic nucleus and electrons. Due to the gravitational force between the particles and the balance of electromagnetic force, electrons which orbit around the nucleus spin around themselves with the angular momentum they gain. This spinning movement carried out by all the particles around themselves is the "Spin" movement. Faruk Erengul claims that this spin movement has a "spiritual" ability. Erengul states that the electrons share their charge of knowledge and love and experiences with the neighbor electrons and that, according to the laws of thermodynamics, the material world constantly loses order and thus sustains its evolution and increases its entropy. As a natural consequence of this, it can be thought that the universe is increasingly getting more disorderly and is dragged into chaos. However, this is not the case. According to Erengul, the force which prevents this is hidden in electrons. Since electrons continuously share the knowledge and love charge they have inside, they create an opposite affect compared to matter in the spiritual world; as knowledge and love increases in the universe, the order is reestablished and entropy decreases. This makes it possible to establish balance in the whole universe. Particles which allow this sharing between the electrons are Tachyons. The spin movement of electrons results in the uniting of atoms and the birth of molecules and the uniting of molecules form living and inanimate structures. Again, due to the spin movement, the evolvement process of all beings in the universe continues and subconscious and conscious experiences gained as a result of all universal activity unite within the universal intelligence. All these formations are proof that we are in a programmed order of evolvement and that these events are never coincidental.

An electron does not emit any kind of information within time and space. Despite this, the sharing of information between electrons does not regard time and space. Quantum science has proven for us that the information an electron attains is attained by other electrons which are of great distance. As a result of the sharing of information of electrons which have an infinite life-style, it is possible for all kinds of information to be accumulated in the universe and transform into a universal memory. Accumulation of information does not only embody the information gained y the brain, but also the love experiences of the spirit. Turkish scientist and an advocator of Esoteric, Ph.D. Faruk Erengul, states that electrons are also the carriers of the soul. Since electrons, which have life power that is a divine gift, have been continuing their existence since the moment of creation, they contain the whole program of evolution. It is because of electrons that the material world which constantly loses order balances this loss and the lost order is reestablished in the spiritual world.

Electrons, which are the main aspects of molecule structures which make up each organ, have been adding new information to the experiences and knowledge they have been achieving for 14 billion years since the Big Bang for 5 billion years on this earth. The information added within life on earth accelerates the feedback mechanisms of beings on earth and the evolutionary process thus continues. This event may be defined as biological and spiritual evolvement as well. The subconscious knowledge has been accumulating in the universe for billions of years. The general knowledge the electrons have are so dense, that they cannot be compared with conscious knowledge acquired within life on this world. Today, knowledge attained consciously is stored in the subconscious and through rebirth they maintain the evolvement process after death.

Erengul states that only 100 billion of 28 digit electrons inherent in a human being are super electrons which carry knowledge and love and calls these "Eons". The majority of electrons which are not eons are those with normal functions, which carry out biological and physiological activities in the subconscious throughout life. When life on earth is lost, while some of these blend in with soil, some others spread to space. When eon electrons enter a new body to provide for the required energy, the acquired skills appear in new bodies. It is apparent that electrons charged with knowledge and love communicate through a common universal language. Electrons, which store the experiences, knowledge and love they gain during their infinite lives both in their closed spaces and share these with universal intelligence, put forward their old experiences when they enter a new body and thus make the evolvement of the individual possible. However, this accumulation of knowledge is never reflected on consciousness and remains in the subconscious level.

The whole universe is nothing but a storehouse of information. All experiences lived in the universe are constantly added to the Supreme Consciousness and the problem of entropy is overcome through the expansion of the universe. How much information can be squeezed to the whole universe as a whole? Israeli physicist Jakob Berkstein has calculated that information is proportional to area. According to the Berkstein Bound theory, the maximum amount of information bite which can be piled up in a system is mass, which is expressed as kilograms of 44 over 10 information bite multiplication system and the maximum width expressed in meters. Therefore, the only thing we need to calculate the information capacity which can be carried by any system that system's (or object's) area and mass. With the Berkstein Formula, it has been calculated that a hydrogen atom's information coding capacity is 4 million bites and a proton's is only 40 bites. Taking this calculation in consideration, an average person's weight is 5 kilos and its perimeter is 20 cm. this shows that if a human's brain is to be used only to store information, it can store 44 over 10 information bites. The most advanced computer's information storage capacity which is being built right now is 14 over 10 information bite.

Astronomers have calculated the age of the universe to be 14 billion light years perimeters. According to some calculations, its width is 156 billion and to some others, it is 180 billion light years. The total mass weight of the universe is estimated as 42 over 10 kilos with the exception of dark matter which has not been identified yet. When this information is applied to the Berkstein Formula, the universe's total information storage capacity is 100 over 10 bites of system level for now. With the addition of dark matter, whose existence is regarded as mandatory, to the Formula, this number will reach higher levels. However, although this number is quite high, it is still a finite number. If we take the age of the universe as 17 over 10 seconds and imagine that it has produced 100 over 10 bites until now, we can say that the total holographic information processing duration capacity, or speed of processing has reached 90 over 10 bites. This explains why the universe has been expanding with more speed. It means that, as information flow increases, the universe's growth rate will also increase. Whether this growth has an end or not and whether the universe will stop at a certain point, or its end will take place with a big tear is not known.

After the Big Bang, the first atom produced in the universe is the hydrogen atom. After the explosions caused by the clustering and compaction of hydrogen atoms, the two hydrogen atoms unite and the Hydrogen atom is produced. The main source of energy in the universe in general is the transformation of the hydrogen nucleus into helium nucleus through fusion reaction. A hear energy is need for fusion to take place. The temperature at the center of these explosions is centigrade. All the stars in the universe have been produced through these explosions. The energy of the stars comes from this fusion. As a result of the force of gravity, which is one of the four basic forces of the universe, the scattered atom clouds produce a movement and orbit around themselves.

All lumps which are not close to the whole because of the centrifugal force are driven outside. These lumps also start spinning around themselves and take orbit around the main object. Thus, the planets are formed. The whole hydrogen is not captive inside these formations. Hydrogen continues its existence in a dispersed manner to the whole universe and each star and each planet send a portion of the hydrogen it has back to the universe continuously. Thus, within the framework of a specific program, the hydrogen atoms needed for new formations always continue their existence in needed amounts in space. Each of the numerous stars and planets which have been born and died and then were reborn until now gain unique characteristics of their own; for an environment which will allow living beings to develop in planets, or not depends totally on the position of their orbits.

The space is never a complete emptiness at any point. We cannot talk about absence or nothingness at any point in the universe. During the interaction of each area, the rearrangement of matter takes place at the moment of a certain leap. Absence is mistakenly defined as the shape left behind by matter which constantly changes shape. There are dust clouds in interstellar space. There are particles which amount to 100 million within a cubic meter mass. Even in places where the density is minimum between the clouds, there are 100 thousand hydrogen atoms within one cubic meter mass. Critical density in the universe is the 3 Hydrogen atoms within one meter cubes of space. This density means that there is sufficient force of gravity which can stop the expansion of space at some point. If the density falls to a point which is lower than the critical threshold, it will mean that the expansion of the universe will never stop. This is the open universe model. In the open universe model, as the stars exhaust their fuel, they die one by one and the universe turns into a great cemetery. If the expansion stops at one point, due to the law of gravitation contraction will start and density will gradually increase. In case the density increases excessively, the universe will collapse on itself once again and go back to the point of the Big Bang. This is the closed universe model. However, beyond these two theories, it is also of question that the universe will achieve balance in a planned constant. Gamow claimed that the Big Bang was a result of a great contraction which took place previously. According to this point of view which is in line with Esoteric, it seems inevitable that the existing universe will die one day. Due to the fact that the universe has a predicted time limit, it is a "closed" universe. The death of our universe will be the beginning of a new universe. Why is the universe born and dies and why is a new universe born? Could it be not possible for a single universe to continue its existence? It is possible to answer the question why the universe is born and dies through intuition under the leadership of the mind. God has created the universe not only with his knowledge, but also with his love. All kinds of new knowledge which will be brought together during the life span of the universe will reunite in love, return to God and the same process will be repeated infinitely. The single purpose of these repetitions is evolvement. God continuously transmits his experiences of knowledge and love which emerge from one Big Bang to another in the universal evolution processes. Just like a human's increasing his evolvement running from one life to the other.

The most sensitive issue Deist science, which believes in the presupposition that the universe began with the Big Bang and this has happened only once, is how the universe will end. It has been discovered that the boundaries of the universe constantly expand with speeds close to the speed of light in outer space. Lavoisier claims that there is no increase in matter in the universe at all. If the Lavoisier law were valid, it would mean that the density of the universe is constantly decreasing. In that case, the density of the universe will decrease as the celestial bodies increase their escape speed in outer space. Some scientists predict through their observations that the expansion is constant and that the attraction force of the celestial bodies which get too far removed from each other will be set to zero and the universe will disperse in infinity through a great tearing. However, they cannot find any explanation as to what this infinity in which the pieces will disperse and what will happen to these pieces. This question resembles the question why the creator God has created the universe. It does not have an answer. Only the creator knows the answer. According to Esoteric, the universe came into existence to allow various experiences to be lived and it is finite like all other material being. Only God is without a precedent and is infinite. In fact, everything is one and whole. The pieces which emerge from God are already from him. Therefore, the universe will emanate from God with the Big Bang, contract once again and return to God. However, this is not a beginning, or an end. In order for new experiences to be lived, new emanations will take place; new universes will come into existence, contract again and return to God. All these experiences have repeated infinitely and will continue to do so.

The first galaxies, stars and planets in the universe have first appeared after the Big Bang only 2 billion years later. In 1929, Edwin Hubble discovered that these star islands which are each big galaxies have been getting further away from each other regularly. This discovery has shown that the universe is expanding with great speed. Therefore, the consistent and fixed universe model has left its place to the constantly expanding and developing universe model. The Hubble horizon point is the furthest point which we can see inside the universe for the time being. However, the universe does not end at this point. The cosmic expansion theory shows that the universe is expanding in all directions interestingly in the same manner. The Hubble telescope has proven that the galaxies disperse in space with equal concentration.

Again through Hubble, it has been discovered that the galaxies are getting further away from each other with a speed of about one fifth of the speed of light. The width of the universe which can be calculated for today is 24 over 10 kilometers. The universe expands about 10% each earth year time. It has been calculated that far galaxies get further away from the Milky Way with about 56 thousand km per second. If the speed of the galaxies getting distant continues at this level or increases, it is claimed that the "Thermal Death", which is -273 C will be inevitable. However, the average temperature of the universe is -270 C. -270 C which is fixed at every point of the universe is the temperature where the ideal level of radiation occurs for the continuation of life. The materialist point of view has no answer for this fixed and ideal temperature; however the Esoteric discourse repeats that everything has been programmed for evolvement and expresses that this fixed temperature is a part of the order as well. Since the universe is still very young, its growth just like a human teenager continues speedily. Just like a human being, its growth will stop at some point as well.

What are mobile are not galaxies, but space itself. The universe goes through growth constantly. If the rate of the galaxies getting distant comes closer to the speed of light and galaxies get further away from each other with a greater speed, it is claimed that each galaxy, or galaxy clusters which stand close to each other will be left alone in space. Getting distant does not take place between galaxies one by one, it is between galaxy clusters. The Milky Way, Andromeda, Magellan galaxies and the other 20 galaxies is a galaxy cluster which are bound to each other with the force of gravity and these getting distant from each other is not in question. It seems that getting distant takes place between galaxy clusters. In 1923, Hubble has discovered that Andromeda is not a nebula, but another galaxy which contain billions of stars in it. Andromeda is the largest member of our galaxy group. It is estimated that there are one trillion stars in Andromeda, which is 2.3 million light years away from the Milky Way. The Milky Way is in the second place with 300 billion stars. Constant explosions take place in the universe and new stars and galaxies are formed. On the other hand, as a result of stars turning into black holes, galaxies perish within these black holes. We do not have sufficient knowledge about the reasons or functions of black holes. Scientists claim that matter which gets lost in these black holes erupt from another point in the universe and the material required for the birth of new galaxies are acquired in this manner. Therefore, the hypothesis that galaxy clusters being left alone due to getting distant is not a correct interference. New galaxies which will be needed until the end of expansion are constantly being created. Our Sun is a young star which is 5 billion years old. It has been following a quite consistent progress for 4.5 billion years and will turn into a red giant 8 billion years from now. The universe is full of new born, young, mature, old, dead, dispersed and lost stars. These processes include all times. Everything seems to be functioning in accordance with an order, laws which are valid everywhere and a program.

One of the most important factors in the expansion of the universe is the Quasars. These are stars with very big masses in the furthest distance. The farthest Quasar is 12 billion light years away. The observation of celestial bodies is a voyage through time as well. The smallest bodies are those which are the farthest from us in time. Quasars being very far away means that they have been formed in the early stage of the universe and at its border. Quasars are the proof that the universe is going through evolution. However, the universe does not end beyond these. It is thought that beyond the Quasars, there are hot radiation clouds where galaxies have not been formed yet. There is also the view that Quasars are new galaxies to be born. In other words, the formation and expansion of the universe still continues in the last borders which are known to man.

The black holes in the universe are thought to swallow matter and energy around them and send them to an unknown point. Scientists state that, in other corners of the universe and especially in border points where formation still continues, there might be white holes which are the opposites of black holes and that matter and energy needed for the expansion of the universe might be sent to Quasars through these white holes. It is considered that there is a white hole behind the center of a black hole. Through this white hole, which is thought to open to another galaxy, it is claimed that matter swallowed by the black holes are being thrown. White holes are throwing everything that has been sent by the black holes outside. There pull there is negative. There is levitation and no gravitation. However, the existence of white holes has still not been proven yet. It is claimed that even the Big Bang might have been thrown outside through a white hold. The cosmic egg may have come into existence as a result of another universe in the space completing its life span and being sucked in by an extraordinary black hole. It is possible for another universe to complete its life span, then collapse and allow our universe to be emanated. In this case, it is not possible to talk about a beginning or an end in terms of the universe. Each beginning is an end and each end is a beginning. The question what is beyond that is bound to remain as an infinite series of questions which can never be answered.

The universe has come into existence from matter. God has given life to the universe by blowing a part from his soul. Humans have also come into existence from matter. Humans owe their vitality to the union of their body which is matter just like the universe and the part of God's soul which he blows out. If the universe and man are the same, the universal body will get spoiled during this process and die, just as human body gets spoiled in the process and dies. If the universe is man, there might be numerous other universes beyond our universe, just as there numerous human beings on our world. The parallel universe model put forward by some scientists seems possible according to this point of view. However, it is not possible to prove this within the scope of our current knowledge. The birth of our universe has been possible with the Big Bang. Our universe is still in the expansion process. This process will end one day, however death will not be in question. The universe will die at the end of an average of 80 (billion) years just like man and will find body once again. Thus, the chain of evolvement will continue until eternity.

It is apparent that the universe is a living organism, because it lives continuously. Each moment numerous stars die and each moment the same amount of new stars are born. The cycle of birth and death is valid for stars as well. The Milky Way is 10 billion years old and as there are stars which are the same age in it, there are also young stars like our Sun which are 5 billion years old. The greatest characteristic of the universe is that conditions at one point are different from the others. At some points, while the number and density of stars is high, at some other points they are very rare. This is also necessary for different experiences to be lived. Events at each point in the universe being very different from the other points are another proof of the need for universal experience. Supernovas, which are the great explosions of stars, resemble big furnaces where the required conditions for elements heavier than hydrogen and helium to be formed. Earthly beings, man's 90% is made up of Hydrogen, Helium and heavier elements. This also shows that all atoms in the world and inside of us have come from a star which was once a supernova. Beams which still come from supernovas are used in the acceleration of the evolutionary process on Earth. None of the events which take place in the universe are coincidence. Evolution does not only take place in the macro cosmos, but continuously in the micro cosmos as well. If it is taken into consideration that man is micro cosmos, there is a giant universe inside of us as well and life and evolvement continue in this universe too.

There are billions of galaxies in the universe. It has been calculated that there are about 100 billion galaxies in the universe. The universe is made up of about 1 billion galactic clusters, each of which is made up of an average of 100 galaxies. The number of stars in each galaxy is expressed in billions as well. There are hundred billions of planets around these billions of planets. It is thought that 93% of the stars in the universe have planets. When this is taken into consideration, the number of planets suitable for life is once again billions. It should be kept in mind that only in the observable universe, there are over 100 billion galaxies. Considering the fact that the stars in the universe have 8-10 planets and assuming that there is a civilization in a single planet in hundred thousand stars, we reach the conclusion that there are 100 trillion developed civilizations in the universe. Civilization as a natural process of evolution is a notion valid for the whole universe. Civilizations are points where experiences are lived most densely.

In the Milky Way galaxy, there are over 300 billion more stars. However, 80% of the stars in the galaxy are situated at the central area where life conditions do not seem very probable. The intense X beams coming from the center of the Milky Way show that there are intense star collisions and supernova explosions at the center. Black holes pull everything near them inside themselves through their infinite force of gravity. In 25% of the stars in the galaxy, if it is foreseen that there is a planet where life conditions can develop as in the solar system, then it can be calculated that the number of planets will be about 75 billion. 5% of these are either red giants or white dwarves. Only half of 20% of the remaining ones are of medium size where life can appear. However, only 10% of the stars in our galaxy are similar to the Sun. It is possible for half of these to have a planet each within their livable zones. In short, the number of medium sized stars which have a beneficial ecosphere in the galaxy is 5.2 billion. The number of stars where there is one planet in ecospheres where life conditions may be born is about 2.6 billion.

Then, despite all these realities, could we say that the single planet which accommodates living beings in our galaxy is Earth? It seems more of a possibility that life is not that limited as it is assume, but a more wide spread law. Observing life even in the most extreme conditions where life is not thought to be possible on earth, sustaining of life in every possible environment is like a manifestation of the law of life. Signs of life have been observed in many meteors which have fallen from space to earth. Therefore, the matrix of life has been carved in every point of the universe. Life force can even be found in the smallest nucleoprotein. Even in these smallest lives, it is possible to see intelligence. The smallest living being seems to have a complete evolutionary program it has followed since existence and will follow during its evolution that will continue for millions of years.

Let us continue with the calculation of the possibility of life. Out of 2.6 billion stars, which spin in the useful ecosphere in the Milky Way, the number of those which might be similar to Earth is about 1.3 billion. In half, or 650 million of these, it is possible that there has been life. 92% of these are planets which have had the required time for life to develop. There are 600 million of these. Those planets which are 5 billion years old, thus are sufficient to have multi-cellular life are 430 million. In 415 million of these, there might a rich terrestrial life. If we calculate that civilization has not developed in 40% of these and there has been sufficient time for the development of civilization in 60%, then the number of planets on which there is a civilization makes 390 million. It may be considered that the average duration of stay for the civilization on the planet within a star's normal life is 10 million years. In that case, we arrive at the conclusion that a technological civilization might still be continuing in 530 planets in our galaxy today. The idea that only our civilization exists in the whole wide universe is nothing but an expression of arrogance peculiar to mankind. Evolvement continues infinitely not only through the perfect man, but through different perfect beings that are spread to the universe. Still, when extraordinary distances between the stars are taken into consideration, it is seen that the closest civilization to us might be 250 light years away. In our galaxy, if there is half a million developed civilizations and if the average distance between the two civilizations is at least 250 light years, then even a civilization which has the technology to travel with the speed of light to cover this distance is almost impossible in accordance with our knowledge today.

On our world, communication is carried out through radio, television, telephone and Internet waves which move with the speed of light. With the exception of tachyons, since a greater speed cannot be thought of than the speed of light, there will not be an increase in the speed of communication. A civilization which we get to contact should be knowledgeable about the science of radio astronomy. It is not possible to contact civilizations which do not have this technology. A civilization which is millions of years more advanced in comparison to us will not be interested. Signals with the speed of light have been sent from Earth to the universe for the last 100 years. If we consider that these have been sent in the beginning of 20th century, some signals have covered great distances already. However, it is a very low probability that there are being listened to beings which are aware of them. The widest possible area of the universe is being scanned and listened to by us to be able to receive signals broadcasted by intelligent beings. However, it is very challenging to scan millions of stars using frequency. Therefore, it seems a very low probability that we will establish any contact with any civilization on our level. Universal intelligence is everywhere; however it is very difficult to determine the manifestations of intelligent beings.

The easiest proof of the existence of universal intelligence is to show it in notions we can most easily observe and prove. The location of the world is the most apparent proof of universal intelligence. The uranium and lead ratio measurement in our world's oldest rocks predicts the age of the world as around 5 million years. The world seems to be positioned at a location in a specific time slice to enable life to take shelter on it. The Earth is 149.6 million kilometers away from the Sun. This distance is the most appropriate distance which makes it possible to make the heat of the Sun and light energy suitable for life. A few degrees of deviation in the orbit would cause the world to either overheat, or over cool and in both case, it would means the end of life. If the distance between the Earth and the Sun were 148 million kilometers and not 150, it would be impossible for life to begin on Earth due to overheat. In the same manner, if the distance were 152 million kilometers, the Earth would be at a point which is so cold that life would not be possible. It is as if our world has been placed in this orbit in accordance with calculations in terms of its distance to the Sun.

According to Hegel, there is also a universal consciousness and the whole nature is a product of it. The structure of the universe is the proof of the existence universal intelligence. Everything in life has been planned with thought. This planning shows that the conscious action of a great being is in question. Universal intelligence is a consciousness which penetrates in all atomies of life and plans everything. The balance of nature and its perfection cannot be explained beyond the existence of this consciousness. Man who observes the complicated structure of the universe has no choice but to accept that all this structure is the work of a great intelligence.

The infallible order of events has become active since the first moment of the creation of the world and it still continues. For instance, if there were no explosions on the Sun, the light, heat and energy required to protect the vitality of the Earth would not be possible. What is more, the quality and quantity of these reaching our world is accurately at the needed level. It seems that everything has been minutely calculated to make life on Earth possible. The Earth's orbit being close to circular and elliptic seems like another condition required for the existence of life. This orbit is the most important reason of seasonal cycle. This cycle makes it possible for the required conditions for the formation life to emerge at every point on the world. Nitrogen is formed through microorganisms' in the soil turning nitrate and ammonium into nitrogen. Plant life depends on the amount of nitrate in the soil. Nitric acid is formed through a natural process and soil is fertilized. Each lightening in the sky allows the formation of nitric acid. Carbon dioxide which is the waste of plants is transformed in Oxygen through the plants' photosynthesis and respiration and forms this matter which is necessary of animal life. In the same manner, animals turn the oxygen they use into carbon dioxide and support the cycle. The atmosphere has reached its current ratios 500 million years ago.

The Sun is the world's greatest source of energy. The Earth takes only 1 two billionth of the energy created by the Sun. However, the atmosphere still makes it possible for the harmful beams brought by this amount to be filtered and life to continue. When this energy is stored for 15 minutes, energy need of the world can be met for a year. The amount of energy emitted by the Sun is gradually increasing due to the increase in used fuel each moment. Therefore, a few billion years later, the Earth will become impossible to live on due to this excess energy coming from the Sun. Mars which has an average temperature of minus 50 today will be more suitable for life.

The thickness of the Sun's ecosphere is 10 million kilometers. However, its efficiency reaches greater distances. The Earth is also in this ecosphere. Through the world's spinning within the activity area of the ecosphere, life has been possible. Due to the Sun's radiations influencing carious molecules, it has possible to transform amino acids which are defined as inanimate into living organisms and the first bacteria cells have emerged during the process. The photosynthesis of these bacteria cells created the oxygen needed by evolution and multicellular organism were created as a result of the transformation of some bacteria and using oxygen as fuel. The first forests appeared 410 million years ago and 40 million years after that, the first living beings left the water and began to live on land.

Another effect of the Sun is the vaporization of water due to heat and fall on earth again as rain. Due to this cycle, 17 million tons of water falls on Earth every second. The same amount of water then vaporizes and ascends. 17 million tons of water is only 2.7% of the total water stock. The world's total amount of water is mainly in the seas and it is salty water. The total amount of fresh water is 200 thousand cubic kilometers and is only 15/100,000 of the total water stock. Precipitation is the most important nutrient of the fresh water source. Through precipitation, 500 thousand cubic kilometers of fresh water fall in earth each year. The total amount of fresh water used by the whole world population is around 4 thousand cubic kilometers per year. Since our atmosphere is within the world's force of gravity, it does not escape to the sky and hold water vapor inside.

The nitrogen/oxygen balance in the atmosphere is fixed in the ratio of 80 to 20 and due to oxygen forming the ozone layer in the upper layers; the world is protected from the radiation coming from the Sun and cosmic beams. The ratio of carbon dioxide in the atmosphere is 3%. The balance of oxygen-carbon dioxide can be protected due to two different life forms living together on Earth. Carbon dioxide which is the imperative waster of animal forms is the imperative necessity of plant forms, whereas the imperative waste of plant forms oxygen is the imperative necessity of animal forms. The existence of carbon dioxide in the atmosphere protects the world from a continuous ice age. Carbon dioxide's being more transparent against infrared light in comparison to oxygen and nitrogen creates a greenhouse effect. This greenhouse effect allows the world's temperature at livable levels. Carbon dioxide's doubling in amount would mean the overheating of the world and the melting of all the glaciers. This would drag the world towards an unlivable climate.

By means of gravity, it is possible for beings on earth to continue their lives and not get scattered to space. The main force which provides gravity is the nucleus of the world. This nucleus at the center of the world is liquid due to its temperature. However, right at the center there is solid iron due to high pressure. The spinning of the Earth creates vortexes in the liquid. These vortexes create an electrical charge at the center due to the special structure of iron atoms and iron turns into a magnet. Thus, the iron nucleus creates a magnetic field which envelops the whole world. This magnetic field encloses the world through its force lines which connect the magnetic poles. This example and hundreds of similar examples are proof that everything continues within the context of a program.

The world is surrounded by an electromagnetic field. This magnetic crust is sensitive towards any type of electromagnetic energy which comes from space. The changing combinations and frequencies of these energies directly affect life on Earth. The electromagnetic field which is inherent in every individual functions as a receiving antenna for all the electromagnetic waves which come from the outside. American scientist Leonard Ravitz has proven that the energy area in humans changes in line with mental and emotional activity in the studies he carried out in 1959. The brightness of the wave energy which occurs in the magnetic field, its density and color change according to the person's mood. This electrical field can be measured by means of a super conductive quantum interference device known as Squid. Ph.D. Ruper Sheldrake who conducts a study on the electromagnetic fields of animals states that these invisible energy fields regulate the whole system of the animals. These fields function as a designer of physical form and the physical from of animals seems to be connected to the interactions it is subject to from the outside. The atmosphere of the world is constantly under the influence of a cosmic beam rain which comes from the whole universe. The high energy small pieces which these cosmic beams contain constantly bump into each other and while some of them turn into energy, some others create new particle molecules. In other words, every object in the universe is subject to the effects of the other objects in the infinite process.

Planets do not only send electromagnetic waves to the space. They also have sounds which their unique vibrations produce. When the American satellite Voyager 2 got closer to Saturn, it has directly heard Saturn's voice. The sounds coming from Saturn's magnetosphere were speeded up and played with a synthesizer and it has been seen that the waves produce a specific melody. In the same manner, the sounds coming from the Sun have also been analyzed and it has been discovered that it seems to produce a symphony played by various musical instruments. NASA states that the sounds coming from the whole universe are heard almost like a magnificent symphony. In other words, Pythagoras who claimed that the ratios between the sounds in the music scale and the ratio of one planet's distance to the other is the same seems to be right. Tonoscope studies have proven this fact.

English astronomer Sir Martin Ress states that nothing in the universe is coincidental. Reeds suggests if the force values between the two nuclei inside the formation of Carbon on which all life on earth is based are even nano unit different, then life would not be possible and the same is true for all objects in space. Carbon has attained the characteristics it has today after going through a three step process. Another astronomer Fred Hoyle states that even in case of a 0.4 change, the birth of life based on carbon would be impossible; because in this case, each star would perhaps still be producing carbon and oxygen, but the two elements will never come together. Thus, carbon dioxide which allows life to be born will never be formed. The existence of carbon dioxide is based on a precise physical fixed force between the atomic nuclei

There are a total of 6 physical constants which allow certain conditions to be accurately formed in the sub-atomic world. The emergence of the accuracy condition or life deems it necessary for these six constant variables to be brought together with a very fine tuning. The randomness ratio of this condition is s impossible a ratio as six thrown dices coming out with the same number. Shortly, our being here, our existence depends on the very finely tuned constants of nature and laws of nature which are in harmony. The existence of man has been possible by means of the coming together of uncountable coincidences. Even a 1 degree deviation in the world's axis would be sufficient for the destruction of the world we know and are used to. Are these only a chain of coincidences as some people claim? Those who reject the idea that a purposeful universe is possible as an antecedent have come the point of contradicting themselves at the issue that an accurate universe has been created by chance. Rees states "Our existence and survival depend on the very special adjustments of the universe. The goal of the universe if much wider than we can see". Astrophysicist James Jeans says "The universe is a thought rather than a machine," and support the previous idea.

Mankind is newly developing the knowledge about the universe. We should remember that, our Sun's being at the center of the universe had been generally acknowledged as a "reality" adopted by the whole humanity until strong telescopes came into the Picture in 20th century. It was Giordano Buruno who first expressed in Europe that the universe was limitless. Bruno defended his claim despite the fact that it was against the official approval of the church and was executed by being burned. After Newton, the universe has been regarded as a group of matter which is independent of one another; however quantum physics has shown that the physical reality is much different. According to Einstein's General Theory of Relativity "the universe is made up of the union of Time-Space-Motion-Matter which has come together and has not separated from each other". Quantum science has shown that in the essence of the Universe, there are certain forms of materialized light. Matter and energy, the body and the spirit are a whole. This has been proven with the discovery of the Higgs particle which turns energy into matter as a result of the experiments carried out in CERN. Shortly, we may say that science has reached a point where it cannot no longer deny the Union of Existence.

MIRACLE OF LIFE

The only source which can be used as an example in terms of the formation of life conditions and sustainability of life seems to be the Earth in the present time. However, many findings show us that life cannot be limited with our world and that it may be spread to the whole universe. Moreover, is life only limited with living beings? In accordance with the knowledge we have today and our perceptions, is it possible to accept that beings which we define as inanimate indeed are "living" within the framework of their own natural environment and conditions? In the universe, inanimate beings have a life of their own. Matter's physical and chemical changes suitable for natural life, the spinning of atoms and stars on orbits are each a manifestation of this life. It is not possible to change or remove the natural laws which these depend on. Mankind has not been able to realize even the smallest of change in laws of nature despite his efforts. We cannot even say that we have learned the laws as a whole. Just like everything else in the universe, we are the materialized version of those laws which have shaped the universe. Life is evolving with the rest of the universe.

The principle of sustaining existence by spending minimum amount of energy may be defined as "the principle of existence". Each individual chooses a life-style which will allow him to be comfortable with the minimum amount of effort. In the same manner, since humans are social beings, it can be said that they are in a constant effort to unite. This wish is not conscious; it is natural; because it is mankind's unconscious wish to return to the whole. Individuals' having families, coming together at institutions, founding political parties and finally states are all reflections of this wish. When the unity is realized, work is distributed among everyone and results which a single person cannot achieve are achieved by groups. By means of this work distribution, it becomes possible for people to attain maximum amount of benefit using minimum amount of energy. While small amounts of energy requires an order, excess of energy points out to chaos. Many systems turn themselves into orderly structures in accordance with the principle of spending the minimum amount of energy. Clouds of matter which are scattered around space coming together and forming a star, the stars coming together and forming galaxies, galaxies coming together to from bigger galaxies all take place within the scope of the principle of attaining maximum benefit through minimum energy. In the same manner, due to the decrease in energy because of the expansion of space, the celestial bodies come together and join their energies. The principle of sustaining existence by spending minimum energy is the main principle of existence. The principle of spending minimum amount of energy is observed in animals as well. Behind fish forming schools, birds flying in a specific order while they form flocks is this principle. Since birds and fish moving in different directions will form a different air and water flow resistance, it results in spending excess energy. However, when they move together, there is no air or water resistance; on the contrary, these become supports. All beings, which are both defined as living and inanimate fit this principle for which examples have been provided above. In accordance with this point of view, is it possible to talk about whether objects which move in the same manner as living or inanimate? Where does the living-inanimate boundary begin and end? After which aspects are added to a cell which is defined as inanimate becomes living? It is not possible to say for sure. It is not easy to say whether an existence is conscious, or unconscious. The only reason why consciousness is different in humans is that they are able to storage knowledge in higher levels in comparison to other beings:

If there is no chemical reaction in a substance and this matter does not reproduce by itself, cannot adapt to the changing external conditions, does not Exchange energy, it is "inanimate" by our definition. However, this is nothing by an erroneous observation. All matter which is assumed to be inanimate is in a state of constant change and transformation. They go through a never ending process of existence and destruction. Science defines these as inanimate and thus deals more with the How of the issue instead of the question why. The real secret is hidden beneath the Why's. It is natural that the boundaries of many of today's unknown issues will be overcome in the near or far future, the territories of the unknown will be entered newly and the definition of concepts such as Vitality will totally change. On the other hand, when analysis is made in the atomic level, it is known that although atoms display differences in accordance with the sequence and number of electrons, protons and neutrons, they are the same in basis, in essence as well. Elements are in a constant state of passing from the living to the inanimate and from the inanimate to the living. The border where physical event ends and biological event begins is still not known today in full. For instance, is the DNA molecule which allows the continuation of generations alive or inanimate? Matter being sensitive to external factors is not an indication either. It is impossible even for a rock, or stone not be affected by external factors. The stone is a sensitive matter as well, but since we cannot establish the required communication with it and this sensitivity is not perceived by us, the stone is defined as inanimate. Alchemists claim that stones are living beings. They suggest that, since the life course of stones are very slow, it is not likely to observe them.

The human cell is a structure which embodies the knowledge of reproducing itself. This knowledge is hidden in the DNA molecule. DNA discovered by biologist James Watson and physicist Francis Crick, which is a complex acid molecule, has the knowledge to produce new cells which have its own DNA within itself. Almost all cells of all living organisms contain DNA and only that being's information can be found inside them. Scientifically, it is possible to reproduce a whole organism even from a single DNA. The most definite expression and sign of the continuity of life is the cells' capacity of carrying information.

Knowledge is physical. The building block of everything is not matter, energy or love, but knowledge. Nature uses knowledge for communication through atoms. Beneath every process observed in nature, there is knowledge. The main implementer of knowledge is biology. Biology completely functions through genes which continue their evolution by means of the language of protecting and transmitting knowledge. In genetics science, there is a definition which makes it the easiest to understand what knowledge is. In terms of basic principles, biological knowledge is always universal. Knowledge is DNA and DNA is knowledge. DNA is a molecule. DNA transmits information in a conscious manner to RNA. RNA in return transmits this information to the Amino Acids. The Amino Acids read and understand this information and build various cells. These various cells form group by complying with the plan and create the living organism. The process as a whole is conscious starting from the smallest molecule.

DNA, which defines all living beings, consists of four nucleotide molecules. These are Guanine, Cytosine, Thymine and Adenine. In short, there are four letters in the DNA alphabet. This basic structure is the proof that all living beings come from a common ancestor. The fact that all living beings use the same building blocks strengthens the Single Beginning discourse. The number of genes of a bacterium written with this alphabet is 2 thousand and the number of genes in a human being is 1 billion. Living structures go through change using two methods. The first is DNA mutations and the second is DNA's sexual mix. Mutation is a hereditary change in the nucleotide circles. In sexual mix, a change which takes place in sperm or ovaries can affect the future generations. This change is reflected in all of the cells of the new being. In humans, who are made up of 60 trillion cells, there are 60 trillion identical DNA.

Is it a coincidence that the whole universe has been built based on 4 basic forces and DNA structure consisting of 4 basic molecules? Esoteric symbolized these 4 basic forces as Fire, Air, Water and Earth and stated that these are active as pairs. These pairs are Fire and Air and Water and Earth. DNA has the same structure. Adenine can only pair up with Thymine and Guanine can only pair up with Cytosine. It seems that nature has left very little place for everything to go right. The language of the universe is a language which consists of sequential binary numbers and this language is being used as computer language today. The language of the nature is based on sequential binary number Paris, thus a total of 4 numbers instead of sequential binary numbers. Everyone will be able to the following paragraph, although it is very complicated and has been written with this digital coding system:

"According to a research team at Cambridge University, it doesn't matter in what order the letters in a word are; the only important thing is that the first and last letter be in the right place. The rest can be a total mess and you can still read it without a problem. This is because the human mind does not read every letter by itself, but the word as a whole".

So, why does nature make use of digital coding? Because the binary analogue coding will create an extraordinary need for energy and the possibility of making mistakes is very high. However, despite the digital copying method and all the carefulness, some mistakes remain without being corrected and this is called mutation. Some mutations take existence to a more advanced formation which adapts better to the changes in its environment. These mutations are the foundations of the evolutionary process named "Natural Selection". Natural selection makes it easier to establish a connection with the environment. Those who are to survive are ones who best adapt to the environment. Shortly, DNA's are each a historical records of environmental changes our ancestors have experienced. It is apparent that each DNA which is living will be evolved to a more complex structure in the future, because environmental change and information flow are infinite. Is it not interesting that meaningful information is born mandatorily from each interaction between events which are claimed to be coincidental and the natural selection processes which are claimed to be determinist?

The digital coding mechanism of DNA guarantees the transmission of the universal message which most fits its original. So, where does DNA come from? Is there a simpler structure DNA is evolved in? For instance, could the crystal which are simpler structures than DNA and are formed by themselves be the roots of DNA? This may sound like a rational inference; however it is a mystery how the information embodied by DNA is transferred from crystals. Perhaps, DNA's do not only carry information, but other messages as well. What is clear is that, the root of life can be explained by means of the universal knowledge mechanism. But, how is this information formed? Why does knowledge exist before everything else and how does it come to being from nothingness?

Molecular biology has shown that all life forms on Earth use the same genetic code. The DNA code sequence for the same amino acids in all types is the same. This is even true for amino acids found on meteors. In other words, life has been written on the same DNA code sequences in the whole universe. Although environmental factors cause the differentiation of evolution, all life forms in the universe are programmed in the same manner.

The scientific research have shown that chemical elements which are regarded as inanimate beings turn into "RNA" and "DNA" molecules, which are the building blocks of life, when they find suitable environments. In other words, RNA-DNA molecules become alive as soon as they find spirit. RNA carries all the information it receives from DNA which is inside the cell nucleus to the organelles in the cells and makes the continuation of vitality possible. These molecules have first formed the first beings which are unicellular and these beings have formed other beings with more complex structures by time. Death is the separation of the soul from matter. With death, the border which separates the living and the inanimate is overcome. Is this really true? Is what separates the living from the inanimate the existence of lack of the spirit? As developments are made in the areas of physics, chemistry, biology and medicine, it is observed that the absolute boundary between the living and the inanimate is gradually disappearing. It is possible to reduce nature, all living and inanimate beings down to 92 natural and 17 artificial elements. Beings with cell units are essentially made up of 4 of these 109 elements. These are carbon, hydrogen, oxygen and nitrogen. All kinds of matter which the life of the living beings and evolution need have been prepared on earth and its atmosphere. Despite all our knowledge of nuclear chemistry and biochemistry, there are still no answers in terms of why and partly about why of this preparation. It is possible that, even to the first electron of the first hydrogen atom which emerged with the Big Bang has been placed the whole evolutionary program of the universe and this is not only true for our world, but the whole universe. The program is continued in the same direction for the whole universe through the communication and interaction method between the electrons.

For life to exist, the cells should have the ability to copy themselves. The continuation of cells' life depends on their ability to copy themselves. In one period of the evolution, it can be seen that a molecule has copied itself by suing all the other molecules around it as building blocks. However, using other molecules in the environment for this process requires a special function and intelligence. In other words, when this molecule is specifically appointed, it can reproduce itself by using the other molecules around it. However, due to being appointed, the molecule carries this task mandatorily without the need for intelligence. The appointment is hidden in the information within the DNA's. Coincidences emerge perforce within the framework of existing laws of physics and biology, whereas coincidental mutations which take place out of necessity begin their activity through the DNA's in accordance with a specific plan. Therefore, coincidences have formed life within the scope of laws which created universe, in accordance with a plan.

No living being is alone when it is transmitting its DNA to the new generation. Therefore, there can be no individuals with the same DNA. The DNA of two different types forms the DNA data base of the new individual. Thus, new qualitative characteristics emerge in each new individual. Some individuals are born having undergone mutation. These new individuals are constantly tested by nature and the environment. The produced new individual will pass the test, reproduce or quit the game. In this manner, the continuation of the type is made possible through mutations and natural selection in the most perfect and environmentally harmonized way.

DNA molecules embody information about how a life form is to be shaped and produced. All the required information an out forming a cell, or an organism which is made up of a number of cells is stored in DNA's. Information is in packaged from in the DNA's and these packages are called chromosomes. The number of chromosomes in the human body is 23 pairs. DNA starts working with the single cell it is in. Then, it copies itself identically and forms two cells. 2 cells become 4, 4 cells become 8, 8 cells become 16 and the increase continues in accordance with the information in the DNA through geometrical sequence up to a certain point. This process of increase may be resembled to the expansion process of the universe. It is of possibility that the universe will stop at a point foreseen by its program. It is possible that the universe is expanding in order to reach a certain magnitude. 60 trillion cells are needed to form an average human being. DNA cannot reproduce in the form of a single cell structure. For each different structure, different cell structures are produced. Heart cells for the heart, eye cells for the eye are produced. In short, everything is constructed with an extraordinary mind in its place. It is written in coded form in the DNA how a living being is to be made in its finest detail. This coding is called "Genetic Code". Coding is carried out through the 4 main bases explained earlier. All living being are constructed within the framework of a specific plan by means of the coding of these 4 basic bases. This plan is evident in the same manner in each cell of that being. All beings are of holographic structure. The information pertaining to the whole is evident in the smallest unit.

Quantum physicists have proven that matter and energy are essentially the different manifestations of the same electromagnetic energy. Light, which is a form of energy, seems to be life itself. All beings owe their biological functions to light. Without light, there can be no life. Without light, nothing can be perceived. The energy, which brings everything into existence and makes everything visible, is light. In all discourses about the creation, it has been proven scientifically as well that saying that God has firstly given the "Let there be light" command is an accurate approach. The Big Bang has allowed an extraordinary light to be created.

Nature has established its own quantum computer before man. Through this computer network, all kinds of information everywhere is being shared and presented to the use of those who need it. The name of this computer is Supreme Consciousness, or universal Intelligence.

The best example of the system which makes use of the advantages of the quantum computer is man. Human DNA acts just like the chips of a super conductive computer, which embodies information about life in the highest level. DNA is the information storehouse of a great Quantum Computer. The most important characteristic of DNA, which is a macro molecule, is its ability to exist in different states. All natural processes provide their functionality within the framework of quantum principles. Universal reality seems like the product of a multi-layered, complex quantum calculation. For instance, the photosynthesis process which allows the continuation of life on Earth is completely a quantum chain of actions. Photosynthesis is the name given to the process carried out by plants to soak the Sun's light energy, store it and use later on. Through photosynthesis, the disorderly energy which comes from the Sun is coiled and turned into a more orderly and beneficial standard. With the help of this energy whose structure is changed, plant cells can fully carry out their function. Graham Fleming from Berkeley University in the USA has determined that plants use quantum effects for the photosynthesis process. When plant molecules crash into the molecules of sun beams, the molecular vibrations of energy go through change and energy whose dynamics have been changed makes it possible for the plant's feeding process to begin. In this manner, it has been determined that 98% of the sun beams which carry radiation and reach the plant are transformed and stored. This energy makes it possible for plants to suck the carbon dioxide and give off oxygen. Without photosynthesis, there would not be sufficient oxygen in the atmosphere of the world and living life forms cannot live. It seems that the most basic needs of life can be met by quantum laws.

Scientific realities rebut the claim that life has been formed on its own through some coincidences. All life on earth has been determined to be derived from a single source. If life has started with a series of chemical reactions which developed on their own, why does life have many sources which are based on similar environments and not one? A majority of the chemical elements found in living beings contain elements which are found in fewer amounts in the planet. This makes us think why living structure are made up of elements which are more in number in our planet and from elements which are found rarely. The hypothesis that life has come to our world most probably from space has been gaining more and more followers. Therefore, life is not a coincidence, but a process foreseen by a conscious plan to spread it to the whole universe.

Life is predicted to have begun 1.5 Billion years after the formation of the earth. Microscopic life began about 3.5 Billion years ago on earth and then cells with nuclei which had the ability to do photosynthesis appeared. It is known that the first bacteria like beings have lived 3.5 Billion years ago on earth. The most important aspect of these beings is their ability to reproduce themselves. In the beginning of the Cambrian period, 600 Million years ago, complex and advanced multicellular life was began to be seen. According to the fossils which have been found, the first fish in the world appeared 480 Million years ago, the first amphibians 365 Million years ago and the first mammals appeared 210 Million years ago. Life on earth has started in the sky, but developed in the oceans. The fluid in the living cells of all organisms is basically a type of ocean water. There is no life on earth which is not based on water. Bacteria and viruses can preserve their vitality infinitely in completely dried form, but it is not possible for them to sustain their life in environments where water or another fluid to replace water is not found. Life cannot be continued within a solid environment. The same is true for gas state. The chemical events which create life can only be water based. Multicellular life began in the seas and has remained in the seas about nine tenths of the time until the present time. Finally, living beings moved from the seas to the land about 425 Million years ago. The development of life on the land has been possible only through the increase in the number of plants and the amount of oxygen. In the same process, the ozone layer has also gained strength and began to protect living organisms from the harmful rays of the Sun. The first plants have been seen 470 Million years ago. The first vertebrates appeared 375 Million years ago and the first mammals 210 Million years ago. The first primates were born 75 Million years ago. Hominoids with developed brains were seen about 10 Million years ago and only 200 Thousand years ago Homo sapiens, or humans have appeared. During the 3.5 Billion year time, the total number of living species which appeared and still continue their existence is estimated to be around 35 Million.

Are we, humans, made only of atoms which are finite in the infinite universe, limited in terms of power and potential, destined to break apart and come undone after a physical life where nothing is to be experienced afterwards, that came together by chance and in random? Are Homo sapiens a product of the evolutionary process? Evolutionists state that if the evolution of humankind progresses as usual, then the appearance of today's man will take a couple of million years. However, there has been an inexplicable leap in the process 200 thousand years ago and Homo sapiens was suddenly seen on earth. These leaps bring the question "Is there an Intelligent Design or an Intelligent Intervention?" to the mind. Again, about 100 thousand years ago, there is also a process where a very fast evolution took place in the brain functions of Homo sapiens and almost a quantum leap has been experienced. It has been observed that there is a strong tie between the development of the human brain and the environment lived in. This will be dealt with in detail in the coming chapters.

If we consider that we are all made up of protein, the key to evolution is the changing protein. If change increases adaptation to the conditions of the environment, then great. Otherwise, it would be lost. Different from other living beings, the evolutionary change of humans has more than one dimension. We may say that, tools developed personally by man have given direction to the bio-evolution of humans. Tool making began 2 million years ago. Changing anything which can be found in nature and shaping these to serve a purpose is tool making. It is impossible for a human species to continue his existence in different ecological environments if he cannot make tools. Mankind has evolved as various human species, however with the help of its tool making ability; only one species has survived until today (Homo sapiens). Another reason why Homo sapiens has been able to continue its existence is its use of language. Humans, who learned how to speak with language, have acquired the ability to transfer their thoughts and experiences to the next generation and develop it. The control of fire, agriculture, animal husbandry and writing are other significant factors which contributed to our evolution. Contrary to other living species, only humans are able to shape their environment on a large scale. Sometimes, even if it is to its disadvantage, mankind's fate is in his hands rather than nature.

Life on Earth began with amino acids and proteins. In 1957, Miller put some ethane, hydrogen, ammonium and pure water in a cup and applied electric shock to it. After this process, it was observed that there were amino acids in the cup which are the basic elements of a living cell. Proteins create bacteria and single celled beings and the number of cells have gradually increased. The total number of amino acids in the most primitive multicellular beings is 20. In order for these 20 amino acids to unite to form a living being, it is apparent that they need a pre-programmed structure. The probability of a living molecule group to be randomly born out of a non-living molecule is 1 out of 160 over 10. In other words, it is a probability very close to zero. However, in experiments conducted since 1953, amino acids are acquired frequently from non-living molecules. These experiments have shown that the emergence of life is not coincidental and that it shows a necessity. In the light of this information, it has been determined that the first living molecule has been formed 3.5 billion years ago in the atmosphere and developed under the depths of the ocean and initiated life. The atmosphere is an environment which both provides heat circulation and prevents heat loss. The world's force of gravity has the power to preserve the atmosphere. Neither the existence of the atmosphere, nor the emergence of first life in the atmosphere can be explained as coincidence. Many planets have an atmosphere even if they are of different structures and carbon which is the founding block of living organisms is everywhere. Therefore, the existence of life at many points in the universe is an expected, and even a necessary process.

Carbon is a must for the existence of a life that we know of. The determination of a living being's duration of life is also possible with the carbon test. Carbon-12, which is the Standard Carbon element, has a fixed structure made up of 6 protons and 6 neutrons. Carbon-14 is made up of 6 protons and 8 neutrons. These two extra neutrons are formed as a result of the strike of the cosmic beams of the universe on Earth. The moment any living organism begins life, some carbon elements catch two extra protons due to the effect of the cosmic beams and carbons turn into a nondurable structure. Carbon-14 is radioactive due to this unstable structure. Carbon-14 continues to be formed until the moment it continues its living state. After death, its formation ends as well. Although its reason has not been understood fully, the new Carbon-14 does not enter the body and Carbon-14 which is in the body begins to deteriorate to transform into Carbon-12. Carbon-14 analysis is the best method known to determine the age of dead living beings. By the means of this method, the period in which living beings up to 11.400 years of age can be accurately determined. The life-span of Carbon-14 is around 5700 years. In 5700 years, half of Carbon-14 deteriorates and becomes Carbon-12. In 11,400 years, the total amount of Carbon-14 turns into Carbon-12 and it becomes no longer possible to determine the age of old living beings through this method.

What is the mechanism which makes this possible? How does "time" apply pressure on an atom? The reason is the quantum fluctuations of the zero point field. Carbon-14 deterioration takes place in the nucleus of the atom. The electrons in the atoms pass from a state of energy to another state of energy after death and thus the wave band line changes. As a result of this change, the two extra neutrons achieved from cosmic beams gradually begin to leave the structure of the atom. In 5700 years, the first neutron and in the second 5700 years, the second neutron leaves the atom. So, what is the factor which causes the wave dimensions of electrons to change? Each atom has a diffusion of its own. The cosmic photons which emerge at the zero point field create an additional diffusion to this diffusion by colliding with the electrons in living beings and photons reach a different wave length when they collide with the electrons. Then, the collision number of protons which collide with the electrons increases and Carbon-12 turns into Carbon-14. If there are no more electrons to collide with, the zero point photons' action stops. In other words, with the end of vitality the extra dissemination also stops and the atoms star to move to their previous usual locations. The zero point field seems like a factor which activates universal dynamics.

According to the materialist universe theory, the universe has come into being on its own and in random; life forms which started life out of necessity within these environments which were formed through coincidence and go through evolution on their own and reach their current status. This is called evolution. According to this theory, vitality is something which emerges in random and its root is based on a single cell. This cell goes through evolution in different ways and different environments and as a consequence, life forms which are very different from each other have come into being. However, is the beginning of life a consequence of coincidence?

3.5 billion years ago, as a result of a suitable environment appearing on Earth, inorganic matter turned into organic matter and the first living cell is formed. The time needed for inorganic elements to form a living cell in random is 243 over 10 years. We should keep in mind that the age of the universe is only 10 over 10. The probability of a protein to turn into amino acid is 48 over 10. In other words, the probability of an amino acid to be randomly formed will take billions and billions of years. Since the beginning of life for living being on Earth was 3.5 billion years ago, the claim that nature has provided our world with living beings as a result of a chain of coincidences is left worthless. What is more, an amino acid's acquiring the capacity to continue its existence, producing a virus required for the DNA molecule to turn into a structure which will contain at least 10 thousand information units seems outside all possibilities of coincidence. Above all, the emergence of a human brain which has the capacity to think and create at the end of this process is beyond all calculations of probability. Eccles, who has won the Nobel Medicine Prize for his studies on the human brain, states "The more we discover about the brain, the more clearly do we distinguish between the brain events and the mental phenomena, and the more wonderful do both the brain events and the mental phenomena become. Promissory materialism is simply a religious belief held by dogmatic materialists . . . who often confuse their religion with their science". It is inevitable to accept the existence of a divine program.

In some of the pieces of comets which fall on Earth, water and carbon compounds, amino acids seen in the proteins of living tissues and fatty acids. Amino acids are inanimate matters which are formed with the coming together of different atoms. However, proteins are formed from amino acids and life is born on its own in this process. The evidence of amino acids in celestial bodies means that life will begin in every suitable environment. Life seems like an evolutionary program spread to the whole universe. Cells which make up all living organisms seem to have the capacity to decide their own evolution, in order to be able to adapt to their environment in the most perfect manner possible. How has this ability and information of change placed in cells? Are all living organism cells pieces of a universal intelligence?

The supporters of Creationist theory suggest that nothing is coincidence and everything has been created by the Supreme Creator at that first moment, with their current perfection. Millions of living beings have been created with a complete, perfect and superior design in their first moment of their creation. However, the existence of the evolutionary process is a reality which cannot be denied. All species come into existence in accordance with a specific program, however can continue their lives depending on how well they adapt to their surroundings and the evolutionary process. With Darwin's announcing the Theory of Evolution in 19th century, the Catholic Church which opposed this theory with full force and constantly attempted to prove otherwise was left with no choice but the come to terms with the theory of evolution in the light of all the developments. In 1950, Pope 12th Pius published the Human Generis encyclical, which stated that the theory of evolution has not been proven yet, but was a serious assumption. 1996, Pope 2nd Jean Paul stated "New knowledge necessitates the acknowledgement that the theory of evolution is more than an assumption". The English Anglican Church followed the steps of Vatican and announced in 2008 that Darwin's Theory of Evolution is valid and apologized from the world of science. Meanwhile, the Protestant Church still insists on the Creation Theory.

Esoteric argues that life has developed within the scope of a Divine program, but depending on the laws of evolution. Quantum laws which prove Esoteric state that there is nothing as randomness. On the contrary, randomness is not a notion that can ever be given importance to by quantum physics either. Randomness is an inherent state which has spread both to micro cosmos and macro cosmos, to the whole universe. An adverse state would mean blocking the path of evolution. However, associating all developments with only coincidences is as absurd as denying randomness as a whole. Today, science is in position of bet which is placed on the results of the future. German thinker Immanuel Kant stated that he sees the insistence on the reality of the theories and placing a bet as equal. Evolution has two components: The first is the coincidental mutation in the genetic code and the second is being subject to natural selection by the environment. Therefore, evolution itself depends on multi randomness. If the living systems have into being through the regular operation of information processing, then it is not possible to deny randomness. In the same manner, the universe is being evolved by means of its maximal randomness. However, information should exist in a non-random manner for all this. Everything operates within the framework of a specific program.

Life is a natural result of the long evolutionary process. The species came into being when the simple molecules randomly came together in accordance with a specific plan and forming more complex structures which are different from one another. The Universe is an incident which is based perhaps on coincidences in its every stage, however in the DNA of every being formed, there is information as to what kind of a species it will be evolved in. According to a scientific claim called The Anthropic Principle, the universe has been designed to create mankind every time. This claim contends that a single intelligent life form, the Homo sapiens have reached rationality. This point of view means that, either the world with all the humans on it is the only example in the whole wide universe, or that Homo Sapiens will necessarily come into existence through evolution at some stage at every point where life can survive in the universe.

The evolution of living beings depends on three events. The first is heredity through genes which come from our ancestors; the second is the mix of genes which come with reproduction and the third is variation (mutation) as a result of individuals adapting to the changes in the environment. When the characteristics formed are transmitted to the next generation, genes which transmit differences in the society increase and evolution continues steadily. The most important of differentiation is sexual differentiation. The defects seen in those people whose parents are close relatives are the result of the insufficiency of sexual differentiation. In some living species which reproduce without sex, it is observed that evolution nearly does not take place at all. For instance, blue algae have not evolved for 3 billion years.

The historical development of the evolutionary process is repeated in the mother's womb from simple to complex (ontogenetic development or ontogenesis). Therefore, if development stops or if it is stopped due to a chemical or physical impact, or a hereditary malfunction, the being at that stage begins to display the characteristics of the being which coincides evolutionarily with that stage For instance, it will either have primate or syndactyly, have fish scales, will be born with some sort of tail or a body covered with hide like hair, have more than one breast, have gill slits in the area of the neck, have cleft palate and very functional muscles as to move the skin at some places in its body. If the genes which overcome these characteristics are active, the necessary development takes place and the being takes its final appearance. If these genes can take development only up to a certain level, the baby to be born can only acquire the characteristic of his ancestors which is controlled by that gene. If this characteristic cannot keep pace with the other developed and important characteristics, the being dies. It is a scientific reality that the organs are not formed in a complex manner in the womb and that very simple designs gradually become complex structures and more importantly, each acquired characteristic is controlled by one or more enzymes. Most importantly, the enzymes which control these stages in the embryonic development, thus genes, are the same with our closest relative species which carry this characteristic. This is a very clear proof that beings with new characteristics emerge, branching out from an ancestor.

It is known that the genes and enzymes which supervise these stages have a specific molecular sequence, are similar in accordance with their closeness to their relative and some of the deviations taking place in these molecules prevent the characteristics to emerge, or slide to another characteristic. The most important success achieved by the point science has reached today is that, it is able to determine that an anomaly which takes place in out external appearance, or a function is the result of a malfunction in which molecule. Therefore, during life's progress through the process which we call evolution from simple to complex, takes place with the additions made to the hereditary molecule, some changes taking place and is carried out through selection, has become the founding block of the teaching of biology. To be able to understand this, we firstly need to grasp the diversification aspect of the DNA molecule. To make it clearer, DNA is like dough; structural characteristics may be achieved to its effects and various shapes (characteristics) may be achieved functionally. Those which are suitable (successful ones) survive; those which are not are eliminated and are atrophied. For instance, the Pineal body resembles a primitive retina. The pineal gland resembles a primitive eye crystal, a small eye with its pigment and peripheral cells. It is possible that this brain structure which is called the pineal gland might be the remains of a third eye we used to have in the past. Just like our appendicitis or tail, our third eye might have been atrophied.

IT has been observed that amino acid types, which are the proof that living structures evolve from simple to complex, have increased every 10 million years and new life form emerge at the end of each increase. The first single celled life form which has 3 amino acid types is the ameba. The life form which has 140 amino acid types is primates. The number of amino acid types in humans is 141. Inorganic matter on earth has turned into organic matter, amino and nucleic acids as a result of the formation of suitable environments. Viral beings were formed from these in time. The Creative intelligence has given a piece of its own intelligence to these viruses, because it has been observed that these viruses have the ability to contain life force and to reproduce. The virus was alive and had the consciousness to continue its species. It was feeding, adapting to its environment and developing with its ability to establish a balance of entropy. The virus which was made up of a single amino acid combination created a second amino acid combination after an effort of 10 million years and turned into bacteria. 10 million more years passed and the number of amino acids increased to 3 and the number of electrons to 400 million. The name of this new living species was single celled ameba. During the evolutionary process which took millions of years, due to the intelligence which exists in the DNA molecule of the ameba, changes and differentiations took place which allowed it to adapt to the environmental conditions and multicellular being with 20 amino acids emerged. After that, the world was filled with millions of different type of plant and animal species. The preeminent of these were the primates who had 140 amino acid combinations. About 500 thousand years ago, some of these primates produced the 141st amino acid combination and the first hominoid emerged. While the previous primates' brain capacity was 400 cubic centimeters, the brain capacity of the new species was 1300-1500 cubic centimeters. While the ratio of functional cells in the brain was around 2-3% in primates, this ratio increased to 10% in the new species. The brain capacity of the Cro-Magnon human reached 1500 cubic centimeters about 300 thousand years ago and this capacity did not change in Homo Sapiens which was seen for the first time 200 thousand years ago. The living being who has the highest ratio of brain capacity and weight to the total body ratio is humans in this world. The brain being this big causes the female of the human species to experience pain like no other being during labor. In case the human brain grow larger, normal delivery will become impossible. This might mean that nature is limiting the brain capacity.

The human brain is the most developed tool in the known universe. By means of the brain, 2 million visual and 200 thousand auditory inputs can be simultaneously put into use. Its structure is perfect. A computer uses 1 million units of energy for a single calculation. The human brain spends only 100 units of energy for the same calculation. The required unit of energy to produce a DNA sequence is 1 billion units. The evolutionary process has programmed the human brain to survive. Our brain is full of things like anger, fear and war. We have brains which are designed to manage and direct sudden anger, sudden fear and sudden perceptions. On the other hand, the path to evolvement needs a purified consciousness and a purified consciousness requires us to go beyond the survival program. Reaching a purified consciousness depends on learning to use this perfect structure. It is always in our hands to turn the flow of experiences around by changing through patterns. The individual consciousness of man gives him the competency to direct his own life process. Each person has the potential to create his own life by means of the universal mind. This is called "Individual Creativity Area". Humans are limitless beings. It is possible for humans to progress towards limitless goals with a purified consciousness. The universal intelligence is ready to give us everything we want when we want these. Everything we can think about, believe in and expect with trust takes place for sure. This issue will be explained in more detail in the coming chapters.

140 of the 141 amino acid combinations in humans are the same with the ones in apes. Only 1 of them is different. The differentiation (mutation) process of an amino acid combination has been calculated to be 11 million years. With this point of view, we may say that humankind is 1,5 billion years ahead of algae which is its farthest relative in terms of evolutionary development and 11 million years ahead of apes which are its closest relatives. In other words, the most advanced ape species needs to evolve for 11 million years to be able to reach today's humans' level of intelligence. If extraordinary conditions do not come into the picture for the human species and evolution continues on its normal path, a structural change in the human species will take place 11 million years from now. The formation of the 142nd amino acid combination will take this much time. The acquired skills are preserved through the DNA molecules in the chromosomes. All kinds of information are processed in life codes. The main duty of the human DNA is to prevent all kinds of malfunction and deterioration and if a malfunction is in question, to correct it. However, the question s to how DNA's have acquired this sense of duty and where they have found the required intelligence remains an unanswered question. Evolution takes place through this information. DNA's are the physical tools of raising the information load to the highest level. However, DNA's have been observed to carry emotions along with information.

In biology, beings whose biological characteristics get destroyed when they are divided into smaller parts are called Individuals. Each individual's genetic total is that individual's Genotype. Primates are one of the 33 branches of the mammal group. Humans are a member of the primate branch. The genetic similarity of humans and apes is around 98%. Scientists state that humans and chimpanzees had a common ancestor only 11 million years ago. Therefore, humans are only one amino acid combination removed from chimpanzees. In Africa, in North Chad's Djurab desert, a bone piece belonging to the world's oldest hominid has been found. This being which has been named Toumai (meaning Life Hope in local language) was determined to be 7 million years old. The first hominid who lived outside of Africa is a hominoid named "Ankarapitek", who was determined to have lived in Anatolia, around the city of Ankara 2.5 Million years ago. Today's modern man has been calculated to have emerged for the first time 200 thousand years ago. Researchers, taking into consideration the fact that the rate of mutation in mitochondrial DNA's is 2-4% per1 million years, have determined the emergence of modern man as 200 thousand years ago by turning our molecular clock around.

In our evolution, our separation process from the other primates began with our walking on our two legs. Walking on our legs has allowed our hands to be free and our brain began to develop to be able to use our hands in the most active manner. Humans are one of the largest beings in the world. We tend to think of ourselves as of average size; however we are larger than 99% of animals in reality. Even within our 190 typed primate family, we are the largest primate after gorillas excluding Bigfoot which has not been discovered yet.

The DNA researches conducted on the Neanderthal humans who disappeared about 50 thousand years ago have shown that the DNA of Neanderthals stands between the DNA of humans and DNA of chimpanzees. Therefore, it does not seem very probable that Neanderthals to have contributed to the mitochondrial DNA pool of Homo sapiens. Neanderthals are not our ancestors. Neanderthals and Homo sapiens have become genetically different about 500-600 years ago. This human model which has not been able to keep pace with the evolutionary speed of its homogenous seems to have been wiped from the face of the earth within the scope of laws of evolution. It is apparent that Neanderthals are a human species and behaved just like us. They buried their idea and placed ornaments, flowers and some tools in their graves. Shaping their dead in the fetus position brings to the mind the notion that they may have some sort of belief in rebirth as well. Burying their dead with ornaments means that these are intended to be used in afterlife and this kind of behavior points out a sort of religious belief.

300 thousand years ago, the human population has decreased so drastically for some unknown reason that, a single woman, or a few women who were relatives have become the ancestors of all people. There are about 200 thousand Mitochondrial DNA's in each person. During fertilization, the mitochondrion found in sperm die on the way due to the mother's immunity system. Therefore, mitochondrial genes pass to the individual only through his mother. Genetics scientist Wesley Brown, who has produced a mitochondrial gene map, has discovered that each living person has a quite young, common female ancestor. According to Brown's calculations, everyone on the world descends from one, or a few women who were relatives, who lived 300 thousand years ago. These anonymous woman (or women) is called "Mitochondrial Eve". This result has also shown that everyone on earth is in fact close relatives.

According to Darwin's Theory of Evolution, as a result of the random changes which take place in the environment, mutation and natural selection take place. This point of view seems to be valid up to a certain point. John Haught, the writer of "God after Darwin", expresses this Deist approach saying that God lovingly renounces domineering omnipotence and allows the universe to evolve without divine intervention. This will allow advancement without planning and enrich the process of creation. Random and not predetermined occurrences will provide for the natural course of action. Haught believes that after creating the universe, God has voluntarily given up his infinite power. According to Haught, God does not interfere with the wishes of the randomly formed beings as a result of the creation process under any condition. However, Haught does not have an explanation as to why God has chosen to do so.

It is true that the need for environmental adaptation and random events cause mutation. It is not possible to examine the evolutionary process anyway. However, the universe's only being dependent on coincidences cannot result in anything else, but to drag the universe into chaos. In fact, within the framework of the 1st Law of Thermodynamics, all structures constantly go towards chaos. However, this is not what happens in nature. It if were possible to observe the finches, whose beaks have evolved, or evolved in accordance with the environment, to consume different species, these finches remain as they are. They do not evolve in a species due to mutation. In fact, the building blocks of nature tell them to remain as finches and to continue their existence in new generations. No matter how much evolutionary differentiation increases, a finch will always remain a finch without its DNA going through changes. This is not only true for finches; programmed building blocks in every level of the universe allow chaos not to be dominant in the universal plan and everything to evolve within a certain order. As long as evolution continues steadily, the Divine program will infallibly continue as well. It seems that random mutation and natural selection only allow an infinite intelligence to experience its own latent power.

In evolutionary science, living beings gradually reach more complex forms from their initial simple states. Evolution is the gradual change a species goes through in its genetic structure. However, reducing evolution to mere coincidences and natural selection is as erroneous a dogmatic point of view as saying that everything has been creates as it is today. It is no longer possible to deny the existence of an intelligence which determines the finest details in the building blocks of each being in the world. It has taken hundreds of millions of years for the single celled primitive beings to appear in the world. Various living beings to derive from them have taken tens of millions of years. It seems that it has taken the humanoids to reach today's humans from their first emergence about 1 million years. This is an indication that the evolutionary process is gradually speeding up. Since the evolutionary process is infinite, it is understood that the amino acid combination production capacity is infinite as well; humankind will increase its brain capacity, gradually evolve and continue taking its steps to reach God physically as well. Human intelligence is being transmitted from one generation to the other in a more developed manner. In the last time slice of the evolution, especially humans' social structure has entered a phase of extraordinary change and acceleration. The most important reason for this is the fact that, humans have now arrived at a point where they can interfere with the natural process of evolution. The developments which have taken place in the area of genetic engineering are of unbelievable dimensions.

Intelligence is the ability to internalize the information we receive from the environment and adaptation to the requirements of life on this world. Intelligence is the relationship between the purpose of man and the tool he uses. The meaning of Homo sapiens, which science uses to define humans, is "Intelligent Human". About 20 thousand of close to

20 billion cells located in the Cortex layer of the human brain, which produces the activity of intelligence, are very skilled super cells. Faruk Erengul calls the electrons of atoms which produce these super skilled cells "Eons". 20% of the total oxygen need of the human body is used by these 20 thousand super cells. Only 10% of these functions with full capacity. In other words, we may conclude that the human brain works with only 10% of its capacity. Evolution shows that their capacity is gradually increasing. The civilization to be established by humanity which can use 100% of its brain capacity will be of a level that cannot be foreseen today.

The probability of a shape made up of any 20 pieces to create a geometrical order as a result of coincidence is one in 2.5 million times billion. The probability of the human brain which embodies 20 thousand super cells being created coincidentally is very close to zero. There is no program for coincidence. Coincidence which has no intelligence has no chance of forming the human brain, or establishing the current order of the universe. Bringing together the infinite number of variables in the universe to form an infallible order in the infinite process can only be the proof of the existence of an infinite intelligence and power. There are billions of proofs in the universe, which cannot be proven with the notion of coincidence. The repetition of the evolutionary process of the life of living being on Earth up to humans in another planet seems like a very low probability in scientific terms. However, considering that the universal structure is evolving within the framework of a program and that humans are the most suitable beings for the accumulation of information and evolvement, there is also the possibility that the same or very close genetic codes might have been programmed for the whole universal life. In accordance with the law of the continuity of the species, many living beings involuntarily provide support for each other. The chain of life operates within the framework of a specific planning. For instance, oxygen produced by plants is not produced to be used in any way by plants. Carbon dioxide and sold waste produced by animals are of no use for animals. However, they are each a part of the system and have vital importance in the protection of the order. The plants and animals on Earth have been evolved in sun a manner that, carbon dioxide needed by plants to survive is produced by animals, oxygen needed by animals is produced by plants. And this dual life goes on steadily. The solid waste of one is the necessity of the other. This biological and physiological mutation which has given birth to a very accurate result can only be the result of intelligence. Only the existence of this system shows that all this activity is the result of a conscious planning and that randomness is permitted up to a certain point in this plan. On the other hand, living beings which create a natural balance by eating each other are constantly being evolved. As a consequence of this evolution, some species go extinct and new species which better adapt to the environment come into being. However, evolution goes on without any break. The materialist point of view explains this as "Laws of Nature". However, about how these laws of nature which are observed to be universal initially came into the Picture, they have no answer but coincidence. A problem with so many unknowns to be giving such extraordinary results can only be explained as the existence of a universal intelligence.

Just like the universe, the world order seems to be created in accordance with a specific plan as well. The chain of life resembles the rings in a chain. All species come into existence in accordance with a planned structure and either become extinct or survives and allows the continuation of its species by adapting to the environment. None of extinctions mean that the chain is broken; the environmental order is only evolving towards a new direction. There are no findings which indicate that the information in DNA's is the result of random mutation and evolution. In fact, natural selection and evolution in many animal species seems not to have made it possible for that animal's development in the highest level. For instance, if cheetah, known as the fastest animal, had a structure which could preserve its speed for a very long time, there would no animal to be neither hunted, nor other species. Everything is evolved in accordance with a specific plan and order. Natural selection and evolution of the species makes it possible for that animal only at the level of adapting to the environment and allows its development, but does not permit more. In short, the differentiations which have taken place make it possible for the species' structural whole to undergo change.

The claim that another species is created by means of a mutation that takes place in random in a positive way can only be an assumption. Species come into being not through an evolution they will experience later on, but mutation and randomness which take place during the formation of their first building blocks and adapt to the environment by means of evolution and without going through too many changes concerning their species through the DNA's they have. The existence of millions of species on Earth shows that life is not limited to coming into existence only once as a result of coincidences. Planning is different for each being and it does not seem possible to say that these plans are limited only with our world. As there are numerous DNA's which are very different from each other in the world, there is no reason as to why the same plan is valid for the whole universe. Each cell evolves in order to create its own species in accordance with the written plan in its DNA and will continue to evolve.

Paleontologist Teilhard de Chardin argues that there is evolution, but it is directed in accordance with a specific purpose. In his view, evolution moves constantly towards the "Omega Point". The Omega Point is the final destination all existences will reach as a result of evolutionary processes. The increase which is taking place in our levels of consciousness shows us this reality.

It seems that all the conditions necessary for the sustainability of life have been pre-arranged. For instance, the force of friction is indispensable for the existence of life. If there was no such thing as the force of friction, it would not be possible for living beings to walk, run or even eat on Earth. By means of the force of friction between the objects, mankind can walk, talk and eat. When we walk, we push the ground with our feet and the ground does the same. The surfaces of all things are indented. No object is totally smooth. The height of indentations can never be less than 100 atom height. The movement of objects takes place with this friction effect of these indentations on one another.

The ratio of males-females is amazingly always kept in balance. The sex of the sperm which enters the ovaries is determined among 400 thousand sperms and allows it to carry out its duty within an evolutionary program in order to be able to keep the society's male-female population in balance. God has placed his own being inside the DNA of humans and continues to do so just like he did with the first being. If a gene was not placed inside in the first microscopic living matter which came into being and a perfect and infallible evolutionary program which can be applied for an infinite amount of time in that gene was not placed, would mankind be able to exist today?

Each cell in our body consists of 46 chromosomes, with the exception of reproductive cells. There are 23 of each. In other words, they are each half a human being. Still, these cells have the whole plan. When reproductive cells unite, they complete each other and create a new person. God seems to have fit the greatest life secret of living beings into the DNA molecule. It is only these DNA molecules which transmit the life matrix, program code, evolutionary message and information memory of living beings from generation to generation, solves all problems within the living beings' own structure, programs and manages these. These and similar molecules' supervising and regulating the relationships between all living beings in the universe are a high probability as well.

The science of medicine has solved a majority of the anatomical structure of the human body. It is known that all of the organs in the body are made up of a cell society and that these cells have different characters and structures in accordance with the functions of the organs. The cells in each organ have special characteristics in accordance with the function of the organ. Sometimes, even the cells which have the same duty are observed to get different from the other cells within the same organ. In fact, as in the leaves of a tree, it has been observed that a cell is not exactly the same as another cell. The organs contribute to the liveliness of the body through the power they acquire from the operation of the cells inside them together. All organs' carrying out their duties one by one, completing each other and making the body remain alive and functional allows the continuity of the syndrome called "Life".

Some scientists who observed the operation of the body depending on this cell system argue that there is no other force under the name of "Soul" by considering the cell base of liveliness. They claim that, the power acquired from the body's functioning like a machine has been named soul. According to this materialist point of view, the body is made up of a whole of powers which are acquired from the functions of body cells. The power which regulates the function and operation of organs made up of cell groups, regulates all willed and irresolute bodily forces and allows them to work together in an orderly manner is the brain which is also an organ. The mind which is a brain function is another skill of memory. In fact, the skills of reasoning and thinking are two skills of the soul which emerge in the brain. However, since it is apparent that the soul is a much elevated creative potential beyond the perception capacity of the brain, it is apparent that it is also a force that is exalted and superior compared to all the sum of thoughts. In terms of creativity, only thinking is not sufficient by itself. Creativities which guide humanity always appear by means of the power of intuition.

It has been accepted and announced by scientists as well that the human body diffuses a beam called "Aura" around it. Aura photographs are able to show a person's spiritual or physical health at that moment. In times of death agony, it has been observed that the Aura weakens and goes off completely when death occurs. It is apparent that these Aura lights we diffuse each have a frequency. This continuous broadcast turns us each into transmitting stations. While our experiences and knowledge are sent to the universe in this manner, universal knowledge is received in the same way. We may say that DNA cells are in fact a communication system and a method at the universal level. Aura's disappearance at the time of death is an indication that there is a constant relationship between DNA molecules, Aura and soul. It has been scientifically proven that the cells communicate through a light beam which they broadcast in the UV light frequency. When the cell dies, this UV frequency broadcast ends. UV lights are the communication waves of the system placed in the genes inside the cells. This electromagnetic system which is inside a gene that is the size of a one millionth of a millimeter both does broadcasting and evaluates the broadcasts it receives and allows for the continuity of life within a great order.

The transmission of information takes place within the living cells. These electromagnetic particles each of which are close to infinite smallness in size and create an information broadcast, transmit these information with 300 thousand km speed per second. When any kind of radio wave is given to the particles, a change occurs in the molecular level and in accordance with quantum laws, this change stimulates the atom next to it and changes it as well. When we make an observation using the most sensitive and storm microscopes, we cannot see anything in the cell protoplasm other than a protein matter. Where does this matter take this information and how does it transmit it to the cell next to it? Without doubt, this protein matter gains information and contains the physiological characteristics we call intelligence. The information is sometimes transmitted to the brain and sometimes evaluated within the cell and the necessary action is taken. Therefore, the independence of intelligence is in question. Is an intelligence of this level a specific wave dimension, a vibration with a frequency, or a type of energy? Does intelligence have matter, or is intelligence a substance without matter? We may ask more similar questions. What is thought? What does peace of mind and happiness mean? Are love, pity, sadness vibrations which have a specific frequency or wave length? Quantum laws have one answer to these questions. All. Everything is One and whole.

Humans embody within themselves a skill that is faster than the speed of light. These skills are the definite answer that we are a part of God. It is the speed of thought. Thought covers time and space with an infinite speed. Thought has the ability to travel the whole universe and all times with an infinite speed. The moment we think, we are no different from God. We are a part of God. In physical terms, the speed of thought can be defined as "Speed of Soul" as well. The ability of thought is the proof of soul. Besides thinking, the flow sped of imagination and even dreams have no limit. This speed is much greater than the speed of light. It extends to eternity. Having command over thoughts increases as one gets closer to God. This ability may increase to the point of meeting God at a metaphysical point. This ascension is the expression of man's reaching perfection. In Islam spirituality, it is called the "Hakkel Yakin" rank.

A person who reaches such a rank of interpretation is a person who has managed to be free of daily worries, small calculations of interest and needlessly exaggerated worries. Soul's meeting with God becomes real.

Ontology is the name given to the science of existence while Epistemology is the term used for the science of information. Discovery belongs to ontology, invention belongs to epistemology. Existing things are discovered and it is invented by means of non-existing thought. A long-term memory is needed to discover by taking nature as the model and pass on to invention by thinking. Long-term memory can only be possible with regular repetitions and the storage of information. Repetitions which involve order contribute to the construction of orderly structures in the human brain. No matter how complex human thought is, the things it looks for are balance, peace of mind and serenity. The whole universe has been based on building order out of chaos. However, order is not constant and leaves its place to chaos once again. Both the universe and man constantly produce cosmos from chaos and chaos from cosmos and continue their evolvement.

Even the DNA molecule which forms the orderly structures of living beings contains disorder. DNA's small copying mistakes called mutation cause changes. Thus, instead of living beings that look identical, living beings with little differences come into being. Evolution is possible due to these small mutations. Errors are beneficial as long as they turn into new experiences and new experiences turn into new lessons. It is not possible to learn without making mistakes. The chaotic structure called thought is directly related to these mistakes. Unexpected solutions to unexpected events can only be produced with thoughts. Underneath all thoughts, lies the need to find a solution about oneself, or one's society. From inventing a tool to creating a scientific or philosophical model, all types of thought activity arises from a wish to solve a problem about existence. Solutions may sometimes emerge step by step through the rational mind and sometimes by means of intuitions as a leap. For those who are content with the rational mind, there is no metaphysical dimension of reality. However, the rational mind is not sufficient in explaining the intuitional leap. Intuition takes place as a sudden quantum leap in thoughts.

Bringing the seemingly independent and irrelevant pieces of information, coordinating them and creating a whole have become an area of interest of science today. This branch of science is called cybernetics. According to cybernetics, the universe is intelligent and has a specific consciousness structure. The science of cybernetics is another proof of the esoteric discourse. The formation and developments in the universe take place through the information transmitted by the small particles and waves. In the beginning, the formation of living things in our world emerged as a result of the information Exchange ability of these inanimate particles. Therefore, vitality is a mathematical program. DNA chains are the stepping Stones which transmit this program. Man, as the most advanced living species, is an organism which consists of DNA chains and is a series of program package. According to cybernetics' information is man's adaptation to the external world. What prepared today was the past. And it is today which prepares tomorrow. Free will and thoughts which are created through free will have the essence to adapt to tomorrow today, as was the case in the past.

Nature constantly eliminates erroneous aspects. This is the proof of an evolutionary chain which is gradually becoming perfect. Just as going towards biological perfection, our perceptions are also becoming more perfect under the light of our knowledge. As a result of mankind's better understanding of information presented to us by being synthesized by the laws of nature and its reaching more accurate information each day, the structure of the universe will gradually be better understood as well. Beneath the physical, biological and social principles on which our knowledge is based, there lies such a magnificent mechanism. The universe is an existence which constantly perfects its own order through the small disorders created. Knowledge is everything. Except for our own reality, there is no additional definition we can grasp in relation to the universe. Those who know themselves know the universe and God as well.

Evolution seems to be continuing its normal course for now. On the other hand, the evolution of humans has steered from the biological area to the cultural area. Today, we can fly although we do not have wings and swim underneath water although we do not have gills. Our brain has not grown in size, but we are able to do great mathematical calculations immediately. Our teeth have grown smaller, we do not have paws, but we have the capacity to kill millions of living beings on the spot. As Darwin stated, organisms evolve biologically through natural selection. Those who adapt better live longer. Their genes are transmitted to the next generations. However, today's technological opportunities and developments made in medicine seem to significantly decrease the chance of those of us who are weaker to be eliminated. So, have humans completed their evolution, or is a new evolutionary process going on? Biology is evolution's final fortress "Gamete", or its gender cell. No mutation or another change which takes place in the physical organism can be transmitted to the next generation, as long as it is not coded to the gamete's DNA. However, with the gene engineering studies, this final fortress seems to be about to be lost. Gene therapy is speedily approaching the level which will make it possible for DNA to be consciously changed. When this can be done, it is foreseen that the difference between our biological heritage and cultural heritage can be removed.

However, we cannot even say that the nature of man has totally completed its evolution. The reason why most people experience health problems such as back pain, varicose and hemorrhoid is the fact that our body has still not adapted in full to walking on our two feet in terms of evolution. This is a weakness in our design and these kinds of errors are frequently seen as in many other living beings on our world. Genetic engineers claim that they can correct genetic errors. However, they will experience problems in changing genes artificially. In fact, there is almost no identical match between our genes and our characteristics. There is not a gene which has been appointed to determine the color of our eyes. The same gene sequence determines our other characteristics such as height, appearance and other similar aspects. Attempting to change a person's eye color will result in a change in that person's other characteristics as well and will most probably cause that person to be born with defects. The kind of information which can affect the genetic characteristics of humans in a consistent manner still does not exist.

Evolutionary design shows that what is needed is continuing within the scope of a plan as it should be. All the aspects of the miracle called life seem to be the product of a masterful design. The interventions to be done from the outside look as if they will end in disappointment for now. When we go back from organic evolution (in the evolution of the living beings) and continue to trace the signs of the divine design, we come face to face with inorganic evolution (the evolution of the inanimate universe). If we have sufficient time and interest and go back a considerable amount of time, we will only have a hydrogen molecule made up of a proton and an electron. Regardless of which force, for such an evolution to take place, the hydrogen molecule seems inevitable. If we wish to learn about universal designs, we firstly need to get to know the characteristics of the hydrogen molecule more closely. It is the characteristics of the hydrogen atom which determine the characteristics of today's objective world. Whatever there is in the universe exists due to this atom's evolution (its turning into other elements) and its own characteristics. If you attempt to go even further back in time, you will meet quarks. If you attempt to go back further in time just as it was done in CERN, you will see bosons which create matter. What do you finally reach? Basic laws. Basic laws directly mean God.

ELECTRONS-TACHYONS

Newton physics sets off from the notion that matter is a solid and rigid reality. At first sight, this reality seems to be accurate. However, if we take a look at this solid reality using an electron microscope, what we will see will be 99% emptiness and 1% light. Quantum physics has shown that matter which seems like solid reality is in fact made up of intensified light clusters and not solid particles. Each atom inside of us contains 99% emptiness and 1% energy.

Atom is a kind of manifestation at the micro level of macro universe made up of the Sun and planets. Within the scope of our knowledge today, the basic building blocks of atoms are quarks. Protons and neutrons are made up of quarks. Particles smaller than quarks within atoms are Electrons, Moons and Taus. Tau means "That which belongs to God" in the ancient Esoteric discourse. These small particles among which are electrons as well are not an indivisible whole. It is understood that they each consist of smaller particles and there is no particle which can be defined as "the smallest" and smallness extends towards infinity. Stephen Hawking states that, these particles which are defined as basic particles might have even more basic structural layers.

Basic particles such as protons, neutrons and electrons are aspects which have much more different characteristics from every other thing we know in our macro world. The objects or living being we see and know consist of the union of these basic beings which are not objects and not from the union of micro substances. A proton's mass is 1836 times the mass of an electron.

Electrons move in the speed of light in unstable orbits in accordance with the energy levels around the nucleus of the atom. According to quantum mechanics, the density of the electrons is billions of tons/cm3. The temperature of the photon radiation inside is also billions of degrees. Since electrons' location within the atom cannot be determined, it has not been possible to directly observe electrons until today. There is no information about what is inside electrons. Electrons are the focal points of the secrets of the universe. Within the micro metric dimensions of chromosome cells which are me up of atoms with electrons inside, information pertaining to a fully organized human's material and spiritual perfect structure. A DNA molecule, which is about the size of one thousandth of a millimeter is made up of 210 billion atoms and electrons and contains information which cannot fit even in millions of pages.

According to quantum theory, the universe must have an observer. This observer should be available from the very beginning to the very end. There is only one matter particle in the physical universe which does not fit this definition: Electron. Electrons were created in the Big Bang and still exist. As long as an electron is not observed, it is impossible to know what it is doing. According to the uncertainty principle of quantum mechanics, when an electron acts like a wave, its particle appearance is lost. Contrary to this, when an electron acts like a particle, its wave appearance is lost. Wave and particle behavior can never exist together. An object is either energy, or particle, that is, matter. An object cannot both be energy and matter. Within a certain time slice, only one of these two states can be valid.

Electrons are identical to each other no matter in which atoms they are. The reason why objects which touch each other do not penetrate each other is that the electron clouds outside the atoms which form objects and the negative charge of electrons constantly push each other. According to an assumption which generally finds acceptance, since all the electrons in the universe have been created at the same moment, they are all 14 billion years old. This assumption holds that, electrons have emerged from the first ore, the first energy in the universe. However, it is not possible to prove this. In short, the whole universe is made up of electrons. There is a great space between the nucleus of each atom and electrons. Only Vacuum Energy is present in this space.

All objects in the universe are finite, in other words, mortal. In the material world, the only things that are infinite or immortal are the electrons which emerge through the breaking up of atoms. All particles except for electrons turn into energy. Since electrons are carry both particle and energy characteristic, they do not change. Afterwards, the same electrons are used to form new matter. Electrons have emerged with the Big Bang. In the beginning, nuclear force, electromagnetic force, weak force and the force of gravity which exist together in a cosmic egg separate with the Big Bang and start their activity to take the universe from chaos to order.

In order to be able to understand the true nature of electrons, it would be a good idea to remind Faruk Erengul's hypothesis once more. Erengul argues that all kinds of information is recorded and stored in electrons. Electrons share information among each other through the billions of centigrade degrees of photon radiations which emerge from impulses with speed close to infinity and spin interactions. Erengul makes a reference to universal intelligence and says that humans' individual intelligence comes to being with this information accumulation and common memory at the time of birth; he also expresses that, the information each person acquires during life on Earth is added to the common memory and information bank through the atom particles which are separated with death. What make the immortality of the soul are the electrons. Electron is the atom particle which manages the evolutionary program of the universe. Erengul claims that only 100 billion of the 28 digit number of electrons inherent in a human are super electrons which carry information and love and calls these "Eons". Majority of electrons which are not eons are those which have normal functions and carry out the subconscious biological and physiological activities throughout life. When life on earth is lost, some of these blend in with soil, while some others spread to space. Eon electrons' entering a new body to provide the required energy allows new abilities to be gained and these appear in new born bodies.

Quantum science has shown that, electrons share information among each other through photons with a speed reaching up to numbers with 23 over 1o's per second and that the acquired information is sent immediately to all points in the universe. The speed of photons is much higher than the speed of light. This speed can only be called "the speed of thought". Thoughts and information are both sent all the way to the farthest galaxies and it is possible for all the information to be added to the memory of Universal Intelligence. While some of the electrons which are inherent in our bodies enter new bodies after death, some others get lost in the depths of space and blend in with Universal Intelligence. Electrons are

God particles. All electrons in the universe carry out the function of compiling information and love throughout the life of the universe in one center. Erengul, who reminds us that these particles will continue their existence for periods extending to eternity and even just for this reason, human thoughts, and behavior and information accumulation, should be kept inside electrons and that the immortality of the soul is in fact hidden in the eternal life of electrons.

Each electron has an orbit unique to it. Electrons do not arbitrarily deorbit. This is because the electron energy is quantized, in other words, timeless and can only be found in certain energy values. For the electron to leap from this orbit to the other, it needs to be subject to an energy which is above certain threshold energy. This momentary leap is a quantum leap. If the energy it gets is higher than the threshold energy, then the electron jumps to another orbit, but immediately releases this energy as photon and goes back to its previous orbit. The reason for this is the natural balance law which is related to the preservation of the atom's structure. In line with this law, in order for the atom to continue the existence of its balanced structure, each electron is required to move within the orbit unique to it.

In 1925, French physicist Broglie stated that electrons are wave groups and not objects. All electrons are the same in terms of mass weight and electrical charge. In fact, an electron consists of an electrical charge. Electrons do not occupy place in space. Schroedinger has called electrons "energy packages" for this reason. It is not possible to predict the behavior pattern of an electron beforehand. One of the electrons spinning around a nucleus sometimes jumps outside its orbit. This jump brings an energy out into the open. There is no chance of predicting which electron will jump to which direction and why and transmit energy.

An electron's separation from the nucleus and becoming free is only possible if the colliding photon energy is greater than the binding energy. The free electrons which separate from the atom are called "photo electrons". In 1905, Einstein announced the photoelectric theory (effect) and paved the way for a new quantum age to begin. Through this information, many devices which work with the power of the free electrons have been devised. Doors which open on their own when they are approached, or taps which run when hands are moved underneath them all function with the power of the free electrons.

It is not possible to constantly speed matter up and reach the speed of light. Matter's mass does not allow this. However, by heating matter incandescently, it is possible to create light. A particle which is subject to dense energy, or is heated, may pass from one state to another through a sudden and finite leap. Therefore, it is possible for a particle which moves slower than the speed of light to exceed the speed of light by making this sudden and finite leap. Electron, which makes the leap, upsets the balance of the other electrons which are in the orbit it makes the leap from and thus the general balance of the atom is upset. For this reason, it leaps back to its original position, its previous orbit. Meanwhile, it gives off the energy it takes, or the information it acquires, as photon. In the movement which develops through leaps which are finite, constant communication and interaction takes place in this manner.

Quantum physics has shown us that between atoms, which are a part of systems that have formed strong connections in the beginning state, transmit information much faster than the speed of light, even if the system is not compounded. This is an indication that the whole universe is a Hologram universe. The universe is of a structure which has a strong connection between all its particles from the first moment. Therefore, each electron in the universe shares the information and experiences of an electron at another point which is independent from time. The whole universe continues its existence as a single, whole structure and faster communications faster than light take place between the particles. The Aspect experiment in 1975 seems to show that there is a mysterious telepathic connection between electrons. How do electrons transmit their experiences to each other? How do they receive these mysterious signals and do what is needed with extraordinary accuracy? Science says that no signal can travel faster than the speed of light. In every experiment conducted with photons, photons can only travel with the speed of light. Then, how does the interaction between electrons take place much faster than the speed of light?

According to a theory, interaction and communication is carried out by supra conductors within the moment. It is definite that the communication between the electrons does not remain limited with electrons. The information an electron has newly acquired within the moment and shares with its neighbor is transmitted again within the moment to the electron next to its neighbor and this is how information is spread to the whole universe. Each atom affects another atom it is in communication with and finally all atoms get affected. How is this possible without losing any energy and time? While energy transport by means of classical methods causes some losses, it has been observed that y means of supra conductors which have quantic characteristics, there is no loss whatsoever. The reason for loss to occur is the indistinguishable characteristics of quantum. It is impossible for quantum to be affected from any external factor. Electrons are found in pairs in supra conductors. The behavior of each electron pair is in harmony with each other. Like photons which create laser effect, these electron pairs comply with quantic statistics. What makes communication to be possible is the supra conductive characteristic of the Helium atom.

A Helium atom consists of 2 protons, 2 neutrons and 2 electrons. It turns into a super fluid and Helium atoms gain a surprising characteristic by establishing contact among them. Electrons' sharing information within the moment is a characteristic of Helium establishing this superfast connection. Therefore, Helium which is found in -271 degrees cannot be heated or cooled. Helium in this super fluid state is completely immobile. It is the most common matter in the universe after Hydrogen and is spread to the whole universe. It being the most common matter could be the explanation for the sharing of information. It has still not been determined that the fixed temperature of the whole universe is -271 degrees. The super fluidity state of Helium which is spread to the whole universe could be the explanation as to why entropy of the universe does not increase and its temperature remains fixed in -271 degrees despite its constant expansion.

Electrons which move within the framework of quantum laws are able to turn both clock wise and anti-clock wise concurrently. This doubles the electrons' sharing of information. This super connection state is called "Quantum Entanglement". Einstein has defined this term as "the scary motion far away (in fact, everywhere)". Two electrons which are in a state of interaction mean that they have a super connection in quantum physics. There is a reciprocal "beyond norm" sharing and transmission of information. Two electrons almost turn into maternal twins within the moment. If it is taken into consideration that all electrons carry out such sharing of information with the other electrons next to them, it may be better understood how all electrons in the universe share information within the moment and how they comprise a whole together.

Just like the Earth spinning around itself while spinning around the Sun, electrons spin around themselves while spinning around the atomic nucleus. It is this spinning motion which creates the quantic characteristic (production of photons) of electrons and it is called "spin". As electrons remain in their fixed orbits, they seem to be complying with the Newton laws, but when they share photons, or leap to one orbit to the other, they act in accordance with the laws of quantum. Electrons climb to the next step when they are given the required energy by a photon and descend to the lower step when they give off energy from itself through a photon. The dissension of an electron, which is on the upper orbit (external orbit) to the lower orbit (inner orbit) after giving of photons, is called "Quantum Leap". If photons are regarded as the sharing of information between electrons, then it may be expressed that sharing of information is mandatory for a quantum leap.

An electron does not give any information within time and space. Despite this, the sharing of information between electrons disregard time and space. The meaning of this is that, sharing of information takes place beyond time and space, in the metaphysical world. Quantum science has proven that information acquired by an electron is acquired by others electrons very far away in an instant. Due to this sharing of information by electrons which have an infinite life-style, it becomes possible for all kinds of information to be accumulated and turn into a universal memory in the universe. Accumulation of information does not only embody knowledge acquired by the physical world, but experiences acquired by the metaphysical world as well, such as love, emotion and thought. Let us not forget that Erengul suggests that electrons are the carriers of the soul at the same time. Electrons, which have a life force that is a divine gift, have been continuing their existence ever since the creation and therefore contain the whole evolutionary program. By means of electrons, the material world which constantly loses order and the order lost is reestablished in the spiritual world.

The main matter of the universe is Hydrogen which is a simple element with a single atom and electron. After hydrogen spread to space, the atoms which came together formed great masses and as a result of the fusion which took place, Helium with two atoms was created from hydrogen. Hydrogen clouds which have not undergone fusion spread to the whole universe and created space vacuum. This process has been going on for 14 billion years. The basis of all these formations is the balance created between the atomic nuclei and electrons. The force of gravity between the particles and the electromagnetic force balance allow the electrons orbit around the nucleus and spin around themselves as well with the angular momentum they gain. The name given to this movement as we have mentioned before is "spin". Erengul claims that this spin motion has a "spiritual" ability. Erengul, who states that electrons share their love and information charges and experience with the neighbor electrons, suggests that the force which prevents the universe from experiencing chaos is hidden within the electrons. Since electrons share the information and love charge they contain non-stop, order is established in the universe and entropy is decreased. In this manner, an order is established in the whole universe. The experience gained by electrons which are charged with information and love during their lives allows all these records to be shared by universal intelligence by electrons. All electrons in the universe carry out the function of compiling the accumulation of information and love at a single center.

Matter and anti-matter particles which emerge in the Big Bang interacted with each other and destroyed each other. An extraordinary amount of heat and energy were created from these collisions and the first photons were created. With these first photons the evolvement process began. Physicist Paul Dirac discovered anti-electrons which have the same mass with other electrons and carry positive charge and called these "positron". This anti-electron put forward by Dirac in his Theory of Electronic Relativity has verified the ancient esoteric knowledge that the universal structure is made up of the opposites of its essence. Each particle during the formation of the universe has emerged with its opposite and as a result of these coming together and their explosions, the energy needed for expansion has been created.

Opposition is the foundation of creation. Nothing can exist without its opposite. God has also made use of the metaphysical plan which is the exact opposite of the physical plan to create it. In physics, polarity is essential in the creation of particles. A photon which has sufficient energy can turn into two different particles instantaneously. A positively charged Positron and a negatively charged electron are created by the destruction of a gamma ray photon. Nature is capable of creating an environment without any charge and full of pure and neutral energy. However, this environment can only be possible in a polarized environment where each opposite charge neutralizes the other. When the negative charge of electron and the positive charge of positron collide, photon energy free of charge can be achieved. Matter is formations whose sum of their characteristics re zero. This condition could be the key of the formation which allows metaphysical laws to become visible in the physical plan.

A photon does not have mass and the speed of motion is much higher than the speed of light. Photons are defined as the communication aspects of electrons. If photons are communication aspects and move with the speed of thought, then they are the ones regulating the connection between the spiritual after life and the material world. Today's science has been able to understand all until the time of "Plank Time" which remains insufficient in defining the Big Bang, space, time and matter. The time prior to Planck Time may be defined as an area where Electrons and Tachyons existed together. It is seen that, with Planck Time the soul and matter have started moving separately but as a whole. The definition for beyond Plank Time depends on the experiment capacity of the CERN accelerator. The existence of the charge free Higgs particle which transforms energy into matter and creates mass has been proven at the CERN research center through the experiences conducted in the Large Hadron Collider. In very high energies, it has been observed that an amount of energy turns into matter and a new particle is created. The name given to this new particle is the "God Particle".

Quantum has shown that particles, which are exempt from the limitations of time and space, influence each other much faster than the speed of light. So, how does this "particle" which makes this interaction real and is much faster than the speed of light move? The interaction between two objects always requires a connecting piece, or a wave. This particle needs to move much faster than light. Einstein has stated that no particle can move faster than the speed of light. Is this true? Are there really no particles which move faster than light? Some physicists say that there are some particles which have a mass that is virtual and that this mass consists of a negative number within the root. These particles which we can never detect with our tools that can only see mass which contain positive energy are called "Tachyons".

Tachyons are the focal point of another theory as to how the instantaneous sharing of information takes place between electrons. While events always move from the past towards the future in the physical plan, Tachyons move from the future towards the past. Since Tachyons move faster than light, their thermodynamic laws should be the opposite of the laws which are valid in our universe. All matter in our universe has a constant increasing tendency to create disorder. The constant increase of disorder should result in the dominance of chaos in the universe. However, it is not so. What is valid in the physical world is order. Even if order is spoiled in some way, the Chaos created is evolved towards a new order within a short period of time. It seems that chaos and order constantly follow each other. The entropy of the physical plan where order is dominant is fixed. Then, how come this formation which is against the laws of thermodynamics possible? Since tachyons move exactly as opposite to the laws of thermodynamics, their tendencies should be from chaos to order. They should be moving towards creating an increasing order. The slowest speed of these particles which move with the speed of light will be the speed of light.

Particle physicists acknowledge the existence of these abstract particles which move faster than light. Tachyons are explained as the negative attraction force of electrons. The energy of an immobile object is close to zero. As the object gains energy, it speeds up and when it turns into infinite energy, its speed moves closer to the speed of light. Meanwhile, Tachyon who has zero energy moves in infinite speed. It slows down as it gains energy and when it gains infinite energy, it slows down to the speed of light. No object can go faster than light under any circumstance. No tachyon in return can go slower than the speed of light. The speed of light is a border between these two structures and this border can never be crossed. Photons seem to be serving as bridges between these two structures. Due to the light barrier, since there cannot be contact between particles which belong to two different worlds, information related to the electrons of the physical world are carried by photons to the metaphysical world's tachyons. In other words, tachyons are the materialized states of information and thoughts.

The direction of the connecting particles which transit force is not definite. These particles are shown with wavy lines. Electrons do not move from a particle to the other. They are exchanged between two particles. When two electrons are moving towards each other, they exchange two virtual gamma beams. After the change, the event is immediately ended and each electron returns to its own particle. Since electrons are connected to the nucleus with a quantum force, they do not deorbit. After they carry out communication, they immediately go back to their previous locations. The Exchange of gamma beams which are light photons should be considered as a sudden leap. Information is transmitted in an instant within the framework of this leap. Information which is shared by means of photons are transmitted to tachyons and spread to the whole universe with the speed of thought. This communication is not only limited with electromagnetic interactions. All kinds of information in the sub-atomic level carry out communication in this manner. Quarks, which are defined as basic particles, interact in the same way.

The communication of particles (waves) which separate after they come together faster than light is possible with the infinite speed of tachyons. In short, the electron world can be explained as the physical world and the Tachyon world can be explained as the metaphysical world. As a consequence of the Big Bang, not only the physical world, but a metaphysical world in parallel to it as well. Although it is not possible for us humans who belong to the physical world to perceive the laws of the metaphysical world, it is apparent that ancient beliefs which say that the soul is a part of this metaphysical world and returns there after death. After death, the soul passes onto the tachyon world and returns to the physical world during finding a physical body again. The tachyon world is the physical world's source and the electron world is the source of the metaphysical world's source. Just as the soul and the body forming a whole, the tachyon world and the electron world also form a whole. While our world balances the constant flow towards order in the tachyon world, its own disorder is balanced by the tachyon world and they both can continue their existence supporting each other.

Some scientists with the Materialist or Deist point of view object to the idea that there could be a metaphysical world beside the physical world. According to them, the existence of particles called tachyons is not in question either. Tachyons can only be the subject of parapsychology in their view. It is possible to say that parapsychology is the Science of Metaphysics. Parapsychology is gradually moving more and more towards the area of interest of science today. What is more, the researches to be done about subjects related to parapsychology, scientific researches carry importance as to be a new scientific revolution. Today, starting with Princeton University, parapsychological studies are conducted in may scientific institutions. In the USA, many centers have been established which deal with ESP, telepathy, tele kinetics and psychokinesis and millions of dollars are spent on researches. Extra Sensory Perception (ESP) and Quantum mechanics have many common points. The instant communication particles, quantum realities such as unexplained events taking place shows that this science has the capacity to find intelligent explanations for a majority of these psychic incidences. If the particles communicate with each other instantly, then there must be a certain amount of scientific explanation for thoughts transmitted telepathically from one brain to the other. Only, this has not been proven yet, that is all.

Slowing down in the Tachyon world, where all the laws are in opposition to the laws of our universe, in a manner as to move closer to the speed of light means forming interaction with our universe. Electrons which belong to our universe and speed up to reach the speed of light and Tachyons which slow down to reach the speed of light interact and communicate with one another in the level of the speed of light. This interaction which takes place in the light barrier area is called the "Tunnel Effect". Tachyons which establish communication with electrons create order during this interaction and return to their own universe after they receive information. The interaction ends within that moment. However, it constantly repeats and since this interaction involves an infinite number of electrons and an infinite number of Tachyons, it is indefinite. Therefore, its effects are visible to the eye and it is possible to measure it. Although some materialist scientists who deny the existence of Tachyons state that the events are coincidence, chaos and order constantly following each other and fixedness of entropy points out to the existence of a source energy area.

Since Tachyons move close infinite speed, they have the ability to transmit the information they receive from electrons in an instant to all points in the universe. Thus, they cause the thermodynamic balance in the universe to be formed universally. Tachyons are of a structure which feed and equip the Supreme Consciousness with information. All experiences and thoughts which are an aspect of evolvement i the physical universe become the property of the whole universe through Tachyons. The reason why new orders are formed as a result of changes is Tachyons as well. Due to Tachyons being particles which establish order, it is inevitable that they produce balance both in our universe and theirs. If all celestial bodies which are all the orderly structures we see in the universe are spread in a homogenous manner in the universe, we owe this to Tachyons. The only reason for order is Tachyons. This function of establishing order operates in all dimensions, in the micro cosmos as well as the macro cosmos. It is this infallible balance which makes it possible for the formation and transformation of existing things. The reason why all beings, particularly humans exist as a whole consisting of the soul and the body is again the existence of Tachyons.

When every point in the universe is considered, it is observed that the same cosmic beam exists everywhere in the same density. Our universe and the Tachyon universe are in fact intertwined. Therefore, the interaction takes place in every point and at every moment continuously. One is in a position of the other's background. Therefore, our universe's background i the Tachyon universe and the Tachyon universe's background is our physical universe. The breathing activity our universe performs to sustain its existence, or the Quantum Fluctuations are a proof of the condition of intertwining of the two universes.

While the universe expands, it also gets old. Some scientific circles claim that the constant expansion of the universe will cause chaos and gradually the universe will dissolve. However, the existence of the Tachyon universe shows that this claim is not true and that the expansion cannot go on steadily. By means of the order establishing existence of the Tachyon universe, the universe will remain together as a whole and will continue its existence in the same dimensions for a while after it reaches a certain size. If we consider that the universe and humans are the same, it is inevitable for the universe to die after a while just like humans. They are both matter, thus have bodies. The body dies, but the soul does not. However, the death of the body means that the next birth will embody its own reasons within its own scope. Big Bang taking place in the beginning resembles the big explosion which takes place in the womb as a result of the union of the male reproductive particle and the female reproductive particle. A new physical life begins this way, as the physical body and the spiritual body unite. The physical universe which will be reborn and the metaphysical Tachyon universe will reunite and a new process of experience will begin. Both of these universes being each other's background is an indication that the system can sustain its existence infinitely between the two forces of attraction. As there is no end to the oscillations of the system, life follows death and death follows life in an infinite process. The existence of the physical-metaphysical universes is not an indication of parallel universes. These two universes are intertwined and make up a whole. The existence of the two points of attraction is the indication that the constant vibration movement which is a necessity for the quantum theory will continue infinitely. The development of the body continues infinitely with the help of the soul and the development of the soul continues infinitely with the help of the body. Evolvement is a never ending chain of existences.

The universe consists of existences and deaths which chase each other. Therefore, all matter which make up today's physical world are each a part of the evolutionary process as well. In order for evolution to be continued through an infallible order within the infinite time process, all particle scattered around the great universe should have the opportunity to communicate with each other and implement a program devised only for them in a complete and perfect manner. Therefore, it seems mandatory that the whole structure is managed from a center. In order for this structure to be ready and waiting at every point of the universe, it is apparent that it will need a much faster system than the speed of light. This difficulty can only be possible by God himself being the universe itself and each particle containing the God Particle inside. God is made up of a soul and a body just like humans. God is made up of the whole of the physical electron universe and the metaphysical Tachyon universe. God can only be informed about each speck and order can only steadily continue in this manner.

The divine evolutionary program, which has been created for the evolvement of knowledge and love, being connected to the 80 billion years old universal life is an indication that at the end of each period, a new universe will be created where more developed laws of nature will be dominant by making use of the accumulation of knowledge and love acquired in the universe. The speed of transmission of information and love between electrons and Tachyons cannot be measured. Reaching the speed of communication which is much faster than the speed of light and takes place through photons is unique solely to thought. If the speed of thought is Tachyon speed, then it would not be erroneous to express this infinite speed as the speed of the metaphysical universe. With this point of view, it is inevitable that souls and thus God should have Tachyon speed which extends until eternity. For this reason, God is everywhere and is informed about each of its parts.

Ph.D. Frieting has stated "Today, it has been revealed that matter is nothing but motion and electrons are nothing but a speed race. The motion of electrons, which our minds cannot comprehend, the energy which represents this motion constitutes the real source of all existence". English astrophysicist Jeans has stated "The universe began to seem to us not like great machine, but a great thought, perhaps like a soul. From now on, we cannot regard intelligence as a parasite which has coincidentally entered the world of matter. We think that we can greet it like the creator of the world of matter, its master," and accepted the existence of a Mind, a Soul which regulates the laws of nature. Quantum physics father Max Planck has stated "I believe that relativity and quantum physics rule out philosophies which are rigid, positivist and materialist. Divine rules are manifested in the universe. We have not imagined these laws in our minds. The circumstances are pushing us to discover them. There is an intellectual order in the universe. The universe is the work of a great mind," and expresses a Pantheist approach. Another English astrophysicist Edington has stated "The universe is the manifestation, the outbreak of absolute power as a relative world," and supported Planck's Pantheist point of view.

FIXED LAWS AND FIXED NUMBERS

It is possible to talk about the existence of fixed numbers which show that God is everywhere and has a never changing program. The primary number among these is the speed of light. The speed of light is fixed everywhere and it never changes. The speed of Gravity is the same with the speed of light. In the same manner, God's physical laws are also fixed and active without any change in every point of the universe. For the newly discovered laws and the ones not yet discovered, this reality never changes. The universe's whole knowledge seems as if it is included in a few laws. Leibniz summarizes this situation as follows: "God in hypothesis has chosen the simplest but the richest in phenomenon".

Within the framework of these unchanging laws, each object is the result of another object and each event is the result of another event. Therefore, objects have a place within an infinite connection. This connection is uninterrupted and ceaseless. That is the reason why there cannot be coincidence within the universe. There is no event, a design or voluntary decision that has not been determined by a previous event. The order of the physical and the metaphysical universes are one and thus the soul and the body affect each other. The soul and the body meet in mandatory formation each moment and are located in parallel to each other. Thought depends on a rigid necessity in the events and formation within the soul. What goes on inside the soul comes out of thoughts by means of a mathematical necessity and reflects on the physical world. Events need the laws of nature to take place. Events are documents over which laws are determined. To be able to determine events, mankind should know these laws.

Another proof that nothing is coincidental in the universe is the relationships in the sub-atomic universe. A certain number of protons, neutrons and electrons coming together in nature always produced a certain atomic structure and certain atoms constantly unite with each other and always the same molecules are formed. It is as if an atom chooses the atom it will unite with. For instance, 11 protons + 12 neutrons + 11 electrons always produce the Sodium atom and Sodium always chooses Chlorine to unite with. It cannot unite with Potassium, because their structures are not suitable. Making this kind of a choice is only possible with the existence of knowledge. This knowledge is unique to objects. It is the knowledge in its structure.

All material unions, from the smallest to the largest, or from sub-atomic particles to the community of states, take place as a result of matter connecting with a specific energy or other matter. This structural harmony or accord is knowledge itself. The notion of learning appears in structures which are larger than cells. This means that, temporary information can be temporarily added to the structural knowledge of cells. Learned information cannot change structural knowledge.

The dominant reductionism of modern science grounds all its scientific theories on laws of nature which randomly scatter in a universe, which completely lacks any purpose. However, the laws of nature operate in the same manner in every point of the universe and each has a specific order. The source of these laws of nature point of to the existence of intelligence. How universal consciousness has created matter has been shown with the discovery of the Higgs Particle in CERN.

According to Western science, the events in the universe are based on laws of nature or coincidences. This point of view is based on Newton mechanics. Newton mechanics suggests that indestructible particles move in accordance with foreseeable forces. It claims that, if these basic particles and the forces which have an effect are defined accurately and if there is sufficient calculation power, everything may be known in the physical world. However, Quantum mechanics has proven that the motion of observable particles cannot be predicted. The theoreticians of the classical physical world seem not to have taken much consideration whether their theories are applicable or not. According to these theoreticians, the universe has a completely deterministic and unchangeable structure. However, physics is an extremely dynamic activity. As soon as scientists construct a model to define reality, another theory may be put forward and challenge all the other points of view. Scientific processes and in particular physics is an area full of surprises; in fact, the universe itself is full of surprises due to its nature. The most known example of this has been experienced with Plank in the beginning of 20th century. With Planck's Quantum Theory, the deterministic universe has suddenly collapsed.

Despite the findings of Quantum physics which bring physics and metaphysics together, scientists who advocate determinism insist on regarding the term "Metaphysics" as a doomed term. Scientific circles take great care in writing their scientific researches and articles in an excessive scientific language, in an effort not to make quantum findings to be wide spread within the public and discussed. The reason behind the scientific world's choosing this exaggerated scientific writing style is the instinct to resist. People of this world, who do not readily accept a new theory firstly themselves, spend great effort not to popularize the concept of science.

According to the writer of the book *The Last Wizard Isaac Newton*, Michael White, at the foundation of Newton's thoughts which changed the science world drastically lies the knowledge of Alchemy. His studies on alchemy and scientific studies are intertwined. Newton's spiritual questioning and being very advanced in the science of astrology has led him to discover the Formula for gravity. It is a great discrepancy that today's science world hold him in high esteem while making fun of him for has area of interests. WE can never say that Newton aimed at transforming the course the Western world was taking in accordance with materialism. The development Newton caused involuntarily seems to have paved the way for Planck, Einstein and other scientists who are the creators of the quantum theory (involuntarily for them also) in terms of Esoteric wisdom. However, the physics world for the first time is leading the way which takes humanity to metaphysics, contrary to mankind's historical evolutionary process.

Newton is a scientist who advocates Deism. According to Newton, God has created the physical particles, the forces between them which have an effect in the beginning and has been acting like a machine operated by fixed rules. This mechanical interpretation of the universe has led to a rigid and an affirmative Deterministic view to be dominant in the world of science. Newton, who regarded the force between the particles as the power of God, claimed that no force or effect could disrupt this force God has put forward in the first moment of creation. According to Deism, the Creator God is also subject to the rules he has created. Nothing, including God, can interfere with the universe externally. The system has been designed in a perfect manner and operates that way. Nature has a structure which operates and functions by itself. There is no answer as to what God is doing right now in Deism. Merely for this reason, Deism has been evolved into Materialism and Atheism which means the rejection of God.

The reason why Newton was interested in gravity was the motions of the tides. Newton thought that the Moon was responsible for the tides and the reason was Astrology. The scientists of his time believed that this view was Astrological nonsense. Even Galilee Galileo who proved that the Earth was spinning around the Sun is known to have rejected the effect of the Moon on the tides as "Astrological nonsense". Newton was not aware of any force which could attract the sea towards the moon. He believed that this was an Astrological reality and assumed that such a force existed; he calculated how the system could work. And he called this unknown force, with reference to the force which gives every object in the world a sense of weight, "Gravity". Newton, who based his calculation on the assumption that gravity existed, firstly calculated when tides occur and then realized that he could estimate the orbits of comets. Through the calculations of gravity, he was able to calculate when the Halley Comet would return to Earth. His predictions have proven how accurate this calculation was. Due to Newton, the force of gravity is not regarded as an astrological nonsense today. However, astrology is still considered to be nonsense.

In addition to gravity, another finding Newton came up with is the law of Action-Reaction. This law, which is referred to as Newton's 3rd Law, contends that any kind of action directed towards any system will be balanced by an equal but opposing reaction. Every formation in the universe is being directed with this law. The law says that "Each action creates an opposing reaction equal to it". If this is true, then it is inevitable that an action which caused the Big Bang should exist. Everything in the universe being subject to the same universal laws excludes the idea of a coincidental formation without a reason. Within the framework of universal laws, there must be a precursor reason for the formation of universe itself. This point of view strengthens the hypothesis that each universe which dies with the great collapse is reborn.

The F=ma equation is the cornerstone of Newton Physics. In this equation, it is suggested that the Force exerted on an object is equal to the multiplication of the Mass of the object and its Acceleration. This equation explained in Newton's work *Principia* in 1687 is merely an assumption which seems as if it could be true. It can never be proven. Newton and the physicists, who followed, assumed that each object has a mass. According to Newton, an object's mass is also a measurement of its inaction. An object can only be moved when it is applied some kind of force. In this concept known as the Mach Principle, mass has always been accepted as fixed, however Einstein has proven that mass is relative. There are many more assumptions based on Newton physics whose accuracy cannot be proven (such as the Laws of Thermodynamics and Lavoisier). Inaction is a characteristic which attributes rigidness to an object, however the fact that there is a relationship between the Zero point Field and inaction has been proven by means of quantum physics. When it is moved with the speed of light, the inaction of matter can be traced back to the zero point field. When moving with the speed of light, it is observed that the whole space shrivels in one point. Within the scope of light, there is no definition of space and time. Since light supports the basic reality of our physical universe, all matter in the universe means the derivations of the zero point field.

On the other hand, Newton physics has been tested for 200 years and it has been verified each time. In fact, Quantum Physics does not prove that Newton physics is no more valid. Just like the Laws of Thermodynamics being valid in closed systems, Newton physics embodies laws which are valid in the Macro universe and their validity is not over. Quantum science has shown us that each system has laws unique to it and the effects of the methods of implementation are not direct but indirect on different systems. The laws of nature reach the level of implementation under different conditions. As you cannot apply a law of Newton physics on the quantum world, you cannot apply a Quantum physics laws on the Newton world. The most accurate way of understanding nature requires knowing about Quantum laws as well as Newton laws. The quantum laws of the micro cosmos shape the universe. However, Macro cosmos is deterministic as a whole. The laws of the macro cosmos are the Newtonian Laws.

The fixed laws of the macro universe and the micro universe are different. A solar system and an atom system may seem similar at first sight. However, we cannot say that the Sun, or the planets which orbit around it have a charge. They are all neutral. On the other hand, in the sub-atomic world, electrons are negatively charged and positrons are positively charged with electricity.

The Law of Electrodynamics says that the reason behind electrons' orbital movements is caused by their own charge. The orbits in the macro universe are subject to the Laws of Force of Gravity. In the micro universe, all electrical charges, primarily electrons, lose energy by giving off radiation. While electrons lose energy, they are also constantly subject to the fluctuations of the zero point field. This results in the orbit of the electrons t be unfixed and its locations to be never determined. This totally overlaps with the laws of quantum mechanics. The orbits in the macro universe are fixed as long as there is no eternal interference and totally overlap with the laws of Newton mechanics. Physicist Ludwig Boltzmann has attempted to carry the laws whose validity has been proven in microscopic systems into macroscopic dimensions; however he has not been successful. This reductionist philosophy has brought the end of Boltzmann and the famous physicist has committed suicide under the pressure of scientific structuring. Another physicist Paul Ehrenfest has also committed suicide for the same reason and Robert Mayer has lost his mind. Scientific theory says that the truth about nothing can be proven. The only things Western science can prove definitely are errors. If a theory cannot make accurate predictions, it is erroneous and needs to be abandoned. However, it is very surprising that a majority of Western scientists persist even on errors which have been proven.

The validity of quantum laws only in the micro cosmos never means that the quantum formations do not have effects on the macro cosmos. If we take into consideration that all energy and matter in the macro cosmos is made up of sun-atomic particles, everything that takes place in the world of atoms and electrons directly involve our universe. The only thing which can explain the flow of electricity within a quantic super conductor without any resistance, how neutron stars overcome gravity, a spider's skill in climbing a wall of vertical plane, how we do not fall towards the ground while there is such emptiness between the atoms of our flooring is Quantum Physics. The same Quantum laws embody how developments which take place at every point of the universe spread in an instant and how we can determine our future; shortly, they embody the secrets of sharing information within the moment.

Natural constants show that the universe has been designed consciously as a fine tuned mechanism. If the force of gravity even becomes a fraction stronger, all of the stars will be destroyed as a result of their own nuclear fuel, within a period of less than a year. If the nuclei of atoms hang onto one another even a fraction weakly, the formation of stars will not even be possible. Carbon and Oxygen have been arranged as to form the thermonuclear reactions inside the stars at a specific level. A very small difference in a percentage in the power of connection will either result in the star not being formed, or its being burned and total destruction. Therefore, the possibility that the universe has been formed as a result of coincidence is nearly zero. No theory can explain why the physics laws have such a balanced structure. The theory that such an extraordinary structure has been formed by chance means making fun of the common mind of humanity.

In living systems, order is always on the foreground. When order is established, chaos is always reduced to minimum. In other words, Chaos (entropy) is excluded. Both energy and knowledge is necessary for order. Lehninger calculated that in order to be able to decrease chaos as 1 kcal/mole, information as much as a 23 zero digit number is required. Thus, it has become evident that energy and information can transform into each other. Then, the building blocks of the universe are information, along with matter and energy. Knowledge is Quantum Unity.

Another proof of the Unity of Quantum is the Hologram Law. To refresh our memory, in Quantum philosophy there is a relationship between the particle and the whole. The particle embodies all the information of the whole. What happens to the particle happens to the whole. These two are an inseparable whole. In the energy level, everything is a whole. Everything is energy. An atom exchanges energy and information with all the other atoms in the universe within "the moment". Everything is in interaction with each other. What one atom knows, all the other atoms know. The experiments carried out have shown that an intervention carried out on an atom effects the other atoms. The intervention is known at the same second in every point in the universe. All beings, including humans, the whole universe are made up of atoms. Atom is the universal building block. Each atom carries the reality of being a whole. Therefore, man is actually doing all the evil he does to his environment to himself. When humankind acknowledges that this is so, the path for humanity will be speedily opened.

The Hologram Law is the definite proof of this quantum unity. According to his theory, all units which exist in the universe embody the complete knowledge and appearance of the whole. As long as the appropriate environment is established, each unit has the capacity to reflect the complete appearance of the whole. All knowledge is ready to be used at any time and at any place. The essence of all parts is one and equal to each other. The parts are the same with the whole. The universe is not a machine created by the coming together of different objects, but an inseparable and dynamic whole. God-Universe-Man is the same and whole. The expression that God has created man in his own image has begun to receive acknowledgement from the initiates who discover this reality through their thoughts and intuitions as well as scientists. Even the smallest speck of the hologram embodying all the characteristics of the object's whole is the scientific proof of this reality. Both the universe and man embody Divine characteristics. All living beings or objects are parts of the existing whole. Everything carries all the characteristics, even the essence of the main plan it has emerged from in different shapes and proportions inside. The knowledge of the universe has been distributed to all the units. Multiplicity is nothing but delusion.

There is nothing but God in the universe. What is seen everywhere and in everything is one and the same thing. Until today, these concepts which have been expressed by the advocators of esoteric have now reached the point of being the property of the whole humanity with the influence of the Age of Information. The oneness and singularity of the universe has now become a unit which can be accessed by everyone. Today, everything appears before us as the natural laws of nature. Today, science tells us that everything is connected to each other in the universe, all specks share the information they acquire in an instant with the other specks all over the universe, matter is energy made up of the union of matter with a specific density, we are all parts of the same whole and carry the same essence inside. During a certain time unit, the number of waves which pass from a certain point are called "Frequency". In the frequency plane, time and space are identical. Information is everywhere at each moment.

Evolution consists of existence and destruction which chase each other. Within an infinite period of time, all pieces which have been scattered around in a great universe need to have the opportunity to communicate with one another and implement the program especially prepared for them in a complete and perfect manner in order for the evolution to be continued with an infallible order. It seems necessary that the whole structure is managed from one center. In order for this structure to be ready and waiting at all points in the universe, it is apparent that it will need a very fast system. This difficulty can only be overcome with God being the universe himself.

The word Hologram is formed by the union of the words "Holos" (complete picture) and "Gram" (written) in Greek. It is a unity of symbols where all information is recorded. In the holographic registry, all kinds of information recorded are even evident in the smallest speck. Even if the hologram is divided into millions of pieces, all information can be obtained even from the smallest speck. Universal records are also recorded by means of a hologram technique. The Supreme Consciousness keeps the information of the past and the present time and the plans and expectations of the future together within a holographic order. Therefore, the whole universe communicates at the same time and what the whole knows is known by the smallest speck. Since he whole universe knows what the smallest speck knows, there is nothing hidden in the universe. No emotion, thought or formation can remain removed from the whole.

Hologram means complete record or complete information. Hologram, which may be defined as a method of recording with three dimensions, has been discovered by Gabor in 1947. The hologram technique makes use of the interference of two laser beams, one reflected from the object whose record will be taken and the other directly from the laser device and taking the three dimensional photography of an object. In holographic screening, laser light is separated into two on a mirror which is semi silver. One of the beams illuminates the object and the light scattered from there falls on to a photograph plate. The other beam falls directly on the plate without hitting the object. Due to the laser beam being consistent, these two beams mix together and make an attempt. The plate loses the attempt appearance of the mix of the two beams. In this manner, an object's three dimensional appearance can be seen in the hologram record from all angles. The object whose hologram record is done can be observed from different angles as if rotating around it. The source of the laser beam is a special wave movement of the high energy light. Under laser light, light photons act in unity within a special form within the scope of Quantum mechanics. In laser, the light is strengthened with the stimulated radiation emission. What provides stimulated radiation is the photon energy which comes from the outside. In laser beams, the light energy can be accumulated densely at one point and it becomes possible to attain a very high level of energy at a very small point. In holograms, light comes from all points of an object and it is recorded. Therefore, when the plate the object is recorded on breaks into pieces, each piece contains the record's appearance as a whole. No matter how small pieces the plate is broken into, each speck contains the codes of the whole and has the ability to give the complete appearance of the whole record.

The Hologram Law means that each being contains the "Complete Message". Physicist Bohm, who is one of the founders of the Copenhagen School, states that the universe is a single giant hologram and that what we think we see are not separate pieces but visions which contain the information pertaining to the whole. According to Bohm, everything from sub-atomic particles to giant galaxies, everything is different appearances of the whole and they all have the same information structure. In this respect, the holographic universe is a product of a creation. The holographic design of the universe is the proof that this design is beyond space-time coordinates. Each unit independent of space and time embodies the information of the whole universe since the moment of creation and has the capacity to obtain new information in an instant which are being constantly added to the universe. Information independent of space and time can be found everywhere and at any moment. Fred Alan Wolf who agrees with this says "The universe is a giant hologram which embodies both matter and consciousness at the same time".

If the universe is regarded as a hologram, we may say that there is a main source beyond universal order and each object regardless of living or inanimate that we perceive does an analysis of this main source as much as they can perceive it, in accordance with their own level of consciousness. Thus, everything and everyone can benefit from this main information source in their own capacity. Each cup can take its fill from this ocean. Since everything is a whole, all kinds of experience gained by each piece are shared instantly and each unit constantly takes all sorts of information. We may only talk about the variability of the consciousness levels of these pieces in proportion with their perception capacity. The hologram's method of deciphering the object is very similar to the human brain's method of deciphering the stored information. Both have all the information and are quantum. In other words, everything is one. The characteristics of one are evident in all the other pieces which seem different.

Although we are in the 21st century now, one of the areas which we have had little progress in is the structure of the brain. It has not even been discovered where memory is located in the brain. According to a generally acknowledged point of view, memory is not located at a single point. It is all over the cortex. In the same manner, the universal Supreme Consciousness is spread to the whole universe. The energy waves which reach humans externally form connections in the brain cortex and allow memory to develop. The waves produced by the body and the brain pass through the sensory organs, return to the brain and form thoughts. Memory is a hologram record formed in the brain. The Quantum theory suggests that the observer and the observed form a whole. The hologram records seem to be proving this argument. In hologram records, the light wave which is recorded never collapses. Therefore, no matter how small you make the hologram, even the smallest piece will preserve the whole image. All information is coded as a whole. Similarly, information is fixed in the brain as a result of miscellaneous repetitions and recorded widely in the whole cortex. Even the smallest piece of the cortex contains the whole of the recorded information. In the same manner, all laws of existence and the universal evolutionary program might be recorded in the brain. This is valid for all living beings and not unique to humans. All thoughts and experiences are recorded without interruption both to the cortex and the Supreme Consciousness. Holography is the recording system of the Supreme Consciousness.

According to Quantum Theory, if a structure has formed a whole in the beginning, even if you break down this structure, the main structure information of each piece is hidden inside these pieces. In addition, the interaction between the pieces will continue non-locally no matter what the distance is between them. A connection is definitely formed between the two pieces of a whole. This connection continues its existence free from the difference of space and time between them. However, it should be kept in mind that a whole always has more of a structure than its pieces. By breaking down the whole to pieces, trying to understand the whole from these pieces would mean ignoring many characteristics of the whole. Energetic connections can only be formed if the objects which interact form a holistic system.

Humankind joins the universe with its mind and consciousness. The consequence is both holistic and holographic. Energy which is equipped with holographic information turning in on itself is a necessity for the continuation of beings. Shortly, man is a holographic record of the whole universe. There are information, experiences, images and symbols from the past in man's subconscious. These archetypes are universal images and they only reveal themselves in special circumstances. For instance, there are both manhood and womanhood characteristics which are recorded holographic ally in each person. As long as these characteristics have a harmonious balance with each other, a person will be healthy and peaceful. When one is more than the other, an unbalanced character emerges. A personality mixed with the right balance expresses the ideal person.

Quantum completeness shows itself not only in the Hologram Theory, but in fixed numbers which are valid and the same in every point of the universe as well. It is possible to call these fixed numbers Divine mathematics too. Fixed numbers such as the number Pi, Fibonacci sequence and the Golden Ratio are expressions of Divine mathematics. If fixed numbers are indications that mathematics is the primary building block of the universe, circles, globes, spheres, pentagrams and spirals which we frequently see in the universe are proof that the structure of the universe is based on geometry. The number Pi, 3,14159..., which is a number sequence that extends until eternity is the fixed number found as a result of the division of a circle's perimeter's diameter. No matter the size of the circle, the number Pi is always fixed. It is an irrational and Transcendent number. No number has been seen whose 50 billion digits have been calculated and repeats itself. The globe shape we frequently encounter in the universe is directly related with the number Pi.

The Golden Ratio is irrational like the number Pi. It has a structure which rotates in on itself and it constantly appears before us in the structure of living or inanimate beings with this characteristic. In nature, fixed forces such as the Golden Ratio are seen frequently. These points with force prevent numerous natural systems to get out of control and pull a system which has been dragged into chaos into order. In motions which seem complex, these fixed forces can be observed. There are very small differences between order and chaos and small changes in the fixed parameters allow passage from one to the other. The Golden Ratio is observed in many points in the universe. Some scientists claim that the shape of the universe is like a structure which consists of pentagrams whose 12 faces are equilateral. This shape is named "Dodecahedron" and is a structure that has the Golden Ratio in its basis. The Golden Ratio is almost like the proof of existence of a divine architect. In the distances between the planets, the number Phi is frequently seen as well. The Phi letter in Greek alphabet represents the Golden Ratio.

The Golden Ratio is one of the two numbers which is equal to its square when it is added to the number 1. The Golden Ratio is expressed as 1,61803... It is also known s the Fibonacci sequence. The Fibonacci numbers carry the secret of the golden ratio. Each of these numbers consists of the sum of the two numbers which precede them. The Fibonacci number sequence continues to eternity as 1,1,2,3,5,8,13,21... When you divide a number with the number preceding it beginning with the 13th term in the Fibonacci sequence, we get approximately the fixed number 1.618... This number is the mathematical expression of the Golden Ratio. The Fibonacci sequence is infinite. However, it can be ended with an inter term. At the point where the sequence is ended, a number very close to the golden ratio but not equal to it is achieved. Due to this small difference, it is possible to create structures which are very similar to each other but different. This is the reason why individuals of all species are very similar to each other, but still have different structures.

An area where the golden ratio is seen in nature is plants. If the leaves of plants grew in 180 degree intervals, since the first leaf would be on top of the third leaf in a full rotation, the third leaf would be preventing the Sun and the rain. Therefore, plant leaves always grow as arranged in the style of the Fibonacci sequence. None of the leaves prevents the growth of the other. This most efficient and favorable manner of arrangement is in accordance with the golden ratio. Structuring in line with the golden ratio is seen not only in living beings, but in the structure of atoms, star islands, galaxies and even cyclones. The golden ratio is even present in the ratios in the human body and face. Many systems which seem complex to the eye from the outside have been discovered to be in order due to the golden ratio.

Another proof the universe-man sameness is again found in the Golden Ratio. Just as in the universe, the Golden Ratio shows its existence in the human body very frequently. The ratio of the parts of the body, the ratio of the organs on the face is all Golden Ratio. It is even seen in heart beats. It is possible to find this ratio in fingers, arms, legs and even inner organs. The snail structure in the middle ear is in the structure of the golden ratio. The ratio of a person's height and the distance from his belly to his toes always result in the Golden Ratio. It is known that Leonardo, Raphael, Rubens and Botticelli used this ratio in their paintings. The golden ratio is not only unique to humans. From the arrangement of sun flowers to pine cones, from the leaves of trees to shelled sea creatures, the same ratio is observed in many living structures. Behind all the perfect works of art in the areas of painting, music, sculpting and architecture, there is the proportional wholeness defined as the Golden Ratio. The Golden Ratio is the ratio of the order of the eye. The Golden Ratio has been used since Egyptian architecture in architects and masons in architecture in all periods of history who were the members of the Esoteric schools. The Golden Ratio is observed in Egyptian, Mayan and Chinese pyramids. The base of each of these pyramids' ratio to their height is a Golden Ratio. Architect Sinan has used this ratio in the minarets in the Suleymaniye and Selimiye Mosques. This ratio has been kept as a professional secret for centuries. The Golden Ratio gives the ratio of the length of the side of the pentagram to the side length of the pentagon inside it. The pentagram is a symbol which represents the union and harmony of the four elements with the Soul. The pentagram is generally associated with Venus. For every 8 turns the Earth makes around the Sun, the Venus does 13 turns. This creates an orbital resonance of a 13:8 ratio when the Earth is taken as the center. This resonance forms the shape of a pentagonal star which is close to perfect.

In the ancient language of symbolism, the pentagram is the symbol of the geometrical order of the universe. It tells that the universe is constantly dynamic. The pentagram is the symbol of Order and the hexagram is the symbol of Chaos. In accordance with the Esoteric teachings, the pentagram reminds us that God exists inside of us. The source of light and reality is one and the same. According to Pythagoras, the pentagram points out to the order God has given to the universe through the science of geometry. The word he uses to define this star is Pentalpha. Pentalpha means 5 A's. Alpha is the first letter of the Greek alphabet. When these A's are drawn as to form a star, it can be seen that the A's are in 5 different positions. While each A represents the four basic elements, the A whose point is looking up represents God, who is the source of everything, and his first characteristic, the act of creation. God has created the universe with what he embodies and has allowed the universe to pass from chaos to order by means of the four basic forces. The pentagram symbolizes the final goal as a result of divine arrangement, that is, man. The most known usage of this star with five sides which is drawn as the head, arms and legs is the "Vitruvius Man" by Leonardo da Vinci. In this drawing, there is the head, arms and legs of a human in each arm of the star. The drawing depicts the perfection of man. Inside the pentagram within a five pointed star drawn in accordance to the golden ratio, a new five pointed star can be drawn using the same ratio again. But this time the star is upside down. This process can be continued until eternity theoretically. Therefore, the pentagram is also the symbol of eternity. The hexagram formed right at the center of the six pointed star depicts that a synthesis can be reached from thesis and anti-thesis, each different point of view may reconcile at one point and what is important is to achieve balance. Therefore, the six pointed star is the sign of the chaos of thoughts as well as the fact that an order will surely arise from this chaos. It is also the symbol of human rationality, rational thought and intelligence which looks for reality and understands reality.

Even a single five pointed star drawn with the Golden Ratio is proof of God's existence by itself. Pythagoras stated "Evolution is life's law. Numbers are the laws of the universe. Unity is the law of God". Mathematics is a universal law, which has validity everywhere, including everything from the meals we cook to feed ourselves and all the scientific branches, besides art. The spinning rate of the Earth and all macro cosmos including its distance from the Sun is based on mathematics. The same law is valid in macro cosmos. Each atom's location and state of fixed. Even the smallest deviation would cause chaos. Similarly, the number of chromosomes in DNA which make life possible are fixed and even the lack of one of them would mean disability. All bodily balances which show the functions of life (blood, sugar, cholesterol) are also fixed and deviations are indications of illnesses. Balance is essential for each formation. The Divine expression of balance is mathematics and geometry. It was John Nash who proved mathematically each being's tendency to reach a natural balance through his "Natural Balance Theory".

English mathematician Godfrey Harold Hardi stated "Today, we are discovering that the universe has been approved within the framework of the same rules as mathematics". Kepler stated "Wherever there is matter, there is geometry. What provides beauty in nature are Mathematical Ratios". Physicist James Jeans suggested "The Architect of the Universe must be a great mathematician". Einstein has commented "The only aspect about universe that has not been understood is that it is understandable". Western science's discriminating rationality is evident in mathematics as well. The term infinite which has been used by Esoteric for thousands of years has been used in mathematics only in the 19th century. Another interesting point is the entry of the number "Zero" into the world of mathematics. According to Western science, the concept of "Zero" is not known in the ancient world. Zero has been discovered in India a short time before the birth of Christ and has been brought to Europe by the Persians and Arabs. However, it was not Hindus who discovered Zero. Zero means "Nothingness" and it has been used for thousands of years by all ancient cultures as a symbol of nothingness. This discourse is one of the Cartesian West's dogmas, which suggest that subjective scientific concepts are the works of near history of mankind. The first use of the number zero in mathematics is known to have taken place in the work of a Brahman priest called Brahmagupta: "Siddhanta". Brahmagupta has expressed the concept of nothingness with the "0" symbol and has narrated the rules which showed how to do calculations with this number. Muslim scholar Musa el-Harezmi who worked on Siddhanta has carried the concept to Europe over Andalusia. Harezmi's another work about the same subject has been translated into Latin a few hundred years later and thus, Western scientists have learned about the number zero. However, this does not mean that neither the concept of nothingness, nor the concept of infinity was not known before.

Our perception of the reality through rational assumptions and constructed on their refutation is called the Popper Method. This method has been working non-stop for thousands of years to be able to make better predictions about reality. Scientists and thinkers are constantly making assumptions to define reality in the shortest and simplest manner possible and as these assumptions are refuted under the light of new experiences and acquired knowledge, new ones replace them. This process seems to be continuing in the same manner as long as humanity exists. Experiments and observations are continued to test the reality models. Science is constantly reborn from its own ashes. The methodical research and analysis of science is based on the questioning technique. To simply deny immeasurable conditions with the present tools in the experiments and claim that these cannot form evidences, is an adverse attitude in terms of the questioning mechanism of science. The key to scientifically proving the existence of the soul, whose existence is denied since it is an interest area of metaphysics, is energy, light. Perhaps, the soul being a kind of energy will be proven very shortly. Science will be hand in hand with religion to the extent it will be successful in abandoning its reductionist ideology, remove dogmas of religion and the pair will enlighten the path of humanity.

"Let there be light" discourse of all religions regardless of divine or not and energy (light) created at the moment of the Big Bang in the scientific creation discourse overlap exactly. Therefore, mankind seems to know this reality since the very ancient times; in fact, this ancient allegorical narrative has been scientifically proven today. The first thing that emerged in the beginning of creation was Light. The first period following the Big Bang is a period during which light was dominant. It has been predicted that this period lasted for 330 thousand years. The universe was then full of electromagnetic radiation and solid matter did not exist yet. Visible light is parts of the electromagnetic spectrum and the only difference between microwaves, infrared, visible light, ultraviolet, X rays and Gamma rays in the environment is the wave length of each or the energies they are equal to. In fact, they are all a derivative of electromagnetic radiation. In short, they are all Light. The course science has taken is completely towards proving the existence of God. Today, science has come to the point where the only rational explanation for the universe and creation is the reality that we are all parts of God. Newton's view that universe is a structure left on its own devices has lost its validity, because it has begun to be understood that the universe is continuing its existence as a hospitable structure which has been created through rules which made it dynamic and thus allowed variety of life, steadily continued and constantly evolved.

Hologram and Quantum Theories have proven that all events which take place in the universe are connected to each other and that randomness is not possible. Physicist David Bohm stated "Now, the view that the world can be analyzed by separating it into independent and isolated parts is leaving its place to the unity and wholeness approach. We have reversed the classical "Basic Units" approach. We claim that the universe is made up of an inseparable Quantum interaction. We believe that the units which seem independent are in fact the parts of this whole," and has put forward the Pantheist approach of the Copenhagen school. According to Bohm, the universe is a complex network of relationships which are formed between the different parts of the holistic unity.

The Anthropic principle says that the laws of the universe were exactly as they first were now and that is how they were created. In fact, the laws being different would mean that they are not laws. If the universe is a Quantum Computer based on fixed laws, was the program to operate this computer created first, or the computer itself? Since it would not be possible for the program to operate without the laws, firstly the laws of nature have been considered and designed. The universe which emerged after that was given direction by these laws from the first moment. The four basic forces are the best indication that these laws were active even from the first moment. Shortly, the laws of nature may be said to be the thoughts of God. Therefore, God is the computer programmer who makes it possible for the operation of the universe in a way. So, why is this computer operated? The reason is to create new information by adding new data and advance the system.

THE FOUR HORSEMEN OF THE APOCALYPSE

The four basic laws which keep the universe in balance are The Law of Gravity, Electromagnetic Force, Weak Nucleus Force and Strong Nucleus Force. The first laws of nature which were activated after the Big Bang were these four basic forces. From the first moment of creation until the present time, their effects have continued non-stop. These four basic forces, which took the universe from chaos to order and have been keeping the whole process of evolvement in balance from that moment on have been defined as the four basic elements by Esoteric. The divine religions called these four basic forces "The Four Horsemen of the Apocalypse", or the four archangels

Each speck in the universe creates an area around it and creates force on the other specks. This force may manifest in four different types in accordance with the size value of the speck and the location and state of the other speck it affects. In fact, studies about a combined quantum theory are currently being conducted on these four forces to show that they are the different appearances of a single force. All effects the speck in the universe is subject to contain these four different types of basic forces. In scientific terms, these are The Law of Gravity, Electromagnetic Force, Weak Nucleus Force and Strong Nucleus Force. In terms of Esoteric, they are Fire, Water, Air and Earth. So far, there has not been any event in the macro and micro universes which has not been explained by one of these forces. The definition Fire, Water, Air and Earth is ten thousand years old. Scientific definitions on the other hand have been put forward in the last few centuries. Science has once again verified Esoteric.

Gravity among these four basic forces is the force that has been discovered first. It was discovered by Newton in the 17th century. Electromagnetic force, the second discovered force, was discovered by Maxwell in the 19th century. The other two forces were discovered in the 20th century with the discovery of atom physics. The discourse that there 4 basic forces in nature dictated by Esoteric thousands of years ago was rediscovered only in the light of 20th century science.

In the first moment following the Big Bang, energy is so dense in the nano period of the first second that, the four forces cannot be distinguished from one another. Right after this moment where matter and energy were one, firstly electromagnetic force has become active in the first few second and it was followed by the weak nucleus force (nuclear force) A few seconds later, matter began to separate from energy by means of the strong nucleus force and lastly, the force of gravity was formed between matter. Another claim is that the first activated force was the force of gravity.

According to those whose argue for this, it can only be possible for the Big Bang to take place with the existence of two different poles. Since positive and negative poles attract each other and the Big Bang is created thus, we may say that the first force to be activated has been the force of gravity with existence. The super string theory also supports the thesis that the first force which was created in space-time for the creation of super strings. Since the universe is a universe of light energy, it is likely that the speed of light was in question in the formation of events right from the first moment. In fact, energy spread around with the speed of light. In this environment, the other three forces have separated, become active and began to put the universe that we know into order. As a result of this separation being understood, it will be possible to find an explanation for the "Theory of Everything" science is seeking for today. To be able to understand the background of the separation, it is necessary to accept the existence of the main essence which embodies eternity. IF it is not acknowledge that everything is a whole, it will not be possible to unite the three forces which were possible to be untied and the force of gravity.

Ancient science calls these four basic forces the four forces which took the universe from chaos to order. The first force which became active was water. That is the reason why it is argued that the universe has been created out of water. The most important aspect of water is that, it attracts the atoms it contains to itself and gives them off repeatedly. It is the source life. AS a result of this cycle, it is possible for water to reach every point in the world and that is how it sustains life. Water has the ability to contract and shrink with cold and expand with heat. Another aspect of water is its production of magnetic current. Electromagnetic force also produces magnetic current. The first force seen after the Big Bang, electromagnetic force has the ability just like water to attract and repulse. Atoms and molecules are kept together by electromagnetic force. The negative charge of electrons repulses the other electrons and prevents them from mingling with each other. The existence of atoms and sustaining their lives is possible by means of this force. Objects sustain their existence in this manner. The pieces which carry electromagnetic force are called photons. Photons are the sources of communication between electrons. Electromagnetic force is 38 over 10 times higher than the force of gravity. Due to electromagnetic force, the matter in the universe has always had equal positive and negative charges. Besides atoms, larger objects such as the Earth and the Sun also contain an equal amount of positive and negative charges.

The second force which became active in creation was fire. Fire has the ability to expand. Fire and light contain characteristics which are creative. Fire and light have carried nothing into existence. The reason why light is visible is the existence of darkness. Without darkness, light cannot be seen. Darkness is passive, while light is active. The weak nucleus force is the force which creates the radioactive disintegration in some atoms and allows atom nuclei to separate. This force is thousand times weaker than electromagnetic force and 35 over 10 times stronger than the force of gravity. If there were no nuclear reactions caused by the weak nucleus force, it would not be possible for heavy elements to b created and the universe would only consist of hydrogen and helium. The most known characteristic of the weak nucleus force is its ability to create heat and light, thus energy. The most known characteristic of nuclear reactions is their ability to create heat and light power, the power of Fire. Even today, the continuation of formation, or evolution, is possible by means of the weak nucleus force, or fire.

The third element which was activated is the element of air. This force has acted like a mediator between the forces of water and fire and has taken both of their strong characteristics in its scope. Air has taken heat from ire, moisture from water and joined the two forces. If these aspects did not come together, the continuation of life would not be possible. A majority of the universe is in gas state. What fills the space between masses is gas, or dark matter. Similarly, a significant part of macro cosmos materials with mass seems to have atmosphere. There are gas layers which surround objects and these are the very important functions of the atmosphere. The atmosphere which surrounds the Earth is the most important reason for the existence of life in our planet. The strong nucleus force is the force which allows solid and fluid objects, as well as gasses to remain without separating. What makes protons and neutrons in the atomic nucleus to stay together is the strong nucleus force which is the most important force of nature. Just like air uniting the characteristics of fire and water, the strong nucleus force has been the force which infinitely united the quarks and leptons which emerged after the Big Bang and allowed matter to be born. Without air, we cannot talk about life and evolution.

The most effective element among the four basic elements of nature, but has the least force is the element of earth. The ratios of objects which have mass or earth take up a very small place in comparison to area without mass. So much so that the distances between masses can be measured with light years. All the remaining areas are without mass. However, it is these areas which contain objects with mass that laws of evolvement are densely active. The element of earth has been created with the interaction of the other three elements. Earth as the last force which became active has been created as a result of the interaction of all elements and their solidification. The law of gravity carries out its activities through earth, or masses which have been created as a result of the interaction of the other forces in the macro cosmos. The force which controls the galaxies, stars and planets in the universe is the force of gravitation. This force shapes the structure of the universe. Each speck is affected by this in accordance with its mass and energy. The force of gravity is the weakest among the four forces. The force of gravity always attracts objects to each other. Similarly, the universe stays together by means of this force. If gravitation were weaker than its current state, matter would not be able to get dense and the birth of the element of earth would not be possible. The universe would remain cold and empty. On the other hand, the universe is in a state of expansion because the force of gravity is weaker than the other forces. Our galaxy and solar system have expanded as a result of the force of gravity being weaker than the other forces and has taken its current state. Another area of activity of the force of gravity is that it creates attraction between the centers and surfaces of masses. The densest point of attraction is the center of the mass. As it moves away from the center, the force of gravity decreases. The surface of the earth appears as an area which contains the ideal force of attraction to enable a living being to live.

The four basic forces in the universe continue their existence in four different structural states just like the four basic elements. There is no other basic structure in the universe except for these structural existences. Matter exists in nature only in solid, liquid, gas or plasma states. Quantum philosophy says that nothing in the universe is lost and that they are only transformed. Since everything is energy, all existence which complete their life-span transform into energy. Natter is the solid state of energy. Plasma is its energy state. The four elements of earth, water, air and fire are different manifestations of energy. These four elements constitute the universe of matter.

Such a balance has been created in the universe in terms of mass, distance and spheres of influence through the force of gravity, electromagnetic force, nuclear force and weak force that, the universe has almost immediately passed from chaos into order. All these fine calculations lower the probability of the moment of creation and what happened afterwards to be a coincidence close to zero. Everything is planned and the work of an architect. Einstein has stated "It seems as if there is someone who Knows," and revealed the invalidity of the probability of chance. Strong nucleus force weakens in high energies and electromagnetic and weak nucleus forces get stronger in high energies. All objects produce beams. In other words, all objects have the capacity to produce radiation. The particle of radiation is photon. Photons are sub-atomic particles which do not have mass and travel with the speed of light just like radio waves. Due to the force of gravity being weak, particles without mass can move without breaking apart and in a linear manner, even if their source is billions of light years away. Electrons' influencing other electrons which are billions of light years away is possible through photons. The information photons contain is transmitted to Tachyons and communication with the speed of thought becomes possible through Tachyons which can travel much faster than the speed of light. Science has never come across an event which could not be explained through one of the four force areas known in the universe.

The most visible of the four forces in the macro universe level is the force of gravity. Each particle has a force of gravity in relation to its mass and energy. The force of gravity is valid everywhere and at all times and is universal. The force of gravity can be effective from great distances. Objects falling to Earth, the attraction between the Earth and the Sun, the attraction between the galaxies are all works of this force. The very weak forces of gravity between each of two objects' parts can pile up on top of each other and form a strong force of gravity. Each being in the macro universe spins around itself and creates its own force of gravity; each being also spins around the being with mass in accordance with the force of gravity of the star or system it is dependent on. The same is true in the micro universe. While atoms are pulled to the matter they are connected with, they also attract the particles around them to themselves.

What keeps the universe together and prevents it from breaking down is the force of gravity. This also called the Universal Force of Gravitation. According to the Laws of Gravity discovered by Newton in 1666, each object which has mass in the universe attracts the other to itself. All objects in nature are under the effect of this force. The galaxies, stars, suns, planets and all other objects with mass in the universe are tied to each other with this force. From the cosmos to micro quantum, each object with mass attracts the other through the force of gravitation. The universe itself stays together, without breaking away due to this force of attraction. The force of gravity behaves in the same manner both in the macro cosmos and the micro cosmos. The world of science states that the force of gravity which the galactic clusters have on each other is weak and not sufficient enough to stop the expansion of the universe. Still, it is thought that the expansion will slow down due to the same force. By time, expansion will stop and the size of the universe will remain fixed. The forces of gravity, its areas, and its directions are all proof of a universal intelligence. The mass of the Sun, the mass of the Earth and the distance between them are of such an ideal dimension that due to the force of gravity created through them, the beings who live on Earth are neither floating in the heavens, nor are they rooted to the spot they put their feet on.

The power of the force of gravity is -40 over 10 and it is the weakest among the four forces. Despite this, it is still the force of gravity which has an infinite influence area in the macro cosmos. An object's escaping the influence of the force of gravity and getting further away from a planet and star and going into space is called "The Escape Speed". The Escape Speed for Earth is 11.23 kilometers per second. The escape speed from the surface of the Sun is 617 km/sec. The technology we have today is able to overcome gravity in vehicles sent to space since these can achieve a 14.5 kilometer speed and allows humanity to do research on space.

The force of gravity between two objects seems to be active only in the macro cosmos. The force of gravity is also evident within atoms in the micro cosmos; however it has not been identified yet whether there is a force of gravity between two atoms. The effect of the force of gravity to the micro cosmos may be said to be indirect. The weak nucleus force and strong nucleus force which are active in the micro cosmos effect the macro cosmos indirectly as well through atoms. Electromagnetic force, which is the fourth force, is known to penetrate to all areas and affect them. The studies conducted until the present time have show that other forces except for the force of gravity act together within the framework of Quantum Laws. A theory which ties the force of gravity with Quantum physics has not been developed yet.

The other three forces beside the force of gravity are essentially active in the micro cosmos, or in the sub-atomic world. However, their effects are valid for the whole macro cosmos. Electromagnetic force among these allows each object to remain fixed in its own mass. The force which keeps the electrons of an atom around the nucleus is electromagnetic force. By means of this force, electrons push the electrons of the atom next to them through negative charge and the mixing and breaking up of the two atoms is prevented. The same force keeps atoms and molecules together. Particles charged negatively such as electrons and protons can interact due to electromagnetic force. The force between particles of similar charges is repellant and the force between particles of different charges is attractive. In the nucleus of an atom, the electromagnetic force between the proton and electron is 10 times higher than the mass force of gravity.

Electromagnetic force both has the ability to attract and repel. Attracting and repelling depends on the type of electrical charges. If the charges are the same, objects push each other. If the charges are different, they attract each other. The scientific proof of the Esoteric discourse that opposites always attract each other has been revealed with the understanding of this force. Due to this force, electrons with negative charges remain around the atomic nucleus which is positively charged. In this manner, atoms remain fixed and the creation of matter is possible. The power of electromagnetic force is -2 over 10 and its effect extends from zero to eternity. The particle of electromagnetic force is photon. The electromagnetic force inside atoms overcomes the repelling force between electrons and persuades them to unite. Atoms which unite through electrons create molecules and elements. Elements are only formed from one type of atom, whereas, molecules are created with the union of two or more elements. There are 92 elements in nature. In addition, 17 more elements have been produced in laboratories.

The third force is the strong nucleus force, or the strong nuclear force. The strong nuclear force prevents the breaking away of atoms. It interlocks the particles in the nucleus and the atoms thus remain intact where they are. It is this strong nucleus force which keeps protons and neutrons inside the atomic nucleus together. All objects around us preserve their determined and balanced state with the effect of this force. The strong nuclear force is the strongest of the forces in nature. Its power in comparison to the unit of the other forces is 1. Quarks are the most basic and smallest particle of matter. Each of protons and neutrons consists of three quarks. Quarks cannot be moved, because they are held in place by the Strong Nuclear Force, which is the greatest force of nature. So far, 18 different types of quarks have been discovered. However, the influence of the strong nuclear force is -15 over 10 meters. If the area of its influence were not this small, the force would be applied to all directions and it would not be possible for any object to move.

The fourth and last force which is the weak nucleus force or the weak nuclear force is the force which allows the nucleus to break up into pieces under the right conditions. Radioactive reactions can only be possible with this force. All kinds of radioactive activity in the universe find life by means of this force. If there were no weak nucleus, the heavy elements would not be created and life would not begin. The weak nuclear force is the force between proton and neutron which determines the stability of the atomic nucleus. When a proton turns into a proton, it changes its charge and the stability of the nucleus is spoiled. This causes radioactivity. During radio activity, a neutron and an electron stick together and turn into a proton. Meanwhile, an electron with high speed is created. The atom then changes character and turns into another element which has a different atomic number. The power of the weak nuclear force is -5 over 10 and its area of influence of -17 over 10 meters.

The source of energy within the atom is called nuclear energy. With the breaking up of a single radioactive atom, a great amount of energy can be produced. Fusion is the separation of the atomic nucleus into two equal parts. When the nucleus is broken up, some part of its mass turns into energy. From 1 kilo of Uranium 235, energy which can be achieved from 1.5 million kilos of coal can be obtained. Fusion is the collision and breaking up of the naked atomic nucleus which has lost its electrons. If fusion is controlled, the energy created can be used as a source of energy. Uncontrolled fusion creates an atomic explosion. The breaking up of a single nucleus of the whole of the radioactive matter causes all the other radioactive atoms to be broken up as well and an extraordinary amount of energy is created.

In 1938, the idea to bombard Uranium which is a heavy element with neutrons was proposed. As a result of this bombardment, it has been possible for uranium, which has a high number of neutrons in its nucleus, to go under fission and new neutrons to be produced. These neutrons have broken up the other uranium atoms and the fission reaction has taken place. As a consequence of this reaction, an extraordinary amount of energy has been achieved. When a neutron is collided on the Uranium 235 atom nucleus, protons and neutrons in the nucleus separate into two in groups. Therefore, the weak nuclear force which holds them together is broken. The breaking of the weak nuclear force lets out the energy within the atom. 1 neutron which collides with the nucleus causes 3 neutrons to spring from the nucleus. Each of these neutrons hit 3 separate nuclei as well. This chain fission reaction continues until there is no more uranium atom to be broken down.

The weak nuclear force allows the creation of nuclear energy which does not only break down in laboratories but in nature as well and which makes it possible for evolution to take place in the whole universe. The 4 hydrogen atoms which are present in every point of the universe unite and can produce 1 helium atom. While this is taking place, two of the protons become two neutrons with the addition of two electrons. Ther remaining two protons and the newly formed two neutrons shape a new helium atom. This union is called the fusion reaction. In fusion reaction which is created with the sticking together of two light nuclei, the weak nuclear force is broken and energy is created. The energy which is created from the difference in mass of the particles prior to and after the union is extraordinary. In the fusion reaction which takes inside the Sun, 1% of hydrogen turns into energy. Even this 1% energy allows the central temperature of the Sun to reach 15 million degrees. The amount of energy created with a fusion reaction is much greater than the energy created in the fission reaction of the same mass.

There is an extraordinary sensitive balance in nature. For instance, decrease even in the smallest amount in the strong nucleus force may cause all kinds of elements to separate and only hydrogen to remain behind as the fixed element. Similarly, if the weak nucleus force is even a bit stronger than electromagnetic force, an atom nucleus which contains only two protons will become the fixed building block of the universe and it would not be hydrogen. As a result, the universe would display a much different development compared to the present time. In the same manner, if the mass force of gravity were just a bit weaker than 45 over 10 from the weak nucleus force, the universe would be much smaller and its life-span would be much shorter.

When electromagnetic force and the weak nuclear force were United, it has been determined that the pair created electroweak force. In 1983, the existence of heavy particles which made it possible to unite electromagnetic force and the weak force. Currently, studies still continue to unite electroweak force and strong nuclear force. These scientific studies on quantum mechanics have one common goal: To discover the Grand Unification Theory – GUT. The moment this theory is scientifically put forward, the explanation on the common order in the micro cosmos and micro cosmos universes will be possible. If the theory is ever proven, then it will be turn to add the force of gravity to the three forces. For now, including the force of gravity in Quantum mechanics seems to be greatest challenge of quantum physicists. In case the theory referred to as GUT is proven, mankind will reach the point where it can understand the conditions which gave rise to the Big Bang and even what happened prior to it. With this theory, the Quantum Unity will be proven as well.

The universe has essentially been built based completely on quantum mechanics and quantum knowledge. If the universe has quantum knowledge (and it has been proven that this is so), then the deterministic theories will need to be re-questioned. The universe functions as a Quantum Computer which has created our reality as a whole before our eyes. In other words, the foundation of The Theory of Everything is knowledge, and it is Universal Intelligence which forms its super structure.

Stephen Hawking has stated "If a complete unification theory can be found which can be understood by even the person on the street, then the people on the streets, philosophers and we will begin to discuss the question 'Why do we and the universe exist?' in a more conscious manner. If we can answer this question, we will achieve the most glorious victory of the human mind. Because, we will be able to understand what crossed God's mind, what his purpose was in creating the universe and his thoughts". According to Hawking, who is one of the leading advocators of the Deist philosophy, after God initiated the universe, He has not interfered with its operation ever. Hawking who says that only the black holes do not operate in accordance with the laws that we know and adds that "God has the freedom to choose and recreate the events as he wishes only in such places".

Hawking in his work *Grand Design* asks the following questions: "How can we understand this world we have found ourselves in? How does the universe move? What is the nature of reality? Where did all these things come from? Does the universe need a creator?" He adds "Many of us do not spend all our time thinking about these questions; however we all sometimes think about them". According to Hawking, these are philosophical questions, but philosophy is dead. It has not been able to keep pace with the modern developments in especially in the area of physics. In our search for knowledge, the torch of the discoveries is not in the hands of scientists. It is not possible to agree with Hawking's point of view. In fact, philosophy is much more ahead of science and it is very much alive. The philosophy of Esoteric has expressed the realities discovered newly by science and which cannot be accepted by those like Hawking, thousands of years ago.

Hawking in his work *A Brief History of Time* claims that, by means of the discovery of a complete physics theory which explains everything, humankind will be able to know what God thought about. Hawking says that we will even discover those rules which bind God. Universal laws bind everything and everyone, including God. Hawking claims that it is possible to know the physical boundaries of God. In other words, God is surrounded with the laws of physics. With today's point of view, although this discourse may sound right, Hawking has shown once more that the interpretation of scientific developments are important to the degree where they cannot only be left to scientist. In physics plan, it is true that God is bound with his own physics laws, however claiming the existence of the physical universe and there is nothing beyond it would be nothing but having scientific blinders on. Just as every being has both a physics plan and a metaphysical plan, God also has both. The physics universe is God's body and the metaphysical universe which shares the same environment is God soul. The metaphysical universe having unique laws and God being bound by these laws is very likely, however as long as today's science disregards this area, it will not be possible for humankind to reach an accurate conclusion.

The 4 main forces, which continue their existence without losing power today, have been existing since the Big Bang and a gradual change or a change based on great distances is not in question for them. Essentially, these 4 main forces are not separate from each other, but 4 different effects of a force that is the main essence. In the formation of these 4 forces and the particles which carry this force, there is no such thing as coincidence. Time has begun to flow the moment these forces emerged. Therefore, a chain of coincidences based on time in the formation of these 4 forces which have shaped the whole universe has never been in question and will not ever be. In other words, any kind of randomness is not in question in terms of the creation of the universe. During the passage from the zero moment to the first moment, the 4 forces are present in the Big Bang and all events have taken place within the framework of the laws which the 4 forces depend on and in line with it. Hawking also underlines that the concept of time had never had any meaning prior to the beginning of the universe. Even if the existence of any event or condition before the zero moment is in question, it is not possible for this event or state to effect the present time since time did not exist. Time cannot be defined with times prior to its beginning. Similarly, it is meaningless to talk about a space or time outside the borders of the universe. Therefore, Hawking's question "If the universe has been created, why was it necessary to wait before its creation?" has no meaning. In fact, a waiting time is not in question.

As mentioned earlier, it is possible to talk about the four states of matter in nature: Plasma, gas, fluid and solid. The plasma state of matter emerges only in extreme temperatures. It is matter's energy state. Therefore, gas, fluid and solid states which are the other three states of existence are seen as "matter". Quantum physics says that matter and energy is the same thing. Since there is less attraction between molecules in gas state, molecules are able to move independent of each other. If the amount of energy decreases, contact between molecules increases and these molecules may slip on each other. This is the fluid form of matter. If the energy decreases eve more, the molecules become more stable and the matter is then in solid state. The force of attraction between the molecules of solid matter is very high. As temperature increases, molecules gain more energy and firstly turn into fluids and then to gas. If matter is heated even more, lastly it turns into plasma, or energy. Plasma is an ionized matter in very high temperatures, which consists of positive and negative charged free particles. Molecules have more contact in fluid matter. They display a more sparse distribution. While there is contact between atoms in solid and fluid states, there is space between them in gas state. The solid state of matter is equal to the element of earth, to the element of water in fluid state, the element of air in gas state and the element of fire in plasma state. The interaction and transformation of matter takes place in 3 basic areas: 1- Electromagnetic area; 2- Nuclear area and 3- Gravitational area.

Other than these four elements, a 5th element can also be mentioned. This element is Akasha which makes it possible for everything in the universe to exist. It is the final purpose. The essential purpose of the four elements. Akasha is what is final, absolute, glorious and the most powerful. It cannot be understood. Everything is kept in balance by means of it. It is God's expression. Tibetan priests refer to Akasha as universal intelligence or the Supreme consciousness. Experiences, thoughts, everything acquired as a result of existences and events lived come together in Akasha. It is the expression of universal evolvement. The first element to be born from Akasha is the principle of fire. In the beginning, everything is light. Light is a result of the element of fire. A fireless light cannot be imagined. Fire has characteristics of energy and electricity. The principle of fire has the ability to expand. Each element has two poles. Dominant and passive, in other words, positive and negative poles. While positive always expresses constructive, creative and productive sources, negative expresses all destructive and dissolvent. Light is the expression of fire's dominant aspect. Darkness is the expression of the passive. If there were no darkness, light would not be understood and vice versa. The universe contains neither good, nor bad. Everything has been created in accordance with unchanging laws. The opposite of fire is water. This principle is the 2nd element which has emerged from Akasha. Water has come into existence with fire. Its main characteristics are coldness and shriveling. After the Big Bang, the force which made it possible for the universe to immediately cool down is water. The universe gradually cooled down through water and other forces started to become active. Since water has the ability to shrivel and contract, it produces magnetic current. Fire and water are basic elements in which everything is created from them. Electrical and magnetic currents are the signs of opposite poles. The third element which emerged with the union of fire and water is air. Air forms a balance between water and fire. It takes heat from fire and moisture from water. Without these characteristics, it is not possible for life to begin in some way. Lastly, earth has been created as a result of the interaction of the other three elements. All the other elements' coming together and becoming solid has created earth. The element of earth is electromagnetic.

Elements of fire and water and electricity and magnetic currents which are their expressions are the reason for everything which takes place materially in the world. Everything which takes place in the world of minerals, plants and animals and all chemical processes are determined by these two currents. These two forces complete and transform each other. As electricity can be produced from magnetism by changing the poles, magnetism can be produced from electricity through mechanical methods. Dan is the expression of Akasha in the material world. Dan exists in a compound manner in everything made constructive by fire, enlivening by water, balancing by air and breeding by earth. Every being that contains these five aspects is alive. Akasha is the single structure which does not get affected by the four basic elements. The source of everything that has taken place in the material world, currently taking place and will take place in the future is Akasha. It is the light, sound, color and harmony in each being which has created an area of vibration.

Elements are not only effective on inanimate matter, but also on living beings. The best example to this can be the human body. A healthy body is the expression of the perfect harmony of all efficient powers of the essential aspects of the elements in the body. Besides the electrical flow of the principle of fire, its constructive and renovating characteristic, the disintegration and dispersing of bodily fluids in the magnetic plane characteristic of the water principle and the function of the principle of earth of holding the other three elements together, its ability to revitalize and prompt them into action are the inevitable aspects of health. Health is the requirement for spiritual ascension. Illnesses mean disharmony between elements. A defect which may appear in any of the elements in the body shows itself as an illness. The head is the area where the principle of fire is efficient; the stomach where the principle of water and the chest where the principle of air are efficient. Breathing expresses the principle of air. Earth is the complete body which involves all three with the bones and flesh. The body comes from earth and will return to earth. Depriving the body of matter it needs, or not realizing the needs of intuition, leaves health under serious and dangerous situations.

The fire is the element of the will, water is the element of life and emotions, air is the element of the mind and earth is the element of consciousness of the self. We may hold the elements responsible for the following: the principle of fire from action and passion; the principle of water from conscious and emotions; the principle of air from the ability of differentiation and judgment and the principle of earth from the power to reproduce. Meanwhile, Akasha is the element of intuition and love. It is Akasha which carries the knowledge of experiences to the Supreme Consciousness. In every area of life, it is a holy duty to establish balance. Birth and death events are also the activity area of the four basic elements. The baby is within water in the mother's womb. Birth is man's passage from water to air. After the adventure of life, death is the passage from air to earth for the body and the passage from air to fire for the soul. Death means the separation of the elements. The distributive aspects of the elements take action due to the circumstances and if a sudden separation takes place in the elements, the result is death. The body and the soul separate from each other. While the body joins the material world, the soul passes to the spiritual dimension. The reentering of the soul in a new body and being reborn is the passage from fire to water. Thus, man's adventure of four elements continues infinitely.

In all cultures, fire, water, air and earth are tools of purification. The sign of fire's purification has been regarded as the emergence of new sprouts from the areas it destructs. Fire's sending a part of the objects it burns to the sky with smoke has been identified with the soul's ascension to the sky after death; some part of it remaining in earth, feeding the earth and accelerating the birth of new lives has been identified with the belief of rebirth and thus, fire came to be the most holy being. The constant attempt of fire's smokes to reach the heights of the heavens has led to its identification with the phallus and depiction as an active and masculine being. However, fire immediately extinguishes when it has contact with water. Water is procreative and feminine. Fire is very sensitive towards water with feminine gender and gets extinguished as soon as it unites with it. While air, which makes it possible for fire to burn, is considered masculine as well, the other aspect fire is regarded as feminine due to its procreative nature. Humans have resembled the need these aspects have for each other to the relationship of men-women. Those who burn are active and masculine and those who get burned are passive and feminine. Fire cannot exist without air. Earth gets scorched without water. However, the togetherness of the opposite aspects makes the continuity of life possible. It is necessary for the 4 aspects to act together to sustain life. As a result of fire firstly heating air, then water and finally earth, new life begins. Turks still celebrate this process as the falling of the Cemre (Fire) to air, water and earth. Each being which exists in the physical universe we live in, seem to have emerged as a result of the different mixes of the four basic elements. For instance, iron carries the characteristics of earth in terms of its rigidity, of air in terms of its conductivity and of fire in terms of its magnetism. Storm clouds are under the effect of fire with the lightening they contain; of water with rain and of air with sparseness. In short, similar definitions can be made for all beings.

The oldest common symbol known of the 4 basic elements is the tree of life. Trees are holy; in fact, fire, water, air and earth which are the four basic elements are all hidden within the context of the tree of life. Trees are bound to earth with their roots. It acquires the nutrition it needs through water by means of earth. It burns the carbon dioxide and obtains energy; then, it gives off oxygen. By means of Sun rays (fire) is does photosynthesis and continues its life. Fire is the expression of its spiritual energy, while water is the expression of its life energy, air is the expression of its time energy and earth is the expression of its bodily energy. This is not only true for a single tree, but all living beings.

In fact, all matter in the universe is alive and its smallest parts are the essence of life. In the physics universe, there is no soul without matter and no matter without soul. Matter continues its existence in the universe in seven states, or within seven layers. In the physical universe, the first sub-layer is made up of simple atoms. The second consists of the simple combinations of these atoms and the electromagnetic state of physical matter. The third layer is matter's light, or energy state. The fourth layer is matter's fire state. The fifth layer is what chemists name as the gas state, or Air in terms of Esoteric expression. The sixth layer of matter is its fluid form, or water. The seventh and final layer is solid matter, or earth.

All objects whose existence is observed in the universe have been continuing an order which has been infallible for billions of years through the orbits they follow, the force of gravity, their spinning around themselves, births, deaths and rebirths. The materialist notion that this order does not continue y means of a universal intelligence and that it has developed as a result of coincidences remains helpless in explaining the infallible and unchanging conditions of billions of years. Intelligence constantly puts itself forward through the same unchanging conditions both in the macro and the micro levels. Where are love, emotions and thoughts hidden in the creation process of the Soul? How have these powers placed in the program and codes of the universe? The answer to all these questions point out a being with consciousness. If there is a state of absence in question in the beginning, how has this absence turned into existence? Since the whole universe, which has continued its evolution through an infallible order and in accordance to certain purposes from the micro to macro cosmos for billions of years has not turned into chaos, it seems much plausible to approve the idea of order and existence instead of coincidence and absence.

ASTROLOGY

IS IT SCIENCE OR CHARLATANISM?

Esoteric states that everything in the universe is a whole and everything influences everything else in a non-stop manner. The Aspect experiments have verified this claim of esoteric. Hermes' words "That which is below is like that which is above and that which is above is like that which is below..." implies that the macro cosmos and the micro cosmos are in constant communication. In fact, all differentiations and changes in the macro cosmos (the universe) having great effects on the micro cosmos (atoms and electrons) is a reality which cannot be denied. Similarly, all events taking place in the micro cosmos are immediately reflected on the macro cosmos, because they are all a part of the whole.

The science of communication and interaction between the macro cosmos and micro cosmos is astrology. Astrology has appeared in the ancient civilizations before the flood and is the most studied branch of science. After the flood, the importance of this branch of science has not been forgotten and priests, augurs and astrologers in almost all cultures who could calculate how the events happening above would affect the ones below have been regarded as the most important people of these communities. The importance of astrology has been accepted without questioning until the 18th century. Until astrology left its place to astronomy, it has been regarded as one of the branches of science which scientists showed interest the most for centuries. Even Isaac Newton, who is considered to the father of science in the Western world, was accepted as one of the significant astrologers of his time. He has explained the existence of the law of gravity through analyzing the connections between past astrological events and phenomenon. Leading German astronomer Johannes Kepler has recorded the orbits followed by celestial bodies as a result of the observations throughout the years and has obtained "scientific" data.

In the West, the first country to officially give up astrology has been England. Astrology which has been used frequently until the time of Queen Elizabeth I's Reign has fallen from favor a short time after the queen' death in 1603. The most important reason for this was the increase of the influence of the Royal Society where only scientific data were generally acknowledged. All scientific circles in Europe, primarily the Royal Society, where the creationist theory of the Catholic church was not found scientific and gradually steered towards Deism, have slowly thrown astrology's areas of interest out from science, in line with their separatist point of view. In fact, this separation began with Kepler's discovery of the planets' laws of motion. What is interesting is that, Kepler's purpose was to analyze Astrology and base it on scientific grounds. Kepler, who was a professor of mathematics, has put forward three laws which explained how planets moved in 1596. These laws are still being used today in the calculation of direct orbits of satellites. Kepler is regarded as the father of science of modern astrology due to his studies. The science of astronomy has become totally independent of astrology by time and while astronomy came forward as a science, astrology has been abandoned in the area of interest of metaphysics.

Western science which is built on the hypothesis that everything in the universe is a separate structure free of other structures, suggests that there is no possibility for the motion of stars to influence the behavior of humans. One of the famous names in Western science, Stephen Hawking states that "The real reason why most scientists do not believe in astrology is not because there are no scientific proof, but because astrology is not consistent with the other theories tested with experiments." According to Deist scientists, if astrology claims that a person's personality is based on the position of the universe at his time of birth, then it needs to be scientifically proven in what ways the position of the stars at the time of a person's birth influence personality.

How does the state of the heavens at time of birth influence a person's character? Through this question, Western science asks a Newtonian question to a system, which can only be answered with quantum theory. The answers to be given to this question within the framework of Newtonian laws would not carry a meaning other than search for the answer to "What will happen to me?" and read horoscopes through a birth chart. The question as to how the state of the heavens at time of birth influences a person and the search to figure out individuals' characteristic tendencies from their birth dates, are the outpourings of the Newtonian mentality which attempts essentially to determine the fates of individuals. Although this notion seems accurate, this is not the case for the variable questions of Quantum processes. Quantum thinkers will ask "what are the effects of these parts of the whole on each other?" instead of other questions.

According to astrologers, the magnetic changes which come from the universe directly influence the life in the world. These are the expressions of a harmonious universal management, the Supreme Consciousness. Planets whose cosmic motions we can predict act in accordance with the predetermined codes of creation and the evolutionary process. The secret of these codes can only be perceived through the science of astrology. The astrological signs which also include the planets determine the level of electromagnetic forces which reach the world from their interaction. The celestial body with the densest electromagnetic influence on Earth is our Sun. The Sun constantly sends particles and electromagnetic currents to the space besides the rays and heat it emits. Electromagnetic areas accompany the flow of ionized gases which shoot off from the Sun. The name of this formation is solar wind. Solar wind is a mix of hot plasma and an ion charged with electricity, whose source is formed by the hale of the Sun. It hits the magnetosphere of the Earth and disrupts it. This effect exerts a direct power on all life forms. According to the latest researches of NASA, the most frequent times during which heart strokes are experienced overlap with the times during which Sun explosions take place. According to astrology, the Sun rules the sign Leo and sign Leo rules our heart.

While gigantic planetary bodies spread their great electromagnetic energies to space continuously, they influence our personal biosphere. Quantum physics has proven that an electron even in the remotest part of the universe can change everything in the universe. One can imagine how magnificent the effects of planets which are much larger than an electron on people are. Whether inside an atom, or in outer space, the motion of any energy will immediately create its own reaction and show its effects in every part of the universe concurrently. The world is never excluded from such an operation. We are constantly being bombarded by the magnetic forces which come from the space and our environment. Similarly, we also constantly spread our energy which affects the whole universe. It has been proven that the world's magnetosphere is extremely sensitive towards the cosmic waves which come from the outside. All these waves which pass from the world's magnetosphere penetrate into life-forms which have their own special electromagnetic power fields and constantly influence them.

Radio signals are a form of energy. In fact, these signals are light which has a very long wave length. Scientists in the USA have discovered in 1951 that there was a problem in receiving the radio waves. As a result of their analysis, they found out that the radio waves were affected by sunspots. On days during which the Sun forms angles of 0; 90 and 180 degrees, it has been discovered that static increases. Also, the Moon is known to directly influence the Earth with its force of gravity and forms the tides in the oceans. It has been determined that it also influences the activity of the secretory glands in the human body. Many studies proved that women's menstrual cycle is affected the motions of the Moon. The Moon completes its tour around the world in 28,5 days. Women's average menstruation time is also 28,5 days. According to astrology, each planet has a different effect on the world's magnetosphere. American physicist Dr. Jonas determined that the position of the Moon in a woman's birth chart determines the sex of the baby 97% of the time. As a result of his studies, he has observed that while the Moon is passing from the Zodiac's feminine and masculine signs, it affects the "X" or "Y" chromosomes magnetically in 2,5 day intervals. The feminine and masculine signs are of equal number in the Zodiac and it seems to be providing an explanation for the fact that human population is continuing its ratio of 50% women and 50% men. In astrology, the Moon rules the Cancer sign, which is the sign that rules motherhood and birth.

Findings of astrology are most of the time are accurate to the degree it should not be that accurate. If astrology had been telling wrong things since the ancient times, it would have been abandoned by people a long time ago like the other superstitions. However, despite the persistence of science in the adverse manner, astrology keep sits popularity. Researcher and writer Colin Wilson says "No one knows why astrology makes accurate predictions, but it does... There is nothing predicted through estimation. The positions of all the planets and their relationship with each other should be analyzed... The single thing we can see is personality... It is not the stars which influence human life, it is the position of the planets," in an article published in Daily Mail.

Astrology is so ridiculed in the world of science that, even the smallest research a respectable person would be conducting is met with the outrageous reactions of academicians. Film producer and photographer Gunter Sachs narrates what happened to him during a study he carried out on statistics in astrology in 1994: "I've been subject to a lot of insults and swearing. I had no idea with what kinds of things academicians would confront me. They were not concerned with accurate results". What he has gone through brought to the mind whether displaying a hostile attitude towards those who regard events from different points of view. I remembered the "scientific" attacks made by a zealot under the disguise of a scientist only because I named this book "The Scientific Proof of Esoteric: Quantum". He did not even know about the context of the book.

The number of waves which pass through a specific point within a specific amount of time is called "Frequency". All structures in the universe emit frequencies. We humans are also included. In the physical world, when our inner vibrations are in the same frequency with the vibrations of the eternal world, we may perceive those beings which give off vibrations in the external world. For instance, for our eyes to be able to see an object, it is necessary for that object's source of light to be located within a specific wave length range. Similarly, to be able to hear something, that sound needs to ne within a certain frequency range. The body's and soul's perception of the external world are the same. Just like our body, our soul perceives vibrations which are suitable to its own structure of frequency from the external world and gets to know that thing through its vibrations. The reason why we get along very well with some people and not so well with some others is whether our spiritual frequencies agree with each other or not. Our emotions also have certain frequencies and we attract similar events and situations towards ourselves depending on from which frequency we are doing our broadcast. This issue will be dealt in detail.

Our thoughts give off our frequency and our brain is the organ which produces our thoughts. How are thoughts formed in our brain? The science of nerve dynamics studied by Prof. Walter Freeman have shown that there are probable centers of attraction in the brain's nerve net. The phenomenon which seems to create and host our thoughts is the high level of neuron activities. These high neuron activities establish connections between them and form centers of attraction. In fact, the cerebral cortex, or the cortex as a whole serves as a center of attraction. In these centers, the emotions felt at this moment are shaped using past experiences and thoughts emerge as decisions. Consciousness itself is also nothing but a constantly expanding neuron process. According to Prof. Freeman, brain activity is simply neuron activities which go back and forth between a series of center of attraction.

The formation of the brain begins within the first month of conception. The fetus produced 1 million brain cells in every four minutes in the fifth week of its life. At the end of nine months spent in the mother's womb, it has been discovered that our brain contains the highest number of neurons we can have in our lives. However, the connection between them is very small. It takes two years for neurons to form connection. Neurons which are not used disappear by time. It is claimed that steady connections formed between the neurons, form the personality of the baby. Neurology suggests that personality depends on the past stimulations the brain receives in the development stage. What make the brain conscious are these connections between neurons. Conscious experience is related to a neuron activity which spreads to the neuron groups in different parts of the brain at the same time. It spreads everywhere. For conscious experience, numerous neuron groups interact. If there is n interaction, or if it is prevented, some parts of consciousness may be lost. What is more, birth does not end with the growth of the brain. The growth of the human brains continues until the age of four. When we are 4 years old, our brain reaches about 1400 cubic centimeters. This weight is four times the weight of the brain at birth. Scientists taking these data into consideration claim that consciousness does not develop at time of birth, but gradually in the next 2-4 years. What scientists overlook is that personality traits and consciousness exposing itself are different things.

Consciousness is not the single aspect which determines personality traits. Personality is the characteristic of the soul, while consciousness is the brain's. Personality is in a constant state of development in accordance with the experiences acquired throughout life. It is in constant contact with the universal consciousness and thus, the formations and changes are extremely influential on personality. Consciousness is a tool used for the development of our personality in this life.

The common view of Western science on personality is that, the sum of memories which we form is life-story, or our identity. Our memories are preserved in our brain as neuron connections. These connections are formed through a series of electrical signals which emerge during a process called long-term potential. This process generally begins as a result of stimulating signals which generally come from our senses. Children are born with numerous neurons with no connections. Consciousness is formed by passing through the bodily selection process. This process consists of the elimination of neurons which are not necessary at the stage where the body needs to show compliance to life. While there is a great number of neurons and a small number of connections in babies, in an adult individuals there is a small number of neutrons on the contrary and a great number of synapses which connect them. During the stage of development, all of the neurons in the brain try to form connections. While those who form connections remain alive, the ones who cannot do that disappear. During mankind's evolutionary process, finding ways of making neurons form denser connections might be a way of making individuals more developed beings.

Today's science still does not have sufficient information about the communication between neurons. As far as it can be observed from the outside, neurons give and take signals, using a partly chemical and partly electrical mix. The communication between then takes place in 1/1000 of a second. In other words, communication takes place a thousand times within one second between two neurons. Memories are defined as a series of electrical currents which are repeated in our brain. Memories are connected to the memory connections. For memories to be created, neurons have to be repeatedly fired and imprinted at that moment on the brain. The reactions felt against an event which takes place in the external world form a series of electrical currents and new physical connections are formed in the brain. These connections are also the beginning of the learning process. Each living being has the capacity to learn. The expanse of learning capacity and the ability to make deductions is regarded as proportionate with the volume of the brain. In comparison to its body weight, humans are the living beings whose brain is the heaviest. Except for this difference, there is no difference in terms of the structure of brain cells between the human brain and the brains of other living beings. There is no brain cell or brain protein unique to humans. In terms of cells or biochemistry, there is no difference between the neurons in the human brain and the brains of other vertebrates.

It deepens on external factors which neurons form connections and which ones disappear. It has been observed that, neurons perceive the electrical energies formed by emotions and their connections in accordance with this. Radio energy vibrations are also another external factor which influences neurons. Radio waves may cause neurons to fluctuate and form new synapses. A triggering radio vibration may make it possible to form new synapses and initiate the potential process. During the formation of personality, the planets which affect the free electrons, in the ionosphere with their strong force of attraction form waves and the natural vibrations of the waves directly affect the structure of the brain. When a neuron forms synapses, the length from the nucleus to the synapses remains the same until the end of its natural life. Statistics suggest that the vibrations being subject to at time of birth give way to a successful adulthood. If all of the statistical effects put forward by astrology effect the brains of babies at the moment of birth and allow neurons to form new synapses, only then they can be given a scientific explanation. It seems that the force of attraction of various stars accelerates the formation of the neuron web, electromagnetic waves create new synapses and thus, individuals with different personalities are created depending on the celestial body influencing them.

In order for cells in different places in the brain to influence each other, they need to be in communication with one another. This communication is electrical. There are billions of neutrons which are in interaction with each other in the human brain. Consciousness can develop as much as the brain develops. It has been seen that there is no limit to the change and development capacity of consciousness. The intensity of communication of cells among themselves also provides the permanence of the connections. What is essential is to form permanent connections and learn. There are about 100 billion neurons in a child's brain. It is predicted that each neuron has 15 thousand connections. Therefore, the number of connections is 40 over 1X10. In other words, the capacity of learning is limitless. It does not seem possible that such a structure came into existence out of chance.

It has been seen through the electroshock method used in some heavy psychological cases that neurons' being affected electrically causes diverseness in personality. The experiments conducted have shown that giving electricity to the brain completely changes the personality. An electrical current which affect the neurons in the brain seems to be changing the personalities of people. It has also been observed that personality is connected to recollections, or to memory. A person's losing his memory for any reason causes his characteristics to change as well. The connections between neurons being damaged causes this. The connections between neurons gradually decrease, in particular with old age. In order to prevent this situation, which causes dementia, it is very important to constantly do practice. To continue the harmony between neurons, brain activities to be performed daily will prevent deterioration. The efficient use of the brain will provide remembering, as well as increasing the capacity of learning. The brain is a community which consists of neurons which constantly trigger each other. As the connection web increases, the higher level of consciousness will increases as well the capacity of memory and self-consciousness. During the process of the macro cosmos (Universe) influencing the micro cosmos (Man), it is natural that the Sun due to its closeness and size is the celestial body which most influences neurons.

Both radio waves and light rays travel through a straight line. They both cannot be bent. The ultraviolet radiation of the Sun empties the external electrons of air molecules. The emptied air molecules turn into ions and the broken electrons turn into free particles. Electrons which are set free collide with each other more in thick air layers which are closer to the surface of the earth to be able to reunite with ions. The number of free electrons in the thin layers of the upper layers of the atmosphere is higher. It has been seen that the speed of emptying the electrons increases in sunrises and decreases in noon. The Sun's dense ultraviolet rays snatch the external electrons of air molecules in the upper layers of the atmosphere. What keeps positively charged ions and negatively charged electrons is the high energy photons which constantly come from the Sun. Depending on the heat and the power of photons, different ion layers are form in different heights in the ionosphere. The one known as D layer is only formed during the day. The D layer is formed in the lower layers of the atmosphere, which are 50 to 100 kilometers high and the fastest absorption of the free electrons by ions takes place in this layer. While the D layer is thicker in the equatorial areas of the world, it gets thinner towards the poles. The density of free electrons clouds reaches their peak point on the Ecuador at sunrise. It has been observed that the free electron clouds make great leaps during the process of rising of a planet with a strong force of attraction. Planets with strong forces of attraction cause electromagnetic fields, the free electrons in the ionosphere culminate, the communication between electrons and tachyons increases and individuals with a much higher level of consciousness are allowed to be born during this process. The denser the number of free electrons, the more of a chance of birth of individuals focused on success.

During sunrise, there three different centers of attraction which affect the free electrons in the sky. These are the attractions of the Earth, the Sun and the planet rising from the horizon with a strong force of attraction. These electrons move very fast in the ionosphere where there is a no friction effect that can slow them down. The direction they travel depends on the force of attraction of these three different forces. If the effective forces push the electrons to go to different directions, electrons vibrate and mix with one another. This electrical vibration creates the static sound named "cosmic static". The cosmic static heard when the planets with strong forces of attraction are born before the Sun and the sound heard when these planets form a right angle to the Sun are different. If there were no interaction, static would not be heard either. Shortly, planets with strong forces of attraction being born before the Sun or rising to the peak forming a right angle form radio signals with different wave lengths.

It can be seen that there is parallelism between the density of free electrons and success birth rates. The births of individuals who have a tendency to be successful are directly proportional to the sudden increase in the density of free electrons and in sunrises where the speed of discharge of electrons. During sunrises, an intense electrical activity takes place in the ionosphere. Electrons which separate from ions are in fact photons and directly communicate with tachyons. The universal information received as a result of this contact with tachyons is very influential in the newborn child's formation of personality. Stars which have a rising strong force of attraction prior to sunrise affects the ionosphere with their own energy and allow more electrons to be set free. As a result of the interaction of free electrons with tachyons, the knowledge of the past and the duties of the future are transmitted to the new born child and the building blocks of personality are formed. Of course, the new experienced gained through consciousness provide the suitable environment for the evolvement of personality. Since the communication between electrons and tachyons continue infinitely, each change which takes place in the macro cosmos constantly affects the micro cosmos. The differences which take place in the physical universe affecting the physical body of humans are generally known as astrology.

When the free electron distribution in the ionosphere is analyzed, two phenomenon grab the attention. The first of these is the decrease in the number of free electrons as they get away from the Ecuador. There are three ionized molecule layers in the upper layers of the atmosphere. The lowest of these three layers is the D layers. The D layer in its densest state is located between the 30th latitude on each side of the Ecuador. The D layer has the capability to imprison radio signals which belong to the ionosphere in this tropical area and prevent radio energy from touching the surface. In other words, the D layer functions as a security wall in preventing the cosmic static to reach the human brain. Between the 30th and 60th latitudes, the density of the D layer is less. The area where the ionized signals, which are formed when a planet with a strong force of attraction rises before the Sun, reach the surface of the world the most is the area between these 30th and 60th latitudes. The number of free electrons in this area is still very high. On the other hand, since the density of the D layer is sparse enough, the signals created by these electrons easily ascend to the surface of the world. Therefore, the area between the 30th and 60th Degrees is the latitude range where the signals affect the human brain in the densest manner. It is not a coincidence that a majority of the civilizations throughout the history of mankind have emerged here. There is a strong connection between a society's motivation for success and the latitude it lives in.

The area where the D layer is densest and the radio signal activity is reflected on the world the least is the area between Ecuador and the two tropics. This shield of protection gets thinner below the Tropic of Capricorn and above the Tropic of Cancer. There are very few countries below the Tropic of Capricorn. These are Argentina and Chile in South America, Republic of South Africa in Africa and Australia and New Zealand. The rate of development in these countries is much higher than their neighbors. A majority of countries which remain above the Tropic of Cancer constitute the most developed societies of the world. This is not related to ideology, beliefs or the climate. The great civilizations of the past are all the products of these areas. Many countries, whose ideologies, religious beliefs or life-styles are different, have been able to develop their civilizations independent of these differences in the past and the present time. With a few exceptions, the fact that the most successful people of the past and the present time coming from these lands show that there is a relationship with the thinness of the D layer.

The ability of tool making of the human species has appeared about 200 thousand years ago. After this date, humankind seems to have gone through extraordinary evolution. This must have a reason. Archeologists have revealed the diamond shapes drawn with red ochre in the Blombos Cave located in the southern point of South Africa. The estimated date of these drawings which are assumed to be one of the first cave drawings is 70 thousand years. Archeologists claim that, the departure of humanity whose roots are the African lands from this continent is around the same date. Similarly, the founding date of the Mu civilization coincides with 70 thousand years ago. However, there is no definite data about this. It is a debated issue when these people, who were determined to have the brain weight of the present time 200 thousand years ago, left Africa for the first time. Still, while humanity has shown no evidence of mental or artistic activity during its life in Africa seems to have a greater capability of creativity the moment it ascends below the Tropic of Capricorn, even if it is still the lands of Africa. The reason could be that a human population had left the thick environment of the D layer for the first time. Humans had left the below area of the D layer for the first time and their children's brains had been subject to the radio vibrations of the ionosphere for the first time in their brain development process. The result is the oldest known drawings of the history of mankind.

The archeological findings show that humans first started speaking among themselves 80 thousand years ago, used sharp tools almost during that time and their first orderly settlement centers were founded 65 thousand years ago. The emergence of trade for the first is predicted to be about 60 thousand years ago. Shortly, as soon as humanity got rid of the D layer, it made great leaps in the name of being civilized. The first proofs of human creativity have always been found in societies which lived outside the protection of the D layer.

The electromagnetic environment of the world which remains outside the tropic areas seems to be allowing the emergence of a process of selection which displays a tendency towards brains that can develop language, writing and civilization. The moment Homo Sapiens gets far enough away from Ecuador, it has been observed that Darwinist selections enters the picture and the cultures begin to compete with each other in imitating each other through the genetic transmission of neuron expansion patterns. Our species has been able to strengthen its creative brain structure only at that stage and began to form successful societies. New centers of attraction were formed in the brain of humankind who left the protective shield of the D layer and these centers increased thinking and learning processes. A brain full of ready centers of attraction is brain which is more open to new ideas and thus, more creative and more successful.

The forerunners of our species left the D layer. The energy vibrations of the free electrons rained on them. More folds began to be formed on the relatively flat surface of their brains and their brains were equipped with depths and personality structures with different tendencies. Under these conditions, not only it was possible for innovation and progress to take place but became inevitable as well. The "rationalist mind" which the mind used when reasoning and problem solving opened the way for humanity. In short, due to the human brain getting gradually more complex, the personality traits found more beneficial were able to be imitated and humanity's inevitable quantum leap thus took place.

The average monthly income of a person living in Europe and North America is at least ten times higher than then the income of a person living in Asia and Africa. While 7% of the world population living in North America constitutes 43% of world wealth, only 55% of the population living in Asia constitutes 16% of it. This cannot only be explained through the belief system or natural climatic conditions. Societies which are completely Western are societies who have completed their industrial revolution and live technological developments in the upper most level, but why have they been able to succeed in this and not the others?

The share of national income per capita in countries between the 30th and the 60th latitudes are much higher than the average incomes of people who live outside these latitudes. In the beginning of the 2nd millennium, the monthly average incomes of people who lived between the Ecuador and the 30 degrees latitude was around 1500 US dollars, this number was an average of 9250 US dollars for those who lived between the 30th and 60th latitudes. Shortly, there is a direct relationship between economic development and the location of the country one lives in. The differences in success rates can be claimed to be due to climatic conditions. Or the highness of population could be stated to be the reason. However, the studies conducted have shown that the relationship between the latitude and income is an average of 60% and the relationship between latitude and the number of people is only 2%. Therefore, it is not right to form a relationship between population and rate of success. On the other hand, the economies of countries which have a mild climate in general are observed to be much more advanced in comparison to the economies of tropical countries. Countries which have managed to have strong economies such as Singapore and Hong Kong, which are located at the border of the tropical climate zone, with completely sub-tropical climates goes in opposition to the thesis that there is a connection between climate and success.

People being subject to the radio signals coming from the ionosphere in the highest level seem to be increasing their level of success. In particular the free electron bombardment babies are subject to at time of birth causes them to be very successful people in the future. The more distant a baby grows up from Ecuador, the more his chances of being successful are. The studies carried out on the atmosphere have shown that, the density of the D layer on Singapore and Hong Kong, which is right above the Tropic of Cancer is much thinner compared to the tropical zone in general and that they almost reach the decrease of density between the 30-60 latitude zone during months of winter. Similarly, radar maps show that although they are in the tropical zone, there is relatively less density in the D layer on some countries. These countries are countries like Ethiopia, which have been successful in creating more advanced civilizations compared to their neighbors. In short, countries where individuals who are subject more to the effect of the planet which rises prior to the Sun display a relatively much faster course of development in comparison to others. Throughout billions of years during which humanity continued its existence in African lands, it has not displayed any kind of development, but the moment it left behind the Tropics of Capricorn and Cancer following great migrations, it has entered a period of an extraordinary development.

The vibrations of stars and planets which change momentarily have the potential to create various effects on the brains and manner of feeling of all people not only for the moment of birth, but within an infinite process. These momentarily changing vibrations constantly change the feeling and perception potential of the brain. In case a planet which affects personality at time of birth creating these vibrations again later on, it interacts again with the connection which has been created in a suitable length for this vibration, activity in that part of the brain increases and emotional reactions are seen. When the same planet rises again next to the Sun, the initial vibration patterns which trigger the brain connections cause these connections to be re-fired. The duration of effect of the celestial bodies seem to be dependent on their durations of existence on the Zodiac at time of birth, or their speed. While the connection of a majority of faraway stars and signs are relatively fast on the brain of a child, if larger planets which relatively move slower such as Jupiter and Saturn are in question, the effects of the synapses change continue for a few months during which the first connections of the child's brain are formed. Other planets which have strong forces of attraction and move faster repeat their wave patterns intermittently but more frequently in the child's critical growth stage and the neuron connections are more complex due to this. What is in question is the physical effect which changes the brain's structure, thus personality during the development stage of the brain.

Science says that a child's personality develops through the changes in the brain structure and that the brain structure changes and develops as it learns new thoughts. Memory, which is acquired later on, is the physical characteristic of the brain and develops through neurons which are fired altogether and form connections. Science remains silent in terms of the influence of the rising stars on the formation of personality traits of children at time of birth. Meanwhile, astrology claims that personality traits change in accordance with the position of the stars at the moment of cutting the umbilical cord.

Ph.D. Michel Gauquelin who is a leading scientist in the analysis of astrological data statistically has analyzed the relationship between success and birth maps. Gauquelin has discovered that during the hours famous people, who have achieved success in different occupations, were born at some planets were in similar positions. The positions of planets at time of birth are seen to be in an inexplicable relationship with the personalities of important people. During some of the birth hours of a significant number of famous people, it has been observed that Mars or Saturn was rising or was in its peak position. Successful people seem to be generally born while a bright star is rising. The statistical researches Gauquelin carried out in middle of 20th century have shown that the children of people who are born when a bright star is rising have their children mostly when a bright star is rising as well. The only seemingly repetitive aspect of this finding is that, a majority of successful people have been born rather when the Moon, Venus, Mars, Jupiter or Saturn were rising or were at their peak points. Gauquelin's research has shown that, the personality traits of children who are born when the Moon, Venus, Mars, Jupiter or Saturn are rising or are in their peak points carry characteristics which help them be successful throughout their lives.

English writers and researchers Christopher Knight and Robert Lomas have discovered that the star named Shekinah which has been seen during many successful events in history is actually a union of the rays of the stars Venus-Mercury and this Venus-Mercury overlap takes place every 480 years. Knight and Lomas have shown in their study on Shekinah that, a belief system that "successful" people are born under the rays of the bright morning star in the east, before the Sun rises, has been existent for thousands of years. It has also been discovered that the dates on which Shekinah rose overlapped with the peak points of civilizations. The Shekinah belief shows that the realities which were revealed by Gauquelin have been known for thousands of years.

Another researcher and writer David C. McClelland has analyzed the behavior patterns of successful individuals in his work titled *The Achieving Society*. As a result of his study, he has shown that people with high levels of success prefer to take rational risks and have a standpoint which allows them to use their skills in the best possible say while doing this. He has put forward that these kinds of people prefer goals whose success possibility is of medium difficulty or potentially achievable goals. These people who in general know how to motivate themselves in terms of success are never gamblers. Rather than leaving the area they choose to chance, they find it more rational to solve problems with their own abilities. They take medium scale risks and by doing this, they create the greatest effect. This study also showed that this type of people do not care much for money. Earning money is merely a symbol of success. What is important is to be successful. Income is the testing of skills and one of its expressions. These people have been determined to invest their income always to new rational and medium scale risk businesses and as a result, gain greater profits.

MIT Cognitive Neurology President Prof. Steven Pinker says that the cosmic rays are effective during the development process of the brain. Pinker states that even brains of identical twins may develop differently due to momentary cosmic changes and that a single DNA strand which will change its course because of the change can cause this. Through this point of view, we may say that the unstable radio vibrations triggered by planets with strong forces of attraction can reshape the brain neurons. Cosmic effects are an important factor in the shaping process of the brain and this can explain the difference between identical twins. Electromagnetic waves change the synapses formation process and neurons interact with the signals coming from the heavens and form new synapses. These synapses formed at time of birth also have a direct relationship with personality. Statistical data shows that, electromagnetic waves easily changing the synapses connections in the brain during the ion storm caused by the rising planet and the rate of successful people's births are parallel to each other.

If radio waves transform matter to visible patterns and if each magnetic wave have effects in human life with specific consequences, then the vibrations, harmonies and resonances which are constantly emanating through the sounds created by all the suns and planets in the universe have serious effects on life in the universal level. Through the effects of these sounds, it is apparent that the necessary planning has been done for life to come to being on all planets similar to Earth. Perhaps, for life to begin in the first oceans of our world and for the universe to continue within a specific plan, we may talk about a creative effect of the universal symphony on biochemical matter. If we take into consideration that our solar system is a great structure made up of numerous organisms which interact in many planes, each solar system, each galaxy and the universe itself is a living organism. As a consequence, it would not be wrong to call God the "Grand Composer of the Universe".

Another point of interaction between the objects in our solar system is the differences these create in gravity. Gravity is also effective on the activities of free electrons like radio waves and magnetic effects. Another proof that gravity has significant effects on free electrons and free electrons have significant effects on the brain's neurons is the changes created on the brain by the full moon. A research carried out in the USA has shown that there is a serious connection between the full moon and emergency services workload. Connection between neurons takes place through the senses. Connections being formed between the suitable areas of the brain emerge with the neurons which are fired together for the first time. By means of synapses neurons form among them, the parts of the brain create a structure which resembles a simple radio device. Parallelisms have been observed between the stages of the Moon or the different forces of attraction it forms and the firing process of the brain's neutrons. The interaction between the moon's area of attraction and neurons causes neurons to be fired. The reason is that, the resonance of the neurons and the radio waves created by the rising of the Moon have the same length.

Four critical areas have been discovered where the attraction areas of the Moon and the Sun overlap. These critical areas appear when the Moon rises with the Sun, the Moon rises directly opposite of the Sun and the Moon rises with a right angle in front of or behind the Sub. Each of these four positions creates four different patterns which are made up of changing positive and negative vibrations. The New Moon and Full moon phases are phases during which the strongest vibrations are given off; because the areas of attraction either move together or in total opposition to each other. Spring tides take place in the new moon phase. The direction of the Moon's force of attraction is the same with the Sun's. As a result, water moves more toward inland and pulls back a greater distance. However, the tides in the Ion fluctuation do not resemble the tides of the sea. The reason is the force of friction. Water molecules form tighter connections and are much heavier in comparison to ion molecules which form the ionosphere. The number of free electrons between water molecules is very limited. The mass of a free electron is smaller than one millionth of a water molecule and the force of attraction between them is accordingly denser. The probability of ion molecules producing free electrons is much higher. There is a reverse connection between the existence state of objects and ther ate of disseminating free electrons. While solid objects disseminate the least number of electrons, the dissemination of free electrons in matter's loosest form plasma (energy) state is the densest. Since ion is a derivative of air, which is the second loose form of matter after energy, the amount of free electrons are accordingly higher. Free electrons do not stay together. The negative charge they have causes them to push one another.

Free electrons form a very loose cloud from in the ionosphere. In new moon phases and full moon phases where they push each other during which the force of attraction of the Sun and the Moon unite, these electron clouds sway back and forth and create a sort of tide. On the other hand, it has been discovered that a positively charged electrical signal does not have any effect on the brain's neurons. Whereas, all kinds of effects with a negative charge causes new synapses to be formed or the firing of the ones which exist. This back and forth dance of electrons with negative charges creates radio vibrations and these vibrations trigger the synapses connections. Since the attraction forces of the Moon and the Sun neutralize each other in the new moon phase, the positively charged signals are denser and that is why they have no effect on neurons. In the full moon phase, the attraction forces are opposites and thus, the negatively charged signals become denser. Therefore, during full moon where the directions of the forces of attraction of the Moon and the Sun are opposites, denser brain activities appear.

What needs to be paid attention is that, this reality is only valid or the northern hemisphere. While negatively charged signals appear in the northern hemisphere during full moon, this is the time where the positively charged signals are denser in the southern hemisphere. In other words, the force of attraction which influences brain neutrons in the southern hemisphere is not the full moon phase, but the new moon phase. The reason for this adverse interaction is the world's magnetic field. While the magnetic flow direction is clock wise in the northern hemisphere, it is the opposite in the southern hemisphere. There is a direct relationship between the direction of the flow and the load of the signal. Therefore, while brain activities increase in the North during full moon phase, the opposite happens in the southern hemisphere. During full moon in the North, the work load of the emergency services and the cases of animal bite increase. It has been observed that cases of animal bites in the North are much higher during the full moon phase in comparison to the other phases of the moon. In the South, the calmest periods are experienced. The time during which the South makes a peak is the new moon phase.

Lunar in Latin means the Moon. The word "Lunatic" which means "crazy" in English and the word Lunar coming from the same root is a result of the differentiation of the brain activities of all living beings in the North in the full moon phase of the Moon. The majority of the human population living in the northern hemisphere has led to the birth of many legends about the full moon phase. While the time during which all kinds of madness are experienced in the North is the full moon, it is the new moon phase in the South. According to the gravity fluctuation theory, the period in which the negatively charged static radio signals formation is densest in great mounts in the full moon phase in the North; it is the new moon phase in the South. As it has been explained above, since what triggers neuron activity is negatively charged activities, the situation manifests in different ways in two different hemispheres.

THE SUPREME CONSCIOUSNESS-AKASHA

The universal intelligence is a universal data bank which consists of the emotions, thoughts, experiences and knowledge accumulation of all beings which have existed from the first moment of the universe until the present time. This structure, which embodies the knowledge and experiences of all living beings from the smallest to the biggest, can be called Universal Intelligence or Divine Intelligence. Quantum science has proven that, electrons in all points of the universe have the capacity to share the knowledge and experiences of an electron at any other point. Therefore, the fact that the storing of knowledge at a universal level is continuing has been proven with today's science as well. Hermes has given the name Emerald Tablet to this universal intelligence. The name of the same data bank in the Qur'an is Levh-i Mahfuz. Tibetan priests calls these record "Akasha". The name of the acacia tree which is the symbol of immortality comes from the word Akasha as well. Just like all other beings, each person is in contact with this Akashic library. Although these records operate as the recording of the experiences of all living beings including humans, these records are also used in special circumstances to inform humanity by the authorized people. Both revelation and inspiration have their source in the Akashic records. No work that exists in the world can be created without using the Akashic records. Behind a painter's painting, a musician's composition, a writer's book or a scientist's invention, there is always this universal intelligence.

Another definition of the universal intelligence is "Supreme Consciousness". Communication with the Supreme Consciousness generally takes place involuntarily. People who are able to establish this communication voluntarily are those who have reached an advanced stage in terms of spiritual evolvement. An individual who has made serious progress in terms of reaching Perfection, does not only establish communication with Supreme Consciousness, but can form a whole even when he is living with it. The rank of Aynel Yalin in Islam spiritualism is the expression of this unity. However, a majority of people do not have sufficient knowledge to realize this guidance. Therefore, these kinds of perceptions are usually called "Inspiration" and are evaded.

The common ground in which individuals meet with the whole humanity and the universe is the universal consciousness. All layers of consciousness swim within the universal consciousness ocean. The subconscious is like a living archive which embodies man's experiences as a whole. Previous lives are also included in these experiences. If we guide it properly, the subconscious allows the knowledge we want to reach us through the Supreme Consciousness. We can consult it for anything we want to know. The sub consciousness immediately directs the information we want to us. It is the bridge between consciousness and the Supreme Consciousness. The information our consciousness needs are firstly transmitted to the sub-consciousness and then are directed to the Supreme Consciousness. Even if you do not consciously follow it, the information you need inherently appears before you on time. However, extending your arm and taking it requires a skill and accumulation of knowledge. In psychology, this skill in attaining this information which appears before us and meets our need is called "serendipity". The sub-consciousness shapes our wishes visually and turns the meanings attributed to thoughts and words into visual materials. A person who perceives what this visual material is has reached the reality to some extent.

The goal of all living beings in the universe to continue their lives in an orderly manner is called "Instinctus" in Latin. This word has come to the present time as intuition. In living beings, the intuition ability is innate. As a result of the perceptions coming from the sensory organs and the operation of the hormonal system, intuitions begin to be active. The intuition of all living beings has common goals such as protection and sustaining generations. Darwin claimed that intuitions are gradually created as a result of hereditary habits. However, intuition is a mechanical event. IT is a reflex. Only meeting the need makes intuition stop. It cannot be satisfied in any other manner. Plants also continue their lives relying on intuition.

Each person is an extension of the holistic area of energy. Man constantly exchanges energy with its environment just like other beings. It is the bond of energy between the bodies which allows interaction of the bodies. For those who have materialistic beliefs, the body of energy is interpreted merely as a product of imagination. However, the body of energy is in continuous interaction with the holistic energy field as well and not only with the other bodies of energy around it. According to quantum theory, the whole is greater than the sum of the parts. Even if the parts which constitute the whole break up, they continue to interact with the whole. The pieces cannot exist completely free of the whole. As there is interaction between all the pieces, it is inevitable that there is interaction among the pieces as well.

When knowledge is coded by God and squeezed in to laws of nature designed in a suitable manner, it is possible for us to grasp our reality within the framework of this knowledge coded into these laws. On the other hand, the laws have to be an integral part of this big Picture which constantly evolves. If not, the universe would remain imprisoned in an infinite cycle. Therefore, the universe is a Supreme Consciousness, a data processor which has limitless opportunities, in other words, an extraordinary quantum computer. The universe is constantly expanding. Within the framework of the laws of thermos-dynamics, the reason for this expansion is the constant increase of information accumulation. As information flow increases, it means that the universe's expansion speed will increase as well. Where does this information flow come to the universe, so that the universe has to expand in such a Grand manner? Galilee Galileo answered this question as follows: "Philosophy is written in this gigantic book (the universe) and it is always right before our eyes. However, it firstly cannot be understood without understanding the language used in this writing. This book has been written the language of mathematics. The typeface consists of triangles, circles, squares and other geometrical figures. Without these, man cannot a word in this book and dwells in darkness". As it can be understand from these words, the realities of the universe have been coded in mathematics and this coding process still continues in each speck. It is now known that the information in biological systems comes from the building blocks of DNA, the molecules. Molecular behavior gains functionality through the laws of quantum physics and when considered in this direction, the quantum laws function in the same manner for all beings and not only for living beings. Quantic knowledge is spread to the whole universe and is innate. This knowledge is Divine knowledge.

Einstein who stated "Behind all the discernible concatenations, there remains something subtle, intangible and inexplicable. Veneration for this force is my religion. To that extent, I am in point of fact, religious.

If the structure of our universe has been arranged within the framework of quantum laws and if these are laws of reality which rule everything and even our actions are guided by them, how much of a free will can we talk about? The answer is to be found in the capacity of our free will in controlling our actions. Esoteric suggests that our free will firstly has a predetermination period. It is our free will which determines the conditions of a life, which will provide the development the soul needs before rebirth. Within the life we live, it is our free will which also provides our methods of carrying out predetermined duties and the environments which makes them possible. In fact, what makes the evolvement of the Supreme Consciousness and carries this new information acquired from different experiences to the Universal Intelligence is our free will. If everything developed within the scope of predetermined laws or fate, then it would not be possible to talk about evolvement in such an environment.

It can be seen that the universe is a field of energy and that every existing thing forms different levels of density within this field. Each human body is a package of energy, which is made up of different densities. Other than the five senses, we have a point of perception which is sensitive against the energy waves that influence us. This point is called the "point of junction". When man's body of energy enters resonance with the energy waves which reach the point of junction from outside of the body, it is possible for a person to take whatever information he wants from this subconscious source of energy. However, each person does not have the structure to succeed in this transmission. Although this ability is present in each person, it needs to be worked on and developed. If not, the information coming from the universe remains only in the subconscious and cannot reach consciousness. In order to strengthen the point of junction, we firstly need to push the rational mind a bit to the background and loosen up the ties with the world. An individual who activates his intuition becomes successful to the degree he uses this skill under the leadership of the mind. The activation of intuition can only be possible if the consciousness layer leaves the control of the brain on its own free will to the sub-consciousness.

Consciousness shows itself in three different levels. The first of these is the sub-conscious. This kind of consciousness is seen in all beings. Intuition is the result of this type of consciousness. Sub-consciousness plays many roles in our lives. Intuition keeps our body health in balance and preserves and sustains the healthy state. That is why our body has the capability of healing itself naturally. The basis of alternative medicine is to activate these natural skills of our intuition. In addition, it is our intuition which protects our body from dangers in every emergency situation, as they move reactional. Sub-conscious also functions as man's memory bank. The results of all experiences acquired throughout life are stored in the sub-conscious. All kinds of experiences which our sub-conscious decides to keep are kept there. The sum of these experiences forms various belief mechanisms and all sorts of conditions and things in line with these beliefs are drawn to the person. Our sub-conscious is in constant contact with the Supreme Consciousness through our sub-conscious. The point of contact with our Supreme Consciousness is our intuition. The moment our consciousness transmits our desires to the sub-conscious, it transmits these to the Supreme Consciousness. The Supreme Consciousness then takes action to realize the desired or believed thing. Everyone's consciousness is connected ultimately to the Supreme Consciousness. We are all connected to each other at the level of the Supreme Consciousness. In other words, our Supreme Consciousness is common and one. All formations and information is sent to us from there.

Our consciousness is the part of our body which produces thoughts. People use the power of consciousness in all their problem solving and target reaching notions. However, the power of our consciousness is limited with our mind in comparison to the other two types of consciousness. The most important power consciousness has is the power of making decisions. Consciousness decides about all kinds of information to go to our sub-consciousness. However, most people are not able to use this power. Instead of consciously using this power, most people sometimes let unnecessary and sometimes harmful and negative information to enter the sub-conscious. This unnecessary information which fill the sub-conscious like a garbage bin influence people's lives in the same manner and causes them to experience negative things. Whereas, our consciousness has the power to re-program the sub-conscious. It changes old, useless and even harmful beliefs and has the capacity to interfere with the events a person might experience in life. The method to do this, to erase the wished beliefs, is to constantly repeat the notions which are to replace them and thus, establish them. Through repetition, the beliefs programmed in your sub-conscious become automatic and it becomes possible to erase and get rid of events which cause problematic results.

Another method of programming the sub-conscious is hypnosis. Firstly, the mind is relaxed and Alpha waves are spread. During this process, it is possible to reach the sub-conscious. Once a person reaches his sub-conscious, he finds himself in an endless pool made up of memories, experiences and information. When a person is conscious, it is not possible for him to hear or see the atoms which spin and vibrate inside him. However, including the atoms in the human body, it has been scientifically proven that all atoms vibrate and have a resonance of their own. There is a spiral energy and world of light in our bodies. Our minds are in constant contact with this micro world which is outside our normal perception. This awareness can only be increased by reaching the sub-conscious. A hypnotist guides cognitive attention from the left brain to the right and from consciousness to the sub-conscious; in this manner, he can reach those parts recorded in the sub-conscious which the person who puts under hypnosis does not reveal in his normal conscious state. Hypnosis is the method of overcoming the limitations and borders of our conscious mind. After hypnosis, it is possible for the person to reach a new and stronger level of consciousness. Hypnosis a person applies on himself also provides great benefits in terms of change and development. In many countries around the world, there are self-hypnosis courses today.

The brain's Alpha waves are in physiological contact with the eyes. Closing the eyes allows the production of alpha waves needed in the brain for the state of trance. In addition, turning our eyes above, to the middle of our forehead where the brain epiphysis is, or to our

Third Eyes will accelerate the formation of Alpha waves. The brain epiphysis located right in the middle of our forehead is referred to as the "Third Eye" in Eastern Esoteric. The third eye has been accepted as a center of contacting the Supreme Consciousness. In trance, focusing on the Third Eye causes the Alpha waves to increase. Therefore, during trance or meditation, you need to close your brain completely to the material world and increase the Alpha waves by touching the middle of your forehead.

American Ph.D. Daniel Kirsh who has been working on electro medicine since 1972 has developed a technology he calls "Alpha Sim". Kirsch sends the neurons in the brain signals of different dimensions in accordance with the illness, fine tunes the brain waves and allows them to operate within their own range. Through this method, symptoms such as insomnia, depression, stress and pain can be overcome. Another American doctor who studied people's brain waves during the treatment period, Ph.D. Beck has discovered that the brain waves of healers during a treatment are between 7.8 and 8.00 hertz. These waves are known as the Schumann Waves. Beck observed that during the séance, both the healer's brain and the patient's brain synchronized on the Schumann Wave length. Beck is sure that the healers take energy from the world's magnetic field. Those who practice Reiki also state that the healing energy is taken from the universe and given to the patient.

People who go under trance through any method say that they lose their concept of time. They experience an infinite, timeless but a dynamic present, instead of the linear sequence of the moments. In fact, quantum science has also shown that the time expressed as the 4th dimension does not exist, everything always takes place in an infinite "present time" and the past and the future are different perception types of the present time. Deep sleep state is the time during which the brain function the slowest. The brain in this state can only emit Delta waves maximum up to 4 hertz. The second process is the dream state. The Teta wave length the brain emits is between 4 to 7 hertz. The third type of wave is the Alpha rhythm. These are seen in extreme relaxation, meditation and hypnosis and are between 8 to 13 hertz. The time during which the brain functions the most is the time of wakefulness. During this state, which can also be called state of complete consciousness, the brain emits Beta waves and these range from 13 to 30 hertz.

It has been determined that, the nerve cells which are activated when the brain is awake produce more oxygen compared to those which are not active. Constant activity of oxygen consumption at an area in the brain is an indication of the formation of new nerve connections in that area. The stimulations which are constantly repeated in a special area form these new nerve net paths. When you being a new work in almost all areas, the process which is quite difficult and slow in the beginning gradually becomes easier, even routine when the new nerve nets produced by the brain come into the Picture in accordance with the need. When certain duties are repeated again and again, these nerve nets gradually become a part of the permanent nerve net and become permanent themselves. No matter how much time passes, this is the reason why learned skills and information are not completely lost. For instance, once you learn how to ride a bicycle, you do not have to learn it all over again.

The brain is a finite matter. It cannot have a life or consciousness without energy. The moment the brain is deprived of energy, its functions immediately stop. The human consciousness has been limited for a purpose. The reason is to keep the body where the brain is located in a functioning state. However, the learning capacity of the brain is limitless. The best example that our brain capacity has no boundaries is Daniel Tammet's skills of calculation, which is referred to as the "Autistic Scholar". Tammet can list the decimal units of the number Pi until the 22.514th digit in the presence of a notary. It has taken 5 hours to complete this experiment which is also a world record and the Autistic Scholar listed all the digits from memory and without any mistakes. Even this single experiment shows that the individual consciousness is in constant communication with the universal consciousness and that it is even a part of it.

Although Western medicine believes that thoughts are only created by the human brain or preserved y the human brain, many findings gradually show that this is not so and that the whole universe acts within a framework of a specific consciousness. Thought is not a concept peculiar to humans. It is the foundation of the universe and perhaps as mathematician David Chamler says, it is the same with matter and energy. Plants may not have brains, but it has proven many times that they do have a consciousness. All beings in the universe which have electromagnetic energy are consciousness in a way. Since every physical from in the universe has an electromagnetic power field, it may easily be expressed that consciousness is a notion spread to the whole universe. Besides humans, animals, plants and even all material which we define as inanimate constantly emit positive or negative energy to their environment in accordance with their state of existence. They all have their own electromagnetic fields and are in constant communication with one another in the sub-atomic level.

Consciousness is not only a brain activity. The fact that consciousness does not need an organ organized in the upper most level to reveal it can be seen from the reactions plants give. Each plant knows the beneficial or harmful environments for itself even if it does not have a brain. The ability of judgment and consciousness can be in question even in a single molecule. This ability seems to be coming from the data bank of each living building block. In other words, consciousness is the common result of the building blocks spread to the whole universe and is in constant and direct contact with the Supreme consciousness. There is no need for a special structure for the Universal Supreme Consciousness. It shows itself everywhere, in each electron and cell. The Supreme Consciousness is the source of all knowledge and all beings which embody it. Creating a certain order and carrying out activities within the scope of a specific plan requires a Supreme Consciousness. Cells follow the pre-existing Supreme Consciousness plan and establish order. Shortly, consciousness is evident in all mechanisms from the smallest to the most advanced. A scientist who has lived hundred and fifty years ago, Arthur Eddington stated "Consciousness is a complete order which emerges on its own in nature in a later stage of evolutionary history".

On the other hand, an individual who can control his consciousness has a different role in the quantum universe. The awareness of self is the only notion which develops a new objectivity as a requirement of the observation it makes and attributes a new alpha function to the object. Humans are the only beings who do not have to act in accordance with the law of physics and a conscious mind is the only thing who has the authority to reduce wave packages. Physicist Niels Bohr expressed the following on consciousness: "In the sciences of physics and chemistry, there is not a single thing everyone agrees on consciousness. However, we all know what consciousness is, because we all have it. Therefore, consciousness should be a part of nature and reality. Consciousness can have a completely different set of tools from physics and chemistry". Psychologist William James defines the intellectual knowledge which influences the Supreme Consciousness as follows: "The thoughts in a state of normal wakefulness which we perceive as intellectual information or consciousness is only one type of holistic consciousness. It is quite apparent that there are states of consciousness which totally function in a different manner from intellectual consciousness". The common expression of these consciousness is the Supreme Consciousness.

Another name for Supreme Consciousness is infinite mind. There is only one Supreme Consciousness and the consciousness of every existence is connected to this Supreme Consciousness. Defined also as the universal mind, the Supreme Consciousness has infinite intelligence and embodies all the answers. The possibilities are endless and they will all be realized. The source of inventions is the Supreme Consciousness. Great inventors, creative geniuses, those who create their works with, inspiration all contact with the Supreme Consciousness and have achieved these. The Supreme Consciousness allows you to reach your goals. When you transmit your goals to the sub-conscious, the Supreme Consciousness will begin to reply in a suitable manner and create the suitable events and conditions to achieve results. The right people and opportunities will and enter your life and opportunities and lessons which will allow you to evolve will be presented to you. Nothing you experience is chance or coincidence. Your beliefs are the laws of your sub-consciousness. Everybody attains what they accept and believe in. Consciousness gives consent and the sub-conscious believes it. The power of the sub-conscious communicates like a magnet with only the things it believes in and attracts the right people and events to itself through the Supreme Consciousness. This is a universal law and is valid for everyone. Praying is the most common know method of establishing contact with the Supreme Consciousness.

The least dense energy type which can be measured and calculated experimentally is heat energy. However, although we are not able to measure the existence of some types of energy which are less dense in comparison to heat energy, we need to acknowledge them. For instance, the Energy of Thought. It cannot be measured, but can be accepted widely as a type of energy which is less dense than heat energy. Humans have still not learned how to use the energy of thought.

In fact, only the mind and rationality are not sufficient to activate the energy of thought. Humans would learn ways of going beyond the mind and rationality and activating emotional and intuitive intelligence as well.

Thought is a way communication of energy. Everything we think about have a direct effect on the vibrations of our inner energy and this energy directly affects our physical body. Thoughts are always in a state of motion. They jump from one subject to the other. Consciousness is the tool used by thoughts to focus on certain subjects. All created thoughts interact in the environment of energy in the universe and open the way for new interaction. All kinds of thoughts and the resulting experiences are recorded in the Supreme Consciousness, while the information about the experiences accumulates in the memory of the world itself. The DNA of all beings on earth constantly mix with earth, water and air and this information create their own memory. Our world shares both this information and its own experiences continuously with the universe. The Universe in turn continuously records both the thoughts and the material experiences.

Electromagnetic fields are made completely of ions, free protons and electrons. Quantum science has shown that what seem like solid objects in the physical world are in fact beaming energy areas, protoplasm forms and thought structures. The mind and the body are attempted to be redefined through the quantum point of view. It has been discovered that the protoplasm area of all beings consists of a great amount of energy and the particles which constantly separate from this energy radiate towards space. These are thoughts. It has now been understood that the single thing which causes the protoplasm area in humans to fluctuate and radiate are thoughts. Human emotions and thoughts for today are only being acknowledged in the area of interest of the science of psychology; however this point of view is in a slow process of change.

Dr. Carl Gustav Jung is one of the most important names in the science of psychology. Jung, who is also an advocator of Esoteric, has conducted studies in the sub-conscious mind. According to Jung, some parts of our brain are not directly under the control of our consciousness. The sub-conscious mind which sometimes becomes inaccessible for consciousness plays important roles in the life of an individual. Jung believed that all people have a common sub-conscious and the mind o this common sub-conscious embodies universal archetypes. These archetypes exist independently of the world. Only the sub-conscious mind has the capacity to know them directly. In times of crisis, the reasons why many people display the same sub-conscious behavior are these universal archetypes. Deep truths which are not known to ordinary consciousness are presented to the service of humanity through these archetypes. Jung has also criticized the fact that the characteristics of the human soul was not given much thought to. According to Jung, the most important tool for the evolvement of man is the soul.

An individual who has awareness has a different role in quantum physics. The awareness of self is the only notion which can attribute a new wave function to the object as a result of developing a new objectivity through the observation it makes. Man is the only being who does not have to behave depending on the laws of physics and a conscious mind is the single competent thing in the reduction of the wave packages.

Each being is tied to the universe through an invisible tie in sub-atomic levels. Some ties are stronger than others and some messages reach their destination faster in accordance with the wave length power of the sender. Each individual is both the transmitter and the recipient of thought, light and sound. The reality which lies behind the telepathic communication observed between some people is this. However, a majority of humankind has either forgotten to use this skill which potentially exists inside them, or has not reached the evolutionary level at which they can use it.

Extra Sensory Perception (ESP) has many common characteristics with quantum mechanics. Quantum realities such as particles' communicating in an instant and manifestation of inexplicable events show that this science has the capacity to give a rational explanation for a majority of these psychic events. If the particles communicate with each other in an instant, it means that there is a scientific explanation for thoughts to be transmitted through telepathy from one brain to the other. American physicist Sarfatti has analyzed the findings of quantum physics as a proof of metaphysics and claims that unidentifiable hidden variables may play the role of "psychic" variables and parapsychological phenomena such as telepathy and psychokinesis can be explained through quantum mechanics. According to Sarfatti, what makes it possible for electrons to communicate among themselves regardless of the distance is the telepathic communication between them. This unidentifiable hidden variable allows seemingly independent system to communicate. Those who concentrate on metaphysics and especially spiritualists claim that they constantly have "astral travels". According to them, astral travel is the method of an individual's directing his mind to the upper levels. In this method, the individual opens his mind to the energies which come from the above and allows his consciousness to travel in time and space. Those who state that they have experienced astral travel say that this travel is rather a projection and not a spiritual journey. These types of issues, which cannot be interpreted in terms of their validity or invalidity through the current substructure of science today, face humanity as issues which need to be analyzed together with areas of metaphysics such as telepathy, telekinesis, etc. And other areas for sure.

Parapsychology, which can be defined as the science of metaphysics, is gradually becoming more a part of the area of interest of today's science. The latest scientific developments have led many scientists to consider the interest areas of metaphysics, which has been regarded as "charlatanism" in the past. In some universities in the USA and England, studies on the interest areas of metaphysics have increased in number. The researches, scientific studies to be carried out in parapsychology carry great importance as to be considered a new scientific revolution. Today, primarily in Princeton, numerous studies are being conducted in scientific institutions on parapsychology. In the USA, many centers have been founded on areas of parapsychology such as ESP, telepathy, tele kinetics and psychokinesis and millions of dollars are being spent on researches. In Scotland, at the University of Edinburg, a first has been realized and the Parapsychology Platform has been founded. The areas currently being studied by the instructors, professors of this platform are areas such as ESP and telepathy, which were once belittled. CIA and DIA offices in Fort Mead have founded special units to carry out studies in this area. In projects in which psychic experiments are the area of study, especially studies on accessing the sub-conscious are conducted and the information exchanges between consciousness and the sub-conscious are being analyzed. Ingo Swan, who has taken part in one of these studies, states "It seems that, a part of the mind in the sub-conscious level is trying to communicate with the other part of the mind through imagery and emotions". Another researcher describes the situation as "It is as if our sub-conscious is trying to open a channel in the mind to reach information".

While our consciousness is used to acknowledge a thought or an idea, our sub-conscious transmits this acknowledgment to the Supreme Consciousness and the Supreme Consciousness begins to attract suitable people and to create suitable events in terms of this acknowledgment. What we experience in our lives is the reflection of our beliefs in our sub-conscious. When you change your beliefs, you change your life as well. You may observe what you believe in through your past life and experiences. Your reality today is the mirror of your beliefs. If you are not happy, it is in your hands to re-program it through your thoughts. Thoughts which are an activity of the brain are in a way a type of physical energy. Quantum theory has shown that communicating from far distances in an instant is possible. Therefore, it is time to conduct scientific studies on many subjects such as telepathy, telekinesis and clairvoyance which are not accepted in scientific terms today and which are based on the prediction that a physical energy can be transmitted through thoughts. Issues which were once thought to be magic are within the boundaries of science today. What is defined as a dream today might be considered in the same scope in the future. After studies on the cub-conscious and consciousness of the brain, there surely will be a time where studies on the over-conscious and para-conscious will be conducted.

According to Ph.D. Erengul who makes a reference to universal intelligence, the individual intelligence of man is created through the transmission of accumulated knowledge and common memory during birth and each person's knowledge during his life on Earth, are added to the universal common memory and data bank at time of death, with the help of separating atoms. Electrons provide immortality for man. Electrons are the atomic particles which manage the evolutionary program of the universe. Scientists express that, children born today are consciously and perceptively more open in comparison to children in the past. This is a natural outcome. Humanity is gradually evolving and advancing technologically. To be able to deal with advanced technology and its outcomes and carrying these to higher levels requires more open consciousness. Increase in humans' capacity of consciousness is not limited with a development which will make it possible for them to deal with technology. The increasing consciousness will accelerate contact with the Supreme Consciousness as well. Today, such acceleration observed in the flow of information directed at guiding the wide capacity of perception accurately is not a coincidence.

As the number of experiences increases, there is a need for a freer use of will to be able to attain different results from these experiences as well. Humans are being who can use their free-will in the most efficient manner. Although universal rules seem the same for all beings, within the scope of the evolvement of the soul and liberation of the will, there might arise certain differences in the implementation of these universal laws. For instance, the law of gravity has a definite functionality in terms of solid objects. The orbit of no solid object can change without the interference of an external factor or intervention. Therefore, everything remains fixed and in place. Each star system and planet in the macro cosmos is fixed. They have a specific orbit and this does not change. In the micro cosmos the orbit of each atom and particle are definite and fixed. However, the law of gravity operates in a freer manner for humans. The law of gravity which is influential on humans moves freely in accordance with their free-will. As evolvement increases, the ability to move increase and living being are saved from stability.

Man, who can use his free-will in the upper most level, has the capacity to flex the rules of the law of gravity and use it in line with this own evolvement. The orbit of man, or his manner of carrying out the duty he assumes for that life, can change as a result of the decisions he takes with his free-will after his experiences and the journey in the spiritual plan can go forwards as much as backwards. Change is not only in the orbit of spiritual journey. It is possible to make changes in the physical plane as well. Humans can make life conditions more perfect using the law of gravity when they have bodies and open the way for their own evolvement. The brain emits Alpha waves in the stationary level of consciousness. The studies show that, learning accelerates at this time. A person who raises his level of consciousness can rule his sub-conscious more easily and establish a more relaxed communication with the Supreme Consciousness and can change his life conditions for the better. All reflections coming from the essence embody the knowledge and divine light of the essence. However, as the level of evolvement increases, the skill and capacity of using this knowledge increases in the same proportion. This is another expression of the fact that the soul is getting closer to God.

Each being also has a common consciousness unique to its species. In the common consciousness grounds, the I turns into We and the shells of personality are broken. Consciousness in particular used in the migration of birds and fish is this common consciousness. Just as the individual's utmost goal is to evolve, humanity's utmost goal is to evolve as well. The consciousness used to attain this goal is the common consciousness of humanity. This type of consciousness is in constant contact with the universal consciousness. Universal consciousness never loses from its wholeness and unity. Whether evolvement comes from the common consciousness or individual consciousness, it gradually begins to appear more distinct in each life experience. Universal consciousness is never imposing. It always transmits its messages in a soft, clear, calm and unconstrained manner. Universal consciousness is an ocean of knowledge all beings swim in. It is the common territory where all knowledge and power exists. People need universal consciousness to discover their creativity and Divine characteristics. Universal consciousness replies this need with meaningful coincidences or momentary enlightenments. Meaningful coincidences are the warning systems of universal intelligence. Sometimes the answer appears in the form of compelling barriers. When a person feels the wish to develop in his heart and feels ready, the most suitable conditions are created for him in the universe. The key that activates universal consciousness is in the person's hands. When he is ready to take it and is open to understand it, as much knowledge as he can understand is transmitted to him. The capacity to understand is very important. To give a person more knowledge than he can understand might even make that person lose his mind. To increase this capacity, creating harmony between the layers of consciousness is necessary. This harmony also facilitates the cooperation between each layer. Knowing when to use your consciousness and consult your higher self means that a complete inner coordination has taken place.

Your sub-consciousness is the memory bank of the body, where things which are not in your consciousness are also remembered. You are always in cooperation with an infinite and limitless universal mind. Universal intelligence is the infinite mind we are always in cooperation with. When you wish to remember something or learn a new thing, let yourself free and relax. Think very clearly about what you want to know and your goal. If the answer is in your sub-conscious, you will immediately know what it is. If it is not, then the universal consciousness will make it reach you in some way. Sometimes a conversation you hear, sometimes a book or an idea and sometimes in the form of an emotion or inspiration. Trust that great mind, it will definitely find a solution. The more positive the message you send to the universe, the more the only thing that will appear will be harmony and beauty. The universal intelligence will always make experience events that will allow you to advance and develop. If you live a life of harmony with the universal intelligence, then the events will take place right on time, right on the moment where you can understand them and in the most suitable manner. This is what is required by the quantum life philosophy.

QUANTUM LIFE PHILOSOPHY

Quantum theory has shown that universal intelligence is informed about each moment and each event. All information is included in the universal intelligence at each moment and all events are recreated and organized by it. The law of gravity is one of the most powerful tools the universal intelligence uses to create the future. IT holds each atom and molecule together. It is the law of gravity which keeps solar systems and galaxies together. It can be seen everywhere. What attracts bugs to flowers and allow their continuity is the same law. Plants feed from earth. The female and male of all animal species attract each other. Homogenous animals create flocks because of it. The force of gravity of the world prevents the scattering and disappearing of all things on it. Just as the Sun's pulling of its own planets and the planet's pulling their own orbiters. Each object we use stays together due to its own force of gravity. The law of gravity is the most efficient law which keeps everything from a single atom to everything else together. Everything operates within this law. The force of gravity is valid both in the physical plane and the metaphysical plane.

Esoteric says that, nature operates within the framework of Quantum laws and through this point of view, that God and the Universe are the same with man. Both the universe and man have a dual nature which is made up of physics and metaphysics. The body as the manifestation of physics may dies at any moment and change, but the soul which is the manifestation of metaphysical structure cannot ever die. A person cannot imagine not existing. You always existed and will continue to exist; because you are all a part of creation. There has never been a time where you did not exist. There will never be a time where you will cease to exist. What happens when a person dies? The body does not disappear. Nothing disappears. The body only separates into elements. The soul it carries never disappears. IT only passes onto another body. You are immortal beings, who live temporarily in the human body. When you leave your body, you pass onto the most glorious frequency of pure love. That is the frequency of your existence. Heaven or hell is experienced on this world, not when you die. Heaven is the frequency of your own existence. It is inside of you. You can find it through pure love and happiness. You are an immortal being. You have all the time in the world to experience everything. There is no time limitation. You are eternal. You or anybody around you or any person who has lived in the past has an end. Until the time you reunite with God. Even that is not an end.

The individual should firstly know himself to be able to find heaven inside of him. A person who knows and loves himself naturally loves the universe and God, because man is the same with the universe and God. A person who is aware of this will understand that the architect and creator of everything is himself. Each person is a God who serves himself. He may ask for anything he desires from God. God will give him everything without limits. God is your consciousness in the evolvement stage. A person's purpose in life is to reach the consciousness of the universe and God. This purpose is the summary of man's search that has been going on for thousands of years. When dreams become active, anything is possible. Dreams embody all the powers, principles and rules to enable you to declare your kingdom n the heaven of the world. There is no holy war as to defeat oneself. The greatest victory is to exceed your own borders. Wholeness is the healing process of existence. Man is a small universe. The inside of your body is exactly the same as the universe.

With the Big Bang, Oneness seems to have first turned into duality and then to multiplicity, where is multiplicity has turned into chaos. Although it seems that the process in nature is constantly evolving towards chaos, the opposite is true. The passage from the complex structure to the orderly is the ordinary method. Individuals evolve as much as they get rid of chaos and pass onto order as well. The way to get rid of chaos is to get away from the dual system of thought and progress step by step to oneness. The complex structure does not show the dominance of coincidences. On the contrary, chaos is a strong part of the process of evolvement. Without the complex structure, change is not possible. Progress within order is possible only up to a certain limit. Living systems evolve by creating similar structures. Therefore, we need to talk about both continuity and discontinuity together. Disorder means new experiences and new experiences mean evolvement.

The relationship between chaos and order is not a cause and effect relationship. Therefore, it is not possible to predict the future. For instance, the cause of a macro disorder may be a chaotic event which took place in the micro level. Chaos exists in all levels. Although every existing thing doing alternating repetitive acts to be able to continue its existence seems like order, the small differences between these alternatives can turn into complex environments which are impossible to completely predict beforehand. Sustaining existence for living things depends on order. Breathing, the continuous beating of the heart and blood circulation is all results of order.

Scientists have seen that, no matter which example they take in any given area, chaotic notions are very similar to each other. There were many common aspects between various scientific branches and it was necessary for science to be analyzed as an integrated structure. In 1975, Holland published a work called Harmony in Natural and Artificial Systems. This harmony in question was about individuals who display chaotic behavior to display orderly behavior altogether due to natural genetic algorithms. The passage from disorder to order was being observed both in the biological development and social structure of man. The development of the brain, cells, ecology and fetuses in nature and development of culture, politics and economy all involved the passage to the same order. There was not a central structure which managed this harmony. As there is no Master Neuron in the brain, the models of behavior in societies were dependent on individual acts. The control of harmonious complex system was difficult. However, there was hierarchy in such systems. Numerous levels of organization were present and each sub-element group formed another higher level. For instance, proteins and nucleic acids formed cells, cells formed tissues, tissues formed organs, organs formed organisms and organisms formed the ecological system in nature. On the other hand, as experience increased, it was observed that the building blocks changed and reorganized. This was evolution, or the process of evolvement.

Essentially, evolution, learning and harmony were the same things. The only way to sustain life in any system was harmony. The harmonious and complex systems always had future expectations. Holland says that these expectations are beyond the predictions or even the consciousness of man and it is coded to the genes of all living beings starting with the simplest bacteria. He even argues for the existence of a template such as "this being can be successful in these environments". He even goes further and says "Harmonious complex systems always evaluate the information they receive from the external world and make predictions in accordance with their innate model. These predictions determine how the organism would behave in the future". In other words, it can be stated individual behaviors which may be defined as chaotic form a behavior pattern of a higher level and that this behavior constantly moves forward. In this real universe, an evolution which moves steadily from disorder to order is the proof that there is evolvement.

Sheldrake says that, organisms learn, develop and establish harmony through a method called "Morphic Resonance". This process of establishing harmony does only consist of physical and chemical reactions. There are regulating and creative factors behind these reactions. So much so that, each level of the development stages point out to a structure that is more than the sum of the elements a level below. Sheldrake calls this process "Morphogenetic". However, this process is not unique to biological beings. All systems display differences in terms of shaping all kinds of formations and chaos.

Dawkins reminds the fact that DNA molecules produce themselves and continue by increasing and claims that there is a similar structure in the cultural plane as well. Replicators, or structures which increase by copying themselves, are also present in humanity's culture and evolution soup and each thought contributes to the evolution of humanity in this manner. Thoughts and ideas such as genes sustaining their existence by travelling between organisms develop and advance humanity by passing on from one brain to another.

Another issue which is as important as evolvement is knowledge. It has existed before humanity. As the knowledge of life is evident in each being, it is also evident in human electrons. Knowledge is humanity's indispensable asset, which cannot be transferred. Knowing means existing. Knowledge is inherent in each person and cell already. All the books of the world cannot store knowledge in a single atom of a being. Man evolves to the extent he comes closer to this universal knowledge. However, experiences acquired in life make it possible for evolvement to take place not only in the individual level, but also in the universal plane through the addition of new knowledge to universal knowledge.

Knowledge within a book turns into a tangible being. The same knowledge is of abstract structure through the bites on the Internet. In a way, just as photons carrying both particle and wave characteristics in quantum mechanics, knowledge and thoughts can also be of tangible and abstract structures. The universe by itself is neither tangible, not abstract. From the beginning, there is the relationship between matter and energy. This relationship has reflected on the basic units similar to the particle and wave duality. As the complexity of the units increase, this dual structure also gets more complex. Therefore, social evolution in a way reflects the development of this duality.

For a real scientific approach, it is necessary to take into consideration both aspects of events and facts and analyze them. Neither classical science, which reduces everything to some sort of linear relationship and runs after merely mechanistic solution, nor metaphysical belief systems which accept everything without questioning and understand them are sufficient on their own. Everything in nature goes through a process. This process called evolution never ends. The process always passes from disorder to order. In this passage, all orders brought on the chain of evolution are more complex in comparison to the previous one. However, no matter how complex it is, a higher level of behavior or evolvement is observed at each stage from the previous one.

No existence and its place in the universe are coincidental. It is not a coincidence that to be able to get sufficient amount of heat and rays for life, the Earth is positioned at a distance towards the Sun. Laws of nature is strong energies which do an equal process for everything. These laws which are active in the universal level have not changed since the beginning. Life shows how compelling universal principles are. The quantum thought technique is based on the idea that, living in harmony with these universal laws will always bring success. Disregarding a universal principle does not end its effect on us. Laws of nature never show favor and protection. They are valid in equal terms of everyone. Realizing these laws and being in harmony with them increases our power. They allow us to reach our targets easily and speedily. Laws of nature are our natural alliances. Going against these principles, try to act in opposition with them is like going against the current. Universal principles are the rules of life. Each law of nature is a kind of balance system and balance is definitely formed in the universe.

In quantum theory, the moment lived is important. The experiences of the past can only be perceived when you remember them this moment. The future will be lived in the same manner, by constructing it this moment. Therefore, what predict, feel and sense at this moment have a very significant place in the formation of the future. Within this framework, interaction with the environment is quite important. The ties between people who enter a relationship of wholism continue their existence even if they get far away from each other; because in accordance with Quantum laws, groups of objects which form a whole and are connected with each other communicate through a single wave function. There is a communication between photons which is faster than the speed of light and is holistic. This awareness can be defined as a sort of sharing of knowledge. Awareness which is unique only to man is called consciousness.

Quantum physics says that the whole universe was born from a thought. The Universe and Man are the same. Man also creates as he thinks. You are the entire Universe itself. You are not separate from it. Therefore, all the laws valid for the universe are valid for you as well. The law of attraction is one of the strongest laws of the Universe. This law began with the Big Bang, always existed and will continue to exist. The law of attraction is a law of creation in the metaphysical plane. The secret of everything is in this law. It is you who attracts everything which enters your life. You do this with the images in your mind, your thoughts and feelings. You attract the things you think about. This law operates in your life, just as it does in the whole Universe. You create your life by means of your thoughts the law of attraction. The moment you realize this, you will also realize that you have an extraordinary power. You will be able to create your life from that moment on by only thinking. Your mental attitude will attract the conditions suitable for its own nature. Thoughts are magnetic and they have frequencies. When you think, your thoughts spread to the Universe and through their magnetic powers; they attract all similar things in the same frequency like a magnet. Everything sent returns to its source. You are that source. You are all centers of broadcasting. You are the strongest transmitting station of the universe. The frequencies you transmit shape your life, while your life shapes the world. The waves you emit extend to the universal intelligence through electrons and tachyons and the universe makes the necessary arrangements in line with these waves.

The law of attraction gives everything without exception back to you based on what you want. Whatever you think and feel, the law of attraction answers you with the same accuracy. Everything in the universe is magnetic and has a magnetic frequency. Your emotions and thoughts also have magnetic frequencies. Good emotions are indication of positive frequency, while bad emotions are of negative frequency. What you feel determine your frequency and attract the people, events and situations in the same frequency like a magnet to you due to the law of attraction. The perfect order of the universe determines every moment of your life, every experience you have in accordance with this law. No matter who you are, where you live, while your life is shaped by the law of attraction, the omnipotent law operates through your thoughts. You are what activate the law of attraction. You do this using your thoughts.

Quantum Theory has shown that the universe is not a cluster of physical objects, but a network of relationships where everything is connected to each other. In modern physics, an object's own characteristics are the results of the interaction between the object and the observer. What is observed is not nature itself, but the answer nature gives to our question. Quantum theory has shown that the universe is a participatory universe. In the same manner, intuitional knowledge is the kind of knowledge which can never be achieved merely through observance, but with man's full participation in the event. Quantum theory has included man's consciousness as well to its definition of the world. The universe is great network where mental and physical relationships influence each other. Quantum explains this network of relationships through the connections with the whole. Since everything is a whole, all kinds of experience acquired by each part are shared in an instant and each unit receives all kinds of information in an instant. We may only talk about the differences in the perception of the levels of awareness of the parts in proportion to the capacity. Quantum laws have shown that electrons constantly share information. Humans just like these electrons share information. However, electrons do not have the luxury of not sharing information. Information must definitely be shared. If humans do not want to share information, they do not, because they have free-wills. Therefore, people make their own decisions and determine their fate themselves up to a certain point.

Similar things always attract each other. Scientifically, this is called the Law of Analogy. According to this law, "similar things attract each other and create similar things". The Law of Analogy, which is the most basic laws of the universe, was first put forward by Greek philosopher Anaximander. According to this law, our state of existence attracts the suitable events to itself and these events allow us to relive the same conditions that we are in.

The reason for the constant repetition of the same events is that nothing changes. Only will power can break this vicious cycle. Thinking is creative. Events are the visible states of our thoughts. Events may seem as if they are taking place outside of our will at the first glance. However, the only reality is that we are the ones who create them. We are the ones who unknowingly make things happen. Positive or not, human thoughts are always creative. Thoughts always create the environment where the chain of events will take place. Our thoughts attract events which correspond to thoughts, just like invitations we have written with our own hand but have forgotten. Problems, mishaps, failures and all unwanted events knock on our door in the most unexpected moments as manifestations of our negative thoughts. The reason why we think they happen for no reason, or all of a sudden is that, we are not aware of our own negative emotions or have completely forgotten these negative thoughts. What is unexpected always requires a long period of preparation.

Word is a command given to man's Divine being. Humans form their lives with their own words. Therefore, a strong awareness needs to be formed about the use of words. We might need to work on this as if we are re-learning how to speak. It is essential that we know how to reconstruct words to be able to arrive at the desired results in the shortest way possible. Your prejudices about yourself or others are your greatest barriers. For instance, a person who thinks that he is clumsy is not revealing a truth every time he expresses this. He is only opening the path to do more clumsy things in the future. This is a sort of self-fulfilling prophecy. When you say "Life is very difficult", quantum reality will make you face everything which makes life very difficult. The same thing is true when you say "I'm done with everything". It you wish so, then you will not be able to anything. If you think that you cannot earn more, you will not be able to earn more. Thus, you determine your preferences and in return the consequences yourself. Limitations may appear in every area. Limitation about time, age, physical circumstances... Universal intelligence cannot perceive whether you want something or not. It only realizes the though you focus on. Therefore, only focus on and think about the things you want. Universal intelligence does not consider anything to be good or bad. Thoughts are only frequencies which need to be realized. The law of attraction takes your thoughts and sends them back to you as life experience. Negative sentences will always end with negative events. As the elderly say, this is the reason why the things you fear become realities.

By neutralizing our negative emotions and interfering with our thoughts, we not only correct the negative reactions which will come from the external world, but also change the nature of our future in the positive manner. The most important requirement to get rid of our fears, anxieties and worries is to get rid of the psychological conditions which cause them. Excusing, legitimizing ourselves, putting the blame on an un related event or a person, not accepting that the reason is our deficiencies mean not understanding the quantum structure of thinking. Not understanding this is the indication that we will repeatedly live the same things. Through this attitude, we lose the chance to be free of these negative events. Quantum thought is based on studying ways of forming speech styles which are the most appropriate to reach targets. The sentences to be formed for the targets should be clear. Sentences which indicate wishes are bound to remain as wishes. When you form "If…, if only…" type of sentences, know that your wishes will not ever come true. In the same manner, if you are transferring your targets to the future by saying "This will happen, this will be done," these wishes are bound to always remain in the future. Or if your sentence has a negative aspect, you make it impossible to achieve the result you want. If you say "I do not want to hear... anymore," know that the thing you do not want to hear will appear repeatedly. Instead of this, you should say "I want to hear..."

People have the tendency to put the blame of inequality on fate. The equality between people actually results from the fact that they belong to different inner levels of responsibility. The different aspects of the levels of evolvement place people vertically on different planes in the stairs of existence. The real difference between people does not have anything to do with wealth, belief and race. The inner hierarchy between people results from the difference in their manner of existence. This difference is one that is evolutionary and progressive which is based on evolvement. Rising between the stages is only possible through a radical change in the thinking and perception style. This process is the evolutionary process towards the unity of existence. The differences which take place in existence will carry people to higher levels in freedom, enlightenment and evolvement. Each person has the capacity to develop. Activating the ability to develop is the result of free-will be given to people. However, since many people find activating this ability very difficult, they perceive the conditions they face as accidents or fate. A person who knows himself and recognizes his abilities is also aware that an energy concentration is in question through the quantum thinking structure and realizes that he can change fate with his own choices as a person who has become one with the society and nature up to a certain point. While man interacts with his surroundings, he constantly makes interpretations and assumptions. In particular, when he needs to define and determine something, he makes use of dual opposite concepts. In this dual structure determined with rules, reasoning is called the Syllogistic Logic. New oppositions constantly confront people in accordance with the necessities of life. In this respect, man becomes more entangled in the complexity of multiplicity and gradually gets removed from the idea of oneness. To be able to evolve, the Syllogistic Logic should be abandoned and quantum thinking technique should be developed.

The most important propellant power of evolvement is to imagine. By using your power of imagination, it is up to you to live whatever you want. As Einstein said "Logic will take you from point A to point B, whereas imagination will take you everywhere". Imagine and pretend as if what you feel is real. Scientists have discovered some special mirror cells which become activate in our brain when we imagine something. They determined that, these cells perceive what we imagine as if these are real and gave reactions to what we want as if we are already living these. When you dream about what you want, the law of attraction perceives it as the present time. There is no time for this law. There is only now and this moment. To be on the same frequency with what you want, you need to feel as if you already have it. When you put yourself in the same wave length with your dreams, whatever you desire will be real.

The law of attraction has an extraordinary intelligence. This intelligence knows with which tools and with which dosage it needs to apply its power and arranges this in the best possible manner. Humans may delay this attraction with their free-will, accelerate it or slow it down, but cannot stop it. It is the fate of humans to carry out duties which have been foreseen for him. However, beyond these mandatory duties, you can elevate or degrade yourself at any given moment. This is completely up to you. Each of your thoughts, attitudes and words indicates at which level you are and how free you are. At those difficult times, where you have to accomplish those mandatory duties, you need to learn how to act and think to be able to reach a relaxed state once again. Applying the quantum thinking method means holding the key of evolvement in your hands. Everything from the atomic nucleus to the borders of the universe, displays change in accordance with the fluctuating motion. Life is also a wave motion which has not beginning and end. Events which do not go well may confront at all times. It may feel as if something is always urging you to call it quits. What is important is to take action knowing that this feeling is temporary and remove the negative things from your mind. As a result, dealing with the negativities which confront you and successfully complete your task through lessons learned is the essential issue. The completion of the task is the messenger of a new level in the chain of evolvement waiting for you.

The most effective way of getting rid of negativities that life brings is to practice affirmation techniques. Affirmation techniques involve producing positive thoughts about the issue you want to overcome and reading the sentences which express these thoughts in a certain tempo and slowly in a tone of voice you can hear. It is important to always use sentences which create positive effects and make using positive words a habit. The use of these positive words regularly will contribute greatly to your life and change it in the positive way. Meanwhile, the negative generalizations and false beliefs formed in the sub-conscious need to be corrected. Whatever you concentrate on, you make it real. You should voice the things you want and not the opposite. For instance, when you express that you are not scared, this sentence makes the feeling of fear permanent. Instead of saying that, the use of "I feel secure" expression which creates a positive connotation will allow you to have a tangible result. The dominant structure in the universe is based on goodness and evolvement. Therefore, a positive thought emits a much stronger frequency than a negative one. The feeling of goodness is a signal which spreads from you to the Universe and is attracted to you as it gets greater. How it becomes real is something only Universal Intelligence is concerned with. The universal mind knows the shortest, fastest and most harmonious way between you and what you want to happen. It is sufficient for you to create an image of your target in your head as if it has become real for Supreme Consciousness to do the necessary arrangements.

Whatever a person imagines, it will become reality. It only takes some time for the target to become visible. Of course, you need to accept the necessary effort to make your wishes come true. Shortly, we may say that Imagining + Effort +Time= Reality. We need time to see what we imagine, because universal intelligence needs time to make the required arrangements. However, this does not mean that we sit down and wait for our wish to come true. A person should prepare the necessary environment to make a dream come true, spend effort for it and try to do the best he can. Guiding the universe depends on your efforts. There are dreams in everything you see and touch. In order for a perfect or a horrible world to become real, it needs to be imagined beforehand. Behind every reality there is firstly a dream and hard work and behind every dream there is a human soul and body. Even things which seem negative and destructive consist of the reflections the conflicts in some people's minds.

Those who are willing to work hard and for a long time become victorious. Working hard is the founding block of every kind of success. Without working hard, it is not possible to achieve anything meaningful and permanent. If you want to be successful, you have to deserve it. You need to take the risk of working harder than everybody else. Give your heart and soul to what you are doing. However, no matter how hard you work, know that success will not come as long as you do not want this for yourself. Success is not chance, it is a preference. Many people do not have the determination and patience required to become successful. They want everything to happen right away. However, no event becomes real before its time and before the right conditions are created. Our wishes are perceived by universal intelligence and the process of creating the right circumstances begins; however, we need to give as much support as we can. Our duty is to assume a role which will take our strong characteristics to the highest level and lower our weak characteristics to minimum and spend the utmost effort to form the necessary conditions for our target. Repeating a target on its own is not a sufficient method of making it come true. Preparing yourself does not spend the utmost effort to form the necessary conditions. If we keep on repeating to ourselves that we will be successful, the only result will be fooling ourselves.

We live in a world which is full of many people with different skills and abilities. Therefore, we need to adjust ourselves in a manner which will allow us to be the best in our field. When we compare ourselves in a field we are mediocre in, we may lose our self-esteem. We should always focus on developing a skill we have. People naturally develop habits throughout their lives. As we get older, the dependency to these habits gradually increases. WE do not want to abandon things which make us feel good. It is much easier and comfortable not to change. However, evolvement requires constant change. There is nothing that does not change. No matter how much we resist, change is a requirement. Therefore, we need to stop resisting, look in the eye of fear and overcome it. You are never too late to start doing something to change your life. Trust yourself and achieve what you deserve.

Each person develops certain habits throughout his life. Being addicted is always a personal choice. No one or nothing pushes you to become an addict. Only you can do it. If you feel that you are an eternal prisoner of a tiring job which does not embody any creativity, do not blame others. It only means that you gave up believing your own magnificence. The universe means prosperity. A person has the capacity to achieve everything he wants from the heart. In such a universe, there is no reason to fear scarcity. Only the fear and suspicion you put in your heart may make you poor. Poverty means that a person cannot see his boundaries. Being poor is a person's giving up his right to be creative for a job he does not like and want to do. You are the only person withholding yourself from achieving everything.

No matter what happens to you, only blame yourself. Saying "It was my fault" is the first step of transforming the negative into positive. Quantum thought technique will open you the door of constant learning and evolvement in your life. Living a life of illness or health depends on your internalization of this thought technique. Making our being of essence an area of study, analyzing ourselves without judgment, reaching awareness concerning our situation are the keys of correcting the future. What will make us happier, more intelligent and consciousness is observing ourselves. Observing yourself means correcting yourself. Observe yourself. Scrutinize yourself. Enter the darkest corners of your being. Strangle all kinds of suspicion and fear the moment they start taking root in your heart. If necessary, use force on yourself. Charge yourself with happiness, peace and clarity. The conditions of the world outside of you cannot make you unhappy. Only your unhappiness becomes the source of all misery you see in the world. Poverty is a mental disease. You are the strongest magnet in the universe. The magnetic power you have inside is stronger than anything in the world. What emit this unbelievable force of attraction are your thoughts. According to the law of attraction, similar things attract each other. This means that you attract things which are similar to your thoughts. While you are thinking about an issue that makes you unhappy, did you ever notice that everything becomes even worse? When you preserve a fixed thought, the law of attraction immediately enters the picture and brings you events that will make you form similar thoughts.

Quantum thought technique makes a person realize the negative belief programs. As much as quantum thought system is turned into a life-style, the individual being to have a gradually increasing felling of peace and serenity for no reason. He adapts to the conditions better. His ability to express himself increases. His skills of being "In that moment and right there" increases. He develops understanding and tolerance. He acts more wisely with the security of using the common consciousness of the universe. When he has his fate in his own hands, he begins to do everything in an easier manner. He understands others better and accepts them without judgment. He develops the ability to look at everything from a wider point of view. He does not feel the need to prove himself. His perception and attention increase. He can perceive reality in an instant and without a mediator.

Everything on this planet and the universe remains balanced through the law of opposition. Everything has an opposite created by itself and becomes its equal. Each person remains between his wishes and a power which form a barrier against these wishes. This is a kind of universal friction force. In each leap where you want to accomplish something, you always come face to face with an opposing force. Overcoming this opposition is only possible by having a strong personality and getting your feet on the ground. No one can have a greater purpose than himself. It is always said that there is no limit to what people want. However, each individual is capable of realizing everything he wants as long as he keeps his common sense. If your heart is telling you that you can fight with every obstacle coming your way to make your wish real, then the resources are infinite. The maximum limit of what a person may want from life is determined by the expanse of the capacity of existence. The maximum capacity is the limit of what an individual can be and take.

Quantum man is happy about his state and where he is. For him, the most suitable place at that moment is there. Quantum man is special at every moment. Each person he is with is important. No moment can be taken back. Nothing can be lived in the same manner. A person should know how to be happy. He should never carry the memory of evil and injustice done. He should get rid of the weight of the past on his shoulders and direct his eyes to the future. This point of view always fills a person with new energy and emphasizes a person's creative characteristics. Different approaches are always possible for solving each problem. Everything in the middle of quantum uncertainty will be created the way you want. This creation is always in cooperation with a great intelligence for man. Trusting universal intelligence will always open the path of the individual. The most important aspect of overcoming problems is realities. Criticism is very beneficial since they show the truth. If criticism is not an expression of reality, then it disappears without causing any harm.

For an individual who has quantum thinking, the most important thing in relationships is providing benefits for all sides. In any kind of relationship, the win-win attitude provides the biggest benefit and development. These types of relationships remain permanent and once they are achieved, they are not lost easily. Permanent values are very important. No one can take permanent values such as love, trust and knowledge from a quantum person's hands. The quantum person adapts to time and grounds. He becomes a child with children and an adult with adults. He is flexible. Laughs easily. Laughing is the most important indication of harmony with the universe. When the soul is activated, it brings a person ready for change at any moment. As a person takes lessons from experiences, the mistakes can easily be corrected and change takes place. The chain of thought is different in each individual depending on mental maturity. The more ahead a person is in his own stage of evolvement, the speedier thoughts will from in his mind. The soul constantly evolves in the name of truths. It uses the synergy of differences and variety. The things which seem different from the outside are in harmony and union with each other in their essence. Differences mean variety. Being different does not mean being the other. When something is different, it is not separate from the whole. Since all parts carry the knowledge of wholeness inside, they are separate form the whole. Difference is only variety. God has created even the smallest speck from himself. Reality depends on each person's insight. It is possible to see God's signs in each speck. God is everything which exists, but everything which exists is not God.

A person who turns quantum thought system into a philosophy of life has a soul which is complete, perfect and absolute. Nothing can damage or destroy the soul. It is always there. It is one with everything. Since nothing can harm it, there is nothing to fear. A person who lives in accordance with quantum thought carries the feeling o being one with everything inside. Everything operates in a perfect manner and for the development of humanity. Reality is the most important aspect which develops man. Quantum man is peaceful. He knows that the best solution is reconciliation. Man lives in a world of infinite choices and infinite opportunities. He is in a universe of prosperity which flows, moves and reproduces. He knows that he will receive as he gives. He lives life in full like a festival. He knows that everything he needs is here at this moment. Freedom is the most important aspect. Each being should be free within the framework of its own life. Relationships should be continued on the basis of freedom too. Whether it is a love relationship or a commercial one, as long as individuals are able to express themselves, everything will work out fine for them.

Creativity is the basic instinct of the soul. Individuals' keeping themselves open to change is the most important goal of creativity. Man's greatest work is his own life. Life is the most important duty which should be completed with honor. The most creative basic act is each individual's presenting his unique contribution to the world and the universe. Create an environment which is in line with the new self-format. Firstly shape your external appearance in the manner you wish. You knew self will bring you the opportunities for you to make a quantum leap in the direction you want within a short period of time. When you hear a criticism about yourself, ask yourself "according to whom, what, under which circumstances and when?" The answers you give to these questions will tell you whether the criticism is accurate or a judgment that has nothing to do with you.

You may think that everything in the world has limits. However, humankind is on the verge of opening up to the universe and quantum physics tells us that there are an infinite number of stars and galaxies. Nothing has a limit in the universe. You may think that the world is full of living and inanimate things. However, nothing in the universe is dead, they are all alive. Everything you see is only vibrations of energy in different frequencies. If you believe that aging and getting exhausted, these will happen. Human shave developed a short life-expectancy themselves. We have inherited this from our ancestors. The fact that the average human life is gradually increasing is an indication that this belief is slowly changing. Quantum physics shows us that there is no proof that biological death is inevitable. Our body has the capability of producing new cells for the ones which die. Therefore, it is not right to limit as to how long we can live. This belief is put into our minds during our learning process. To be able to have a healthy and long life, it is very important to feel young regardless of our age. Abandon the feeling and thoughts about your age which are created by your sub-conscious. What you feel about your experiences is only a belief imposed on you. You can change your beliefs.

Very significant changes have taken place within the last century in terms of scientific perception and concepts. The reason is that, quantum perception pushes all old value judgments to be reinterpreted and frequently changes place. Despite this, it does not seem to have changed much in daily life. What most affect us today are not the changes in scientific concepts but the innovations brought on by technological progress. Knowledge is the lock to access the secrets of the universe and its key is question. The right questions may make it possible for people to access these secrets. The life of humans is based on questions. It is in our nature to ask hundreds of questions each day. We need to be vigilant to the answers to these questions. While reading, listening to or imagining something, we can get the answers. Sometimes, the answers come through our intuition. However, if the right questions are now asked, you can get neither answer nor knowledge. Always ask yourself how you attracted the problems in your life and take lessons not to experience these again. You are constantly given messages and information. You have received these messages all your life and will continue to do so. The conversation between two strangers is always a message for you. If you can hear the words they are saying, those words have a meaning in your life. Nothing you encounter in life is reasonless. Everything is a message for you and is about you. Everything you encounter is a tool which will allow you to mature.

Spend effort non-stop to perfect yourself. Always try to expand your horizons. It is you who needs to this inside. No one can do it for you. Wish to be the explorer and creator of your own universe. When you make this wish, the world will give you all you wish for. To be able to ascend to the nest level, you need to destroy the person you have been until now. The next step is always the unknown and unseen. Passage to the higher levels is always a quantum leap made toward the unknown. Everything is in your hands. Limits are only inside of you. A person who believes in himself is capable of achieving everything, including the things which seem impossible. Humans and objects are pieces of a single texture. Each of the cells of the system in universal dimensions is connected to each other. Man by himself can transmit his status, level of responsibility and dreams to the whole universe. The purpose of life is to create perfect works from each one of us. This may take place in this life or 100 lives later, but it will definitely happen one day. This journey is inevitable. There is no other purpose in the universe. Therefore, people need to trust their intuition and leave themselves to the hands of their dreams.

Love is a manifestation of love and since it directly comes from God, the divinity of intuition is indirect. Intelligence is an intuitional and natural notion. It exits in each being from birth. It has got nothing to do with intellect. Intellect can be learned over time and developed. It comes from the outside. All beings are not intellectual, but they are all intelligent. All existence is intelligent. Intellect is the manifestation of the brain. The raw materials of the brain are elements. Since matter is an expression of the universe, we may say that intellect is a more indirect manifestation compared to intuition. It is this divinity that intuition shows the secrets and realities of existence. Energy has a special aspect: It can never stay fixed. It is always in motion. It needs to move. It is life. Therefore, if the energy has no reason to suppress instincts, there is only one place it can go: Up. Energy moving to a higher level of consciousness allows the awakening of intuitional powers and acceleration of the creation and evolvement process.

Intuition is a part of higher consciousness. When you give complete freedom to your intuitions, the powers you have inside will surprise you very much. The brain is separated into two spheres. The left lobe is rational, logical and mathematical. The right lobe is intuitional. It is creative, romantic and mystic. However, education for the right lobe is not possible. It is intuitional and intuition is like a light which suddenly shines. The left lobe needs time to achieve results, while the right lobe achieves the result through a leap. There is no methodology for intuition. It operates through quantum leaps. The left lobe only gives permission to the right lobe when rationality is exhausted. The right lobe is ready to give you the answers which rationality cannot find. If you follow it, many doors will open for you. Great geniuses who only work through their logic have been able to make great discoveries only when their logic has been exhausted. At that point, intuition has entered the picture and has given the right answers every time. The answer comes from the center deep inside of you. Since it is connected to the whole universe and the answer to everything is found in the universe, no answer is a new creation. IT is only the discovery of what is needed.

A person who has reached the knowledge of reality knows that life advances through quantum leaps. Those who are able to do this know how to manage each moment. To be able to do quantum leaps, they evaluate each notion and opportunity, in the direction of the formation of critical affect. They do not feel bothered neither by the technological development of the present time, or the new scientific theories. Because they know that each new formation is a springboard which will contribute to his development and transformation. For a wise person, the Esoteric views present by modern science are as important as the ancient Esoteric knowledge. This point of view is called Quantum Wisdom.

The history of humanity has left behind thousands of ears where thought systems have been under constant pressure. Despite all the pressure, it has not been possible to prevent development. The thought systems have remained under the influence of the divine religions intensely for centuries and all kinds of development has been suppressed by this scholastic point of view. However, despite all these efforts, even the Cartesian degradation method on which the mechanistic world view which was opposed to the divine thought structure could be prevented and this point of view which placed science in front of religions came out in the open with Descartes. It has been observed that the scientific developments of the Enlightenment Age have been influenced by the Cartesian philosophy and that the world of science which completely broke away from the Theist/idealist thought predominantly adopted the Deist/materialist point of view. Since the Pantheist/Esoteric world view which is based on the oneness and wholeness of the universe has been suppressed for hundreds of years by supporters of Theism and its advocators have been destroyed through accusations of perversity, the philosophers of the Enlightenment Age have not given much credit to this view. However, western scientists and the Western society in general who had a great shock after meeting of science with Quantum Physics and philosophy are at the stage of getting to know Esoterism based on the "Universal unity" philosophy today. A majority of today's scientists still have a mechanic, partitioned and impermanent world view due to the Cartesian systems they were educated with. They either do not wish to recognize the fact that the universal realities revealed by quantum science have transcended this state or they simply do not understand.

Sigmund Freud described the blow inflicted by science on Theist belief as follows: "Through the flow of time, religion has been shaken twice by the blows of science. The first of these is the understanding that the world is not the center of the universe. The second is the understanding that man is not a being created in a special manner. In the first, it has been understood that our world is merely a needle point within the system of worlds which are incomprehensibly big, while in the second, the bloodline of humans has been reduced to the world of animals as a result of biological researches." As a consequence of this, 19th century science has abandoned the idea that organisms are created by a humanoid God and has arrived at the conclusion that all kinds of formations have been created as a completely coincidental manner within the framework of natural laws. There is even a physical science which belongs to creation. This is called Deism. The soul is not the root of nature, it is only a product. The soul in the human body is only a result of the development of the body. The God of Deism has been reduced to "The First Regulating Principle" by scientists who have not been able to bring a satisfactory explanation to the idea of universal order.

According to the advocators of Deism today, science is a process which always renews itself. Today, it does not seem possible that the dialectics of Hegel or Marx, Euclidean geometry or Newtonian physics or Freud's scientific rules can explain everything. Science has used these developments as a step and has evolved in its own path. Together with science, it is apparent that humanity has evolved as well. Science shows that the God of theology is gradually being replaced by the God of nature. Theology is gradually becoming closer to physical science, the laws of God to laws of nature, the will and power of God to powers of nature and the order and judgment of God to natural selection processes. In short, Theological determinism is now giving its place to naturalist determinism. However, Quantum science has shown that the universe does not have a deterministic structure at all. Even the advocators of Materialism have come the point of avoiding the term "Material" upon the realities of quantum, because matter itself has ceased to be "materialistic". Quantum has shown that matter is only a derivative of energy. The pure and rigid materialism of 10th century has totally collapse don the face of Quantum science. Therefore, the materialists of the past prefer to define themselves as "Realists" today.

The overlapping of the realities revealed by quantum science and the teaching of Esoteric has created shock in the world of science. Western scientists who insist on not understanding and acknowledging this holistic approach which is in total opposition to the Cartesian approach are experiencing great difficulties. The world needs to go beyond the discriminating mentality.

Scientists who conduct studies on the human body have seen that all the cells which they thought were independent from each are in fact informed about each other. Even a defect in one of these cells influences the other cells and may cause the balance of the body to be lost. Therefore, a cell has become not only for itself, but from the whole. This effort is about preserving the health of the whole. A cancer cell resembles the selfish and Cartesian man who only thinks about his own good. It takes the nutrition of the cells next to it and expands despite the other cells. The cancer cells sees themselves as expanding, however it cuts its own throat. The Western world has been wrapped up by these cancer cells. Today, humanity has turned into a kind of humanity that has been completely connected to each other and informed about the events taking place immediately through all kinds of communication channels. Today's humanity is now a Holographic whole. Individuals or societies that think that they can survive outside this whole need to see that they cannot do this. Those who wish to acquire wealth by exploiting others need to understand that it is in fact themselves they are exploiting. Aristotle, Descartes and Newton approaches need to be abandoned. As much as humans give up fighting with nature, they will be able to grasp harmony and the path for quantum leap will be opened. What is needed for humanity is to use intellect and intuition together.

Strict scientists insist on seeing the term "metaphysics" as a doomed term; however they need to abandon this habit. The Body which is in the area of interest of Materialism and the Soul which is in the area of interest of Metaphysics are a whole. According to this point of view, quantum physics is based not on definite realities, nut our level of awareness of reality. This awareness depends on our level of knowledge. Knowledge is an expression of wave function. In other words, our cognition level about reality is variable depending on our level of knowledge. The discourses of the Copenhagen school overlap with the predictions of this book.

Upon the undeniable realities of Esoteric, the advocators of Theism who take refuge in Materialist Pantheism have been spending effort to defend the concept of "Creator God" through the Pantheist point of view. According to Pantheism, the Creator Essence is a concept which can never be reached and is in a place completely separate from his creations. The creations constitute a whole; however it does not mean that they are one with God. God is beyond comprehension. God can never be reached or comprehended and is of a status which cannot be understand with the human mind and thought. One of Pantheism's advocators in Turkey, Ahmet Kabalcı states that the whole is always greater than the pieces it consists of: "Therefore, no matter what we do, we can never reach His Essence". Pantheism claims that, the individual cannot reach God and only all beings created can reach Unity. Pantheism which seems to be trying to reconcile Pantheism's discourse of the Unity of Existence and the Creator God discourse of the Divine Religions does have any explanations for the reason behind the effort spent to reach the Unity or what will happen when all beings reach it.

Albert Einstein defines the duty of man as follows: "The being called man is a part of the whole named the Universe by us. Man is a limited part of the Universe in time and space. However, individuals experience their thoughts and emotions as if these are separate from everything else. This is a kind of optical illusion his own consciousness plays on him. This illusion is a prison for us. It limits us with our personal wishes and compassion we show to those who are closest to us. Our duty is to expand our circle of compassion to embrace the wholeness of nature in all its beauty and save ourselves from this prison".

The Western world experiences pain between the two poles. Most scientists think that humanity consists of aimless creatures guided chemically in random and emerged as a result of coincidences, while Christian religious functionaries believe that a person is God and try to convince others that he needs to be worshipped.

The basic data put forward by Quantum science are still overlooked by a significant number of people who deal with science, whether they are physicists or not. The general philosophy of the world of science still remains as mechanical materialism. Wide masses of public are uninformed about the latest scientific realities under the influence of traditional religions. Those who are informed try to hide the realities from the public with the fear that their order will be disrupted and pretend as if these do not exist. However, no matter what happens, history has taught us that no one has the power to stop scientific developments. Galilee's scientific finding about the spinning of Earth took tens of years to be accepted by scientific circles and it took hundreds of years to cancel the execution decision due to his discovery; however, this has never stopped the Earth from spinning. Upon these developments, even Papacy is not silent anymore. In 1999, Pope Franciscus has announced those in St. Peter square that hell is actually a break away from God, where is heaven are a harmonious unity with God. In the same speech, a pope has announced for the first time that God is not an old man with a white beard and that God is a Glorious Existence who has both feminine and masculine aspects. Esoteric is taking confident steps in the name of becoming the science and belief of the future.

ESOTERIC FUTURE

Today, it may be claimed that technology has substantially removed the process of natural selection. Until 19th century, while the rule that only strong individuals who could keep up with the changing conditions could survive was valid, as a result of the development in the last two hundred years, it has been seen that people with weak physique have more of an opportunity to transmit their genes to the new generations. In fact, the weak are benefitting from medicine, food and shelter which are the products of technology, as much as the stronger people. This has substantially reduced the difference between the weak and the strong in natural selection. Today, even a large scale change in nature will not create a result that will change the process of evolution, unless it is a change that can put an end to technology. Wolpoff states that "Even if climates change and Ice Age comes back, a process which can change the physical structure of humans will not be experienced. Perhaps, we will blast a bomb to heat the air again or place a giant mirror in space. Today, it even seems possible that by interfering with genes, we will be able to change the basic characteristics or our species or others. Therefore, evolution through natural selection as left its place to evolution through human intervention". Carl Sagan also underlines this situation and says "We have reached a milestone in the history of humanity. We are a species which shapes its own evolution". On the other hand, we should not forget that not only the material change, but also the spiritual change in everything is a process of evolution as well. Humanity's having reached the point of interfering with material evolution is an indication of the level it has reached in its spiritual evolution. This development will never end.

Although the whole universe seems to be consisting of independent parts, it is in fact One and Whole. One point in the universe contains the knowledge of the whole. The whole humanity and the universe are hidden inside a single person. A single person's power in Quantum terms is equal to the power of the universe. When considered from this point of view, whole humanity is a family. The whole body suffers from the defects and faults of some parts of humanity which is in fact a single organism. This interaction is valid between all beings in every point of the universe. Damage given to one person is actually given to the whole universe and a help given to one person is a help given to the whole universe. The universe's indivisible unity is like an infinite ocean. Each of the drops which make that ocean up is in constant contact with one another. At this point, there is no space and time limitation. One change which takes place in one point in the ocean is immediately reflected on the whole. Each drop carries the knowledge and power of the ocean inside.

Everything is connected in the universe. There are no separate and independent units. Matter is in fact made up of energy which has come together in a specific density. Including humans, everything is part of the same whole. We carry the same essence inside. Knowledge is everywhere at any moment. Space and time are equals in the field of frequencies. We may see the universe as a human body and all created beings as its cells. In the light of the information stated above, we may say that: All cells are informed about each other. The wellbeing of one means the wellbeing of all. A defect in one means the defect of all, that is, the body getting ill. All cells are responsible both from themselves and from each other. They are all the same and of equal value. Although their efforts seem to be directed for themselves, they actually work for the wellbeing of the whole. We, just like cells, are parts of a whole. The responsibility of the child who dies of hunger in Africa and the pride of the scientist who makes a discovery in the USA belong to us. This point of view shows how wrong selfishness, the passion to own and ambition are. The only way humankind can sustain its existence and evolve is to change its molded thinking style and evolve in line with the new understanding of economic and social order under the leadership of science. Humankind should abandon its desire to dominate, rape, upset the balance and exploit nature and try to understand and cooperate with nature.

Nothing in the universe is disorderly. Everything continues its existence within a specific order and rules. Even the smallest disorder which may take place is immediately interfered with and precautions are taken to reestablish order. The universe has been formed in accordance with a specific purpose and order contrary to belief. There is never and end in the universe. There is always a beginning. Each end is an expression of another beginning. Each beginning in return is a tool for evolvement. Man is the result of evolvement on Earth and the highest level of reflection. The most perfect reflection of unity and wholeness in the world is mankind. A being's search for perfection can only be possible with its opposite. The opposite embodies the search, meaning and result of the being. Opposition is wholeness. Two being are one.

Man is a being open to progress and development. This is valid both for one person and for whole mankind as a whole. There is surely a peak for each period humanity lives. However, this peak today is gradually getting higher. The difference of our century from the previous ones is that, greater masses are informed about this peak. Technology helps the spreading of the accumulation of humanity and the progress of mankind. In this respect, the number of those searching for the truth is increasing and they are supporting each other in the path of development. Instead of people who try to impose their beliefs through arguments, the number of those who try to understand each other are also increasing. Each individual is in need of the knowledge of the others which came before him for his own personal development. Humanity's development is in direct proportion with the internalization of the total knowledge of humanity coming from the past rather by the individual. Each peak is getting higher with the support it receives from the previous ones and humanity evolves in this manner.

In quantum world, everything consists of atoms and atoms consist of particles. Every matter seems different to the eye, however this difference and variety does not spoil the essential characteristics of atoms. It is impossible to pull an atom from the whole or the universe in quantum physics. None of the particles can be separated from the whole. There is no breaking away or separation. There is only changing states. Variability penetrates to each speck. Every speck in the universe knows about this change. Everything that takes place in a galaxy is felt in the whole universe. The speck is the same with the whole. The distance, difference and variability seen between the speck and the whole are only in the energy levels. Differences are as result of energy density and vibrations. Humans perceive the universe shown to them by their consciousness and brains as different energies and matter. The reality put forward by quantum physics is that, atoms in the macro and micro cosmos communicate and interact with each other. The whole material universe which humans are also a part of is a whole of existences consisting of atoms which communicate and interact with each other in infinite second. The aspects of the micro cosmos or humans are influenced by the formations in the macro cosmos or the universe. The same is true for the opposite. Any choice man makes also influences the universe. The moment we contact something other than ourselves, we touch the soul of the whole universe. Each point we contact is one with the soul of the universe. Therefore, it is in our hands to make all the changes. All changes take place within the moment. Living the moment and taking its energy brings feeding with a magnificent universal energy with itself.

Materialist point of view claims the opposite and argues that each formation has unique characteristics and existence is nothing but coincidence. Being born to a world through coincidence created through coincidence, living life with coincidences and dying one day and disappearing, would neither tie a person to life, allow him to have self-respect, nor make him feel peace and happiness. Man should know that he has come to life with a purpose. In the evolutionary program God has arranged for humans, each individual has a purpose and place. Each individual's soul has come from God and will return to God. Man is the most glorious of all beings. Each individual feels the need for such a belief to be able to feel the love of humanity inside. Materialist point of view wants to determine each problem with experiments and see it with its own eyes. There is no proof to be shown or to be seen. However, proof which can be sensed and felt is infinite. Looking for solutions only using the intellect cannot allow man to arrive at a definite result. Intuition under the leadership of intellect is the strongest weapon in the search for reality. Materialism rejects intuition altogether. Our intuition tells us that, God is a circle whose center is everywhere and its circumference is not anywhere.

Mankind embodies a speed even faster than light. This ability is a definite proof that we are a part of God. It is the speed of thought. Thoughts can exceed time and space with an infinite speed. The moment we think, we are no different from God. We are all a part of God. There is also no limit for imagination just like thought. This speed is much higher than the speed of light. It extends to eternity. The ability to control thought increases by getting closer to God. The chain of thought is different in each individual depending in mental maturity. The more a person is ahead in his evolvement level, the faster the thoughts will develop in the mind. Reality depends on each individual's insight. Each person cannot have the same insight and perception, because each person's level of evolvement is different. Knowledge depends on the maturity of the mind, its power of perception and capacity of making distinctions.

All laws and formulas about existence and life in the universe exist as symbols. To the extent humanity deciphers these symbols; it makes its evolvement possible. Including understanding of universal laws, nothing is created from scratch and everything is transformed through rediscovery. The strengthening of the communication network today results in a change at one point of the world to influence the whole world. As humanity evolves, technology develops and as technology develops the level of reality reached increases. It is seen that there are great similarities between new understandings and all kinds of spiritual messages. All the results arrived at are in fact only the verification of the reality. There is a very strong communication between the world and the universe and every change which takes place in the world affects the universe as well.

Hope and trust, which have allowed humanity to survive since the beginning of the industrial age, were the promise that a development with a limitless source could give man the opportunity to reach everything he wishes. The promise of the industrial revolution was that every person would be the master of his own life. The dominant belief in societies was that, as the speed of industrialization increased, freedom would spread to all the individuals in the society. The level wished to be reached was to provide everyone with an equal and average life-style. The triangle of limitless production, absolute freedom and limitless happiness constituted the basis of the new belief which can be defined as "the religion of development". However, despite all the magnificent development which took place in material areas in the industrial age, it was understood in a short time that this new belief would not be able to keep all its promises. What is more, happiness was not only about realizing all wishes. Our emotions, thoughts and passions were being guided by industry and state powers that were dominant over the mass communication devices. The constant increase of economic development remained only the privilege of rich sates and the difference between them and the poor states gradually reached extraordinary dimensions. On the other hand, technological development caused pollution in the environment and nature as well.

Regarding the only purpose of life as meeting all wishes or all special needs and being satisfied caused an increase in selfishness in the industrial societies and the individuals became lonely. The expectation that the teaching of selfishness, which the individuals had to support to allow the system to preserve itself and continue its existence, to create social harmony and peace was imbedded in history before long. Only thinking about personal gain, greed and the ambition to own enlaced the whole society and social peace remained only in dreams. This social harmony, peace and serenity assumption which was realized to be wrong right from the beginning came out into the light more and more with the experiences lived.

In accordance with speedy technological development and the explosion of production based on technology caused a great increase in population. As of today, the world has the capacity to provide a high quality life to about 3 billion people for a very long time. However, our population is now 6 billion and with the rate of present increase, it is inevitable that there will be more people than the world can handle within a short period of time. While the world population has increased with an average of 3.4 per thousand in each century until 20th century, this number has reached 18 per thousand in the previous century. The total world population in 8 thousand B.C. was 8 million. This number had reached 1 billion in 1800 and 2 billion in 1925. If the increase goes on with this rate, the population which has exceeded 6 billion today will reach around 20 billion in 2100. Even if we assume that 18 per thousand increase rate will remain fixed, in 2200 the population will reach 36 times of the current population unless precautions are taken. This presents the possibility that humanity will destroy itself through environmental pollution even today. The world does not have the capacity to feed a population of 20 billion. Unless precautions are taken to zero the rate of population increase, 3500 years from now we will have a population that will fill all the stars and galaxies in the universe.

Similarly, as long as nature is damaged in the same rate, about one fifth of the animal and plant species of our time will become extinct. However, the point of no return, the hopeless threshold has still not been exceeded. Starting with scientists, the whole humanity is becoming more aware of living in harmony with nature and the new understanding of perceiving the balance, oneness and unity in the universe is increasing in more and more societies. This change which began in the 1950's in the level of scientific understanding is being included in all areas of our lives in higher rates with the contributions of quantum physics and the theory of relativity.

The Western educational system is a system in which an average education which can appeal to all people is given. It destroys the individual's potential to develop himself and tries to create the average human prototype necessary for the system. This system is completely directed at making the individual compare himself with others. Trying to be like someone else is one of the most important barriers in terms of individual development. Comparison is the easiest way of destroying one's own goals and natural potential. Since education is not in harmony with man's natural structure, a majority of Westerners feel lost and unhappy. This is the reason why stress and depression are so widely spread in the West the education received causes the human mind to be confiscatory. As a natural result, human rationality works through opposite concepts. In today's system, people have armed themselves ready to fight at any moment. Today's people believe in an economy focused only on survival. Today's economy is the result of a mentality which pushes mankind to disasters, destruction and conflict, from weapon production to environmental pollution, from organized crime to drugs.

Selfishness is the state of wanting everything for oneself. Owning gives people more pleasure than sharing. When the only purpose is to own, people gradually greedy and ambitious; because the more they have, the happier they assume to be. Thus, a society where everyone is jealous of the other and feels hostility is created. Since the customers he wants to fool, the rivals he wants to force to go bankrupt and the workers he wants to exploit causes one to own lesser things, the selfish person makes enemies out of them. Since wishes are endless, it cannot be imagined that such a person will ever be happy and peaceful. His whole life will pass by being jealous of those who have more than him and fearing those who have less than him.

The Western educational system gives great importance to ego. Such an education supports the formation of a self-centered personality. Beneath expression such as "Express yourself" and "Show yourself", what is really meant is "Make yourself the focus of attention". A person who gives much importance to himself believes in the importance of his decisions in every field and behaves self-centered. In Western societies, around 15% of people are being treated for depression. The only way to get rid of this problem is to abandon Aristotle rationality and make quantum thought system side spread in the whole society. To be able to get used to quantum thought system, we firstly need to get rid of ego and then assumptions and obsessions. For a person to raise his awareness and know himself better, firstly his ego needs to get rid of extremism. Therefore, the thought of "I" needs to be changed into "We". The word "We" symbolizes the holistic sum of the words "I" and "You". The idea of "We" does not give place to selfishness. A society which is made up of individuals who do not put forward themselves but the society they live in cannot possibly not evolve both in the individual and social level. It is impossible to develop a country which is ready deep down inside and has not reached sufficient level of prosperity in the richness of its thoughts and its own system of values. Increasing life standards in such countries, emphasizing the evolvement need of individuals depends on abandoning the selfish beliefs and thought systems which have taken root and prevent the societies from progressing. Change in the level of consciousness can only be made under the leadership of science and quantum thought. A person's, institution's or civilization's level of development is directly proportionate to the scientific level they have reached, besides the value they give to quantum thought system.

Western technology constantly spends effort to develop systems which contain artificial intelligences in line with the framework of Aristotle rationality and exceed human intelligence. Artificial intelligence is based on dual logic system and is bound to its own data base. Artificial intelligence systems are planned in a manner to reach the purpose they have in the shortest way possible. Achieving maximum benefit by spending minimum effort is a product of the ego. Artificial intelligence creating the "I" concept through its inner logic does not seem to be possible for this reason. It cannot distinguish its own existence from the others. If we need to express this within the framework of quantum theory, artificial intelligence needs to collapse its holistic energy wave. Since the concept of "Selfhood" is not an object, it seems impossible for artificial intelligence to realize this. A being produced in a finite manner due to its data base cannot turn into an infinite and undefined structure. It will not be possible for artificial intelligence to reach its own consciousness. However, artificial intelligence products are still in a position to carry out duties given to them faster, more efficient and accurate manner than humans. However, people who use these systems and facilitate their lives are becoming more dependent on reductionist thought. Artificial intelligence produced by means of technical and technological development makes humans be more dependent on matter and push them to pragmatic selfishness. As long as humanity uses technological development and artificial intelligence to take steps in the path of wisdom, it will be able to break free from this dilemma. As it cannot be imagined to limit humans' abilities to discover and invent, technology cannot be left aside either. However, technology should not be a barrier in terms of individual development and should not push individual evolvement in the background. Humanity needs to find ways of sustaining its technological development, while advancing on the path to wisdom.

Societies whose urge to do research are suppressed through education live removed from the positive sciences due to the happiness of assuming that they know the reasons for all of the events they witness and live in spiritual terms. Societies who are encouraged about their urge to do research act with the idea that every event should have an explainable scientific reason and achieve great progress in positive sciences. Western society has firstly become an industrial and then technological society for this reason. Eastern societies who were stuck with dogma have paid a heavy price for this development and continue to do so. On the other hand, Western societies who have reached very high levels in technology are known to have become unsatisfied spiritually in this cause. Until a holistic and non-separatist education system becomes dominant in the world, it seems that this dilemma will go on.

Today's educational system is based on suspicion, fear, hypocrisy, jealousy, prejudice, limitation and compromise. This type of education which targets destroying the mind's free thinking and abilities plays an important role in determining the material development level of societies. A country's economy and material development level is the reflection of the thinking and feeling style of that society. In such an education, it is nearly impossible to raise individuals who will hang onto their dreams, believe in them and assume their responsibilities. If we take into consideration that behind every big project there are the dreams of the people, then it may easily be understood that how such a system which steals the dreams of 99% of the people may have prevented until the present time. Similarly, it may be foreseen what kinds of things can be achieved through an educational system based on quantum thought system. In an educational system where all the dreamers will come together, there will not be any discrimination concerning beliefs, race, color and wealth and the most important thing will be for people to develop their personality, it will be possible for each individual to work on himself, develop his abilities and love himself. Through a world order consisting of people who are enlightened by means of this education, it will be possible for humanity as a whole to make a quantum leap to a new level of consciousness.

Although quantum physics has been studied on for a hundred years and numerous new discoveries have been made which will cause us to change our perception of the whole world, classical physics is still being taught in schools and Quantum physics is not mentioned at all. It is as if there is no such subject for educators. However, for how long can these people bury their head in the sand? The only area physicists give a fight is not education. The science of physics is in need of constant updating. If we take into consideration the changes and new ideas in the last 200 hundred years, the speed of this change is quite fast. There is an urgent need for updating at the moment. It seems necessary to update laws related to the macro cosmos within the framework of quantum information, primarily the laws of Lavoisier and the laws of thermodynamics. It should be kept in mind that all laws are accepted as valid and used until the contrary is proven. No theory which is put forward can be excluded from scientific development. The attempts to hide knowledge from humanity have never been successful and will not be in the future.

Separatist education creates a constant conflict not only on the individual level, but between the classes in society as well. The claim of these systems to remove the classes is not real, because they have built their systems on the principle of limitless consumption and Aristotle logic. Overcoming the system through individual efforts is not possible for the majority. It has been determined that the average for moving up the social ladder through personal efforts and moving from the lower levels of the society to the higher levels is around 10%. As long as this belief system survives, social classes and conflicts between the classes will continue to exist and wars between countries will no gradually cease. Greed, which is the result of separatist education, and peace, can never exist together. A greedy person is the enemy of nature. That kind of a person tries to have the maximum benefit from nature in accordance with his own interest and disregards the necessity that nature has to protect itself. Therefore, we are gradually getting removed from nature to which we owe our existence due to our intellect. We leave aside the union and harmony that should exist between nature and man and try to dominate nature. Upsetting the balance of nature causes it to gradually disintegrate and it is humans who have to face the consequences of this the most. The idea of dominating nature has so blinded us that, we do not see that nature is forced to defend itself against the exploiting attitude of humans. Behind all natural disasters we face today, there is the greediness and selfishness of man.

Our war with nature can only end when we understand that nature and man are in fact and one and whole within the scope of the Esoteric discourse. This kind of understanding which is in accordance with understanding the oneness and wholeness in the universe is spreading among man. Scientific data which support this and their reflection on everyday life is grabbing the attention of more people each day.

Findings such as Einstein's Theory of Relativity which proved that space and time cannot be separated and that matter is in fact a type of energy; Quantum Theory which proved that there are no separate and independent matter in the universe and that everything is connected and identical to each other and The Hologram Theory which suggests that all knowledge is ready to be used at any given moment, are scientifically proving what Esoteric belief has been asserting for thousands of years. Basic concepts and thinking methods which belong to the old dual structure have been becoming invalid. In order to be able to explain new formations and reality, a new thinking style is required. Science acknowledges today that the universe does not consist of particles which are separate and different from each other and that these particles constitute an indivisible and dynamic whole. The laws of the universe have hit us like a ton of bricks. Not only scientific but religious beliefs of the past also need to be discussed in detail and new designs have to be put forward.

On the other hand, the concern that the natural resources are limited and that they will be used up by time and affect the development of humanity in a negative manner is not valid. It is true that the resources of the world are limited. However, humanity has been using these from the first day he existed and has not been able to exhaust any of them. Certain inconveniencies have been experienced as a result of erroneous use and these same inconveniencies are still experienced today. However, making mistakes is a learning method to correct them as long as lessons are taken. Without mistakes, progress is not possible. The quicker man learns that he is a part of nature and acquires the awareness that what he is using is himself, the quicker he will learn to approach everything he uses and nature in a more respecting and balanced manner. Esoteric teaching tells humans to be environmentalists and live in harmony with their environment. What is more, mankind is on the verge of opening up to the universe once more and the resources of the universe are endless. It has been discovered that there is sufficient amount of Helium even on our satellite the Moon which can meet humanity's thousands of years of energy need. As long as today's civilization does not repeat the mistakes of the earlier civilizations and takes lessons from these, it will be much easier for it to unite with the universe.

In Latin, the word University means "Towards Union". It is a purely Esoteric word. The mission of a university is to progress the effort of the humanity to "become one" and guide it in this journey to the oneness of the world. Universities need to be transformed into institutions which can teach rationality and intuition, material power and love together. Those institutions which are not able to do this will not have a place in the world of the future. The universities of the future will educate individuals who have the capacity to assume the responsibility of universal politics and economy and those who have the ability to nurture and magnify the ideal of unity. Real knowledge is always hidden in the essence of each individual. Universities will be institutions which will reveal the knowledge of this reality and allow it to develop. The traditional system of universities is not only old, it is very liable to remain fragile, sensitive and be influenced since it is very dependent. Universities which will be open to all individuals who trust themselves and their dreams will raise all kinds of undertakers humanity of the future will need. The forerunners of the new universities are already being raised today. Their purpose is to create a new humanity. Our civilization is in need of individuals independent of time to be able to do the quantum leap. Changing the mentality is only possible through a structure which has the capacity to realize a revolution in the universal level and which has a vision and high ideals. The idea of creating a world which has no boundaries and is capable of changing everything which limits humanity and restrict all kinds of formation has been the dream of people for hundreds of years.

The inventions made only from the beginning of the 2nd Millennium until today are more than the total of the ones made in 20th century. In fact, the progress made is more than the progress made since the emergence of humanity. Starting from the beginning of the previous century, progress has extremely speeded up. The number of people who took role in this progress and the number of that benefit from this has been increasing incrementally each day. Humankind finally seems to have realized the propellant power and the great potential through team work by using the mind of all people. Despite this, the erroneous institutions and establishments, thoughts and beliefs, narrow-mindedness, which our civilization has created in those times where it beat the air, still continue to prevent humanity from finding the level-headed and bright path of civilization which our civilization. The possibility of an atomic war which can drag the world to a period of standstill, or even decline seems to have become quite distant. However, science and humanity still suffer from the hands of states which have not been able to correct the mistakes of a past which has been erroneously organized, where there is nothing but personal weaknesses, ambition and ego and which are institutions of past times and not of the universal period.

During the process in which the world civilization has opened up to space, humanity has come face to face with the requirement to comply with a conscious and programmed process of evolution and to assume responsibilities like a child who is on the verge of walking. For instance, the purpose of biological information transmission should only be regarded as a type of communication device in time, whose only purpose is to create the gene pool of the future. The target during this process is to optimize knowledge. If not, humanity will begin to insensibly play with the structural codes of chromosomes through gene engineering to overcome death or will come face to face with the risk of creating an artificial black hole by turning matter infinitely dense. If science gives up its aspiration to be God and focuses its attention on the evolutionary process of humanity, these types of dangers will be prevented and perhaps humanity will takes its place in the universe as a proud part of the universal civilization. Systems which are spent effort on to send the maximum amount of knowledge through the least effort possible are not only biological systems. Communication systems and other physical systems need to organize themselves in accordance with the needs of the new age in the maximization process of entropy to prevent the collapse of order.

The technology which makes today's revolution of informatics is based on a "quantic" foundation. Computers which were created by adapting quantic inventions such as semi-conductors and transistors to solid matter physics knowledge and the Internet have placed the whole civilization under a speedy transformation. Inventions such as laser and supra-conductors which gradually increase the speed of informatics are completely products of quantum science. Today, it is possible to send photon particles to kilometers away through fiber optic cables. It is also known that studies are underway for the construction of quantic computers. The relative increase of communication has begun with the spread of newspapers, telegrams and telephones. In the 21st century, fiber optic connections, satellite televisions and the Internet make it possible to reach more people in the virtual platform. It is seen that humanity is speedily flowing to a direction where everybody is able to communicate with the others. Money can travel from one point in the planet to the other in a matter of few seconds. Individuals can do realize the same travel the most in 1-2 days. Humanity seems to have entered a fast process of unification.

It should never be forgotten that humanity has almost destroyed itself as a result of a nuclear disaster. Even the ruling out of this danger is a quantum leap. Humanity has ascended to a new level of evolvement. While we travel to our own satellite the Moon or to other planets of the solar system, we show the utmost care that we do not carry the microbes of the world to those places. This is an indication that humanity has reached an awareness of cosmic duty and love. Just like the level of consciousness humanity had reaching in the process of opening up to the universe; it can easily be assumed that the visits to be made or already made from the outside are carried out with the same care. What the extraterrestrials who will visit the Earth will not understand will be that although the Earth seems as a whole, the nations are still at war and conflict with each other. With the same sense of duty and consciousness, the assignment of humanity now is to abandon all kinds of regimes and ideologies which distance the nations from each other. Humanity will be ready for its cosmic duty to the extent it takes precautions to gradually decrease the differences between less developed-very developed, rich-poor and ignorant-intellectual. Meanwhile, it is inevitable that the whole humanity unites and transforms religious beliefs into cultural differences within the framework of a universal God. The wave of wisdom which regards the world and all species living in the world as identical and that our interests are common is gradually becoming wide spread among humanity. Humankind is beginning to understand the reality that it is the master of its own fate more and more. This is the Quantum Wisdom Age. It is the age which has the foundation to unite Eastern and Western cultures. Physicist Werner Heisenberg states the following on the nature of creativity: "The most productive development in the humanity's history of thought consists of points where two different lines of thinking meet. If there is a real interaction between different thoughts, it can be expected that new and interesting creations will be created". In case the synthesis of Eastern and Western cultures are made under the leadership of the intellect and through intuition, the whole humanity will reach a common consciousness and the quantum age will be lived with all its blessings.

The quantum age man is a person who is able to use all the layers of consciousness in a harmonious manner. Man is complete and perfect in capacity and essence. All kinds of constructive and creative quality are hidden in this essence. The main requirement of personal change and development is the realization of this reality. Man is a thinking being. In fact, the main matter of the universe is thought. Everything is born out of thought. Therefore mankind shapes its fate and life knowingly or unknowingly through the thoughts it spreads. Each event we experience is nothing but a flow of information which allows us to know ourselves. Evolving humanity into a universal civilization is all in our hands.

Mankind has reached a point where it is able to change the direction of its path of development. The cells of this new humanity, or humans should be educated in the individual level. Educated men and women need to be prepared for the new age. To be able to do this, humanity needs new generation educational institutions which will lead it. These will be schools which can open the way for those who have the ability of producing solutions, who are enlightened people with visions and feel the need to evolve. Only leaders who can dream and people who are free from all kinds of ideology and superstition would lead societies. These people may take the societies of the world to a new unity of existence. Bigoted, weak and tempered people need to be replaced with understanding and virtuous people now. Each person deserves prosperity, harmony and beauty from birth. A humanity which has no boundaries, lives nested with nature and is able to view the future with hope and a social unity where no one is afraid of wars and hunger, no one is a slave and everyone can live his freedom in full is the future of humanity. Poverty and war are the reflections of a conflict creating consciousness, of a famine mentality. To the extent these are removed from the brains of individuals who are educated in the new order of the world, they will be completely erased from the surface of the Earth. When all eyes become one eye, all glances become on sight, quantum leap will take place. The new world order with enlighten the light of reality once again within the framework of the plan of love.

The greatest obstacle in achieving this dream until now has been the lack of mentality. The rareness of people who embody these enlightened idea, have the capacity to stand to the responsibilities of a great dream, believe in the impossible, will spends all their energy to making it real and have the awareness that they need to pay the price has been the greatest challenge for the unity of the world. However, humanity knowledge level is increasing day by day and its awareness is rising to a level where quantum leap will be possible. Concepts which have only been voiced by the advocators of Esoteric have now reached the stage where they can the goods of the whole humanity under the influence of the Age of Knowledge. The knowledge of the wholeness and oneness of the universe has become a science everyone can access today. Today, everything appears to us as the natural laws of the universe. Science is now telling us that everything in the universe is connected, each speck shares he information it has in an instant with the other speck all over the universe, that matter is in fact energy which has come together at a specific density, that we are the parts of the same whole and that we all carry the same essence inside. In the field of frequency, even time and space is the same thing. Knowledge is everywhere at each moment.

Today scientific studies are most concentrated on the area of sub-atomic world today. The quantum studies made in this area have shown that all unions from the smallest to the greatest or from the sub-atomic particles to the community of states take place as a result of the connection of matter with other matter through specific energies. This structural harmony or accord is knowledge itself. The notion of learning appears in greater structures starting from the cells. This shows that new information can constantly be added to the structural knowledge of the cells from the outside. Still, the acquired information cannot change the structural knowledge of the whole. As a natural result of this reality, the system of thought in our time is evolving to be more holistic, ecological and organic and the previous century's materialist, deterministic and mechanistic system of thought is being abandoned.

Scientific developments have always given results which verify Esoteric discourse. It is very likely that future science will prove that the process of existence still continues. There is an unfailing order within eternity. This order is a mathematical one. No deviation is in question. Society in the final analysis is the whole humanity. Although the messages given in Esoteric teaching are directed at individuals to develop and transform their personalities and it is targeted for the individuals to turn in on themselves and get to know themselves, it is taught that individuals need to get rid of the dominance of all kinds of prejudice and do all their evaluations as "a universal I". There is nothing in opposition to human nature in Esoteric.

The masterpieces of all periods are the works of enlightened minds who are graduates of Esoteric schools. The future masterpieces will be the works of the enlightened Quantum generations who will graduate from the schools of the future which will demolish the traditional system of education from their foundation and will not let their dreams to be fettered. In such schools, which devote themselves to discovering the magnificence of each individual, the awareness related to the wholeness of humanity will be held in higher esteem than anything else. People who are there will learn how to destroy each breakdown, each shadow and division in existence and how to always challenge themselves. They will be the creators of the freedom and uniqueness of humanity and the leaders of the new world order.

Are Esoteric schools only passive institutions which target individual development and leave individuals on their own, or are they activist and actionist communities which aim at radically changing the society in accordance with their own values and directly contact the society to reach their goals? We as the whole humanity are the pieces of a whole. With this point of view, the wrongness of selfishness and the ambition of possession. It is mandatory for people to change. This change is the only solution for the continuation of humankind and it is beyond the moral, religious and psychological requirement.

As the idea of Esoteric is shared more by people its influence will increase in the same rate and will become the new expression of the evolvement of the whole humanity. The belief system of humanity is Esoteric. Schools which have carried the teaching to the present time will evolve just like occupational secrets have evolved into universities and will rise to the status of the whole humanity's common guides and educating institutions. Thus, the duty of "Constructing The Sanctuary of Ideal for Humanity" will have been completed successfully, the whole humanity will be allowed to meet a new reality and everyone will be taught methods of being the Perfect Man. However, the path to be covered to reach this goal is still very long. Knowledge is at a more accessible point for each individual who wishes to reach it. Both the increase in published materials and the transmission of knowledge to the masses in a more wide spread and easy manner through the Internet will allow the Esoteric teaching to be discussed in length by a highest number of enlightened minds and make its evolvement possible. What should be paid attention to at this point is to avoid information pollution which is observed to be evident on today's Internet. The greatest problem of today's humanity is not being able to reach sufficient material which will make it Access accurate knowledge. Recently, there has been a book rush which rained on us like cats and dogs. The Internet seems to be transmitting all the desired knowledge to humanity. However, both sources are either very technical and scientific, or full of repetitions. If the individual is not able to eliminate the accurate ones from the others, he may drown in information pollution and mix everything up. Information pollution is one of the greatest barriers against evolvement besides the dogmatic belief systems. In the name of reaching accurate information and benefitting from the synergy created by elite individuals who meet in the common ground, it seems that Esoteric Schools will still be needed for a long time. As the elderly say, there are hundred as of method but the goal is only one. All people will eventually understand they will be one and whole with God.

Significant progress has been made in the name of making all Esoteric values valid for all people. It seems that the discourses of Esoteric teaching are becoming the common values of all humanity. All kinds of human rights, in particular concepts such as freedom, equality and brotherhood are now indispensable for all people. So much so that when a dictator takes action to take these rights away in a country, he finds not only his own nation but the whole world standing up to him. In other words, all boundaries have disappeared from the world in terms of human rights. The words of an astronaut returning from the Moon are very meaningful: "When I looked at the world from a bird's eye view, I have not seen a border between the countries." It is possible that, in the near future no one will see a border between the countries and reach a stage where compassion, understanding and love will be dominant between them".

The new life conditions which the whole world is connected to are urging us to more careful within the framework of our thoughts and the decisions we will take. Many things in our lives now seem dependent on the speed of taking decisions. Today, there is a humanity which is more open to sudden social changes. Apparently, the future will be guided in a speedier manner by people who are able to take more accurate decisions. It is not important where knowledge comes from. Knowledge belongs to all of us. The people of the age of information seem closer in reaching a just society where the life conditions of all people will be better.

The understanding of The New World Order devoted to the removal of physical boundaries and the uniting of the world under a single roof is gradually embracing the whole humanity. Policies which foresee the transformation and evolution of the global society in this manner are active all over the world. Starting from the beginning of 20th century, economic activities have been carried to supranational dimensions over time. Meanwhile, international organizations under the coordination of powers which control economy have appeared and make it possible for structuring in this direction to get stronger. In the near future, there will not be a national state or boundaries and he supranational and universal union of humanity will reach its goal. Since the whole world will be gathered under the universal roof of humanity, there will not be any conflicts or ward, problems related to population, hunger and environment will be solved and humanity will realize the quantum leap.

Today, millions are experiencing poverty and hunger in many countries of the world. However, has not this been the case throughout the history of mankind? Millions of people are dying. Have not they died until now? Has the humanity not been under constant threat in the hands of states which are organized on the beliefs of the past and are dependent on the weaknesses, ambitions and egoisms of the people? The final solution to all these is the New World Order based on Esoteric and Quantum philosophy. Until people reach the World Unity within an understanding of brotherhood and equality without being under the dominance of any state; by preserving their ethnical identities through the awareness and pride of being a part of a nation; being free to live whatever they wish through a sense of belonging to any religion they adopt and the denomination within that religion, will be constantly plagued by troubles. What we live today are the labor pains.

There has been great progress in spreading the Esoteric teaching to the whole humanity. It seems necessary for humanity, which is on the verge of opening up to the universe, to become one and leave all differences aside and realizes this unity within the framework of Esoteric belief from the Quantum point of view. It seems inevitable that the global developments which apparently will result with a new World Order will be crowned with an esoteric system of education which will educate all individuals in the direction of evolvement. Esoteric is the future of mankind and Quantum has revealed this scientific obligation in all its transparency.

www.ingramcontent.com/pod-product-compliance
Lightning Source LLC
Chambersburg PA
CBHW060504290526
45791CB00001B/256

* 9 7 8 1 5 1 5 0 3 5 3 5 0 *